Shortc

Spirituality

mastering the art of inner peace

Bob Gottfried, Ph.D.

**Deeper
Dimension
Publishing**

National Library of Canada Cataloguing in Publication

Gottfried, Bob
    Shortcut to spirituality:
        mastering the art of inner peace

ISBN 0-9734189-0-7

1. Self-help. 2. Spirituality. 3. Mental health.

Deeper Dimension Publishing
148 Finch Ave. W.
North York, ON
L3P 1B4
Canada
www.DeeperDimension.com

Publisher's Note
The principles and exercises taught in this book are not intended to replace medical care and treatment. Please consult your physician in the event that you are experiencing a serious medical condition or have any health-related concerns.

Some of the details included in the case studies described in this book have been modified to protect the privacy of the people involved.

Design and formatting: Heidy Lawrance Associates
Printed and bound in Canada

This book is dedicated
to my parents, who taught me that
when I believe in myself anything is possible.

Acknowledgments

I would first like to thank my family for their support and encouragement. I also wish to thank Jackie, Janis, Marilyn, and Sheila for their wonderful feedback, Pat Cody for her creative editing, Christine LePorte for proofreading the manuscript, and those who helped in the production of the book, especially Heidy Lawrance. Most of all, I would like to thank my patients, from whom I learned more than I had ever expected.

Contents

Foreword

There are times when our "striving for" seems like a fruitless expedition that will never result in that illusive inner peace and fulfillment that we all hope awaits us. However, the truth is that our ultimate destiny is not far away. In fact, it is closer than many can imagine. Fortunately, on our search we are privileged to meet or discover gifted guides and teachers who nurture, inspire, and lead us to that place of peace and wisdom. Dr. Bob Gottfried is one of those people. I would like to congratulate him for helping his readers find a shortcut on their spiritual journeys and for providing a means to live in the deep moment so that anyone can find their life's purpose.

Shortcut to Spirituality provided me with a new way of viewing my life. Dr. Gottfried's approach opened my eyes to the wisdom and beauty within and around me. It enabled me to find the serenity of the moment instead of the chaos of the past and the insecurity of the future. I was able to work through complex emotions resulting from an abusive childhood and to grow in ways I never imagined possible. I was also able to break free of thoughts and patterns that prevented me from truly experiencing life in all of its magic and glory. I firmly believe that this book will help you, the reader, to look deep within and to understand who you really are from both a psycho-emotional and, more importantly, a spiritual perspective.

I would highly recommend this book to anyone interested in learning important life lessons that will assist in resolving stress, anxiety, anger, and depression. The book also teaches how to deal with difficult people and conflicts that result in a variety of challenging emotions. Dr. Gottfried's work contains a myriad of fresh concepts about the ways we operate and what really drives us. It was refreshing to find new ideas to help me negotiate the path of my life. I believe that *Shortcut to Spirituality's* unique approach can save years of searching for inner serenity through either meditation or cognitive techniques alone. Dr. Gottfried's stories of experience are filled with meaning and humor, making this book a powerful tool for those wishing to transform their traditional and limiting ways of thinking into spiritual wisdom that is both inspiring and liberating.

If you have ever heard that voice inside of you crying or even whispering, "Mend my life!" then this book will provide you with the light on the path of your journey.

Dr. Jackie Eldridge
—Ontario Institute for Studies in Education
at the University of Toronto

Introduction

Where Is This Book Coming From?

The journey to spirituality is one that can take many turns. It could be a simple and easy process or a long and tedious one. What if you could find a way to accelerate the process, to make this journey much shorter?

A shortcut to spirituality does exist, and I intend to show you, in these pages, how to find it. Let me start your expedition to understanding how to speed up your journey by telling you how this book came about.

I've had the privilege of working with thousands of people who experienced a variety of conditions such as stress, depression, anxiety, chronic pain, burnout, aggressiveness, shyness, workaholism, perfectionism, cognitive impairment, and trauma. In the beginning of my counseling career, I realized that many of my patients' emotional and behavioral challenges connected to one core issue: low self-esteem. Whenever possible, instead of working directly on the problem at hand, I focused first on the person's self-esteem. Once the person developed better self-regard and confidence, resolving the stated problem became easier.

I have always looked for similar shortcuts to personal growth for my patients. We have a phenomenal mind-body system and our ability to positively affect this system is vastly underutilized. Finding

> The real voyage of discovery consists not in seeking new landscapes, but in having new eyes.
>
> *Marcel Proust*

shortcuts to better our health and well-being is always possible.

Prior to writing this book, I worked on a manuscript that dealt with stress titled *The Unstress Process*. It demonstrated how to make the necessary inner changes not only to reduce stress, but also to prevent most of it from happening in the first place. I don't refer to external stressors, which most times we have very little control over, but to how we respond to such stressors and how they make us feel. The Unstress process came about through accomplishing mastery over oneself and consequently one's life.

As my writing progressed, I realized that a spiritual perspective was missing. It occurred to me that a book focusing on spirituality could prove far more effective than one just about stress. Spirituality provided a shortcut to self-mastery. I decided not to combine the two topics because in achieving self-mastery, you also remove most stress from your system.

I set aside the Unstress idea, with its predominantly "psychological" theme and chose to write this one, which is predominantly "spiritual." This shift in focus also reflected the changes I had experienced both personally and professionally.

"Spirituality" is such an overused term that its meaning has become blurred for many people. As you read, you'll find three different definitions of spirituality, each one shorter than the previous one.

Right now I want to tell you how my interest in spirituality started. My path was not the traditional route many take as they search for answers to deep questions, although my search came later. I was perfectly comfortable working in the psycho-emotional domain. I felt satisfied and grateful for the opportunity to help people. Spirituality at the time was too "New Age" for me, too far out to fit my more conventional nature.

A few years ago, while attending a professional conference, I talked with a colleague about different therapeutic approaches I used in my practice. At the time, I worked with individuals suffering from chronic pain, sleep disorders, and cognitive difficulties resulting from trauma or ongoing stress. During our conversation, I realized that I had become tired and somewhat bored with my work. But as we continued talking, an interesting question popped into my mind: *What if I could find deeper solutions to the challenges my patients faced?*

Motivated by that idea, I started to change selected elements of my therapy approach, encouraging deeper awareness within the person. As I did, a notable phenomenon occurred. Many patients began reporting what they called "deep experiences," which in retrospect I realized were spiritual in nature.

I decided to look more carefully into these patterns and work with those patients who were interested in traveling this spirituality path with me. The results were amazing, and I really thought that I had discovered a totally new treatment approach. Later, a few patients commented that my ideas were somewhat similar to those found in Eastern philosophies, which I found worthy of note. As I understood how important and powerful my findings were, I did what I usually do in such cases: sought ways to teach the principles of spirituality and make them as practical as possible.

I have noticed that most books on spirituality have been written by theology scholars, rabbis, ministers, students of Eastern philosophies and practices, or people who have had a profound spiritual experience. I want to clarify that I am not a devoted student of any Eastern discipline, nor am I involved in any religious organization. However, since I began exploring spirituality, I have become more interested in world religions, trying to extract the essence of many of them. It was not too surprising to find that most religions, at their core, aim for the same purpose; they just differ in their approach and technique.

This book is my attempt to teach the spiritual principles that I have discovered, learned, and taught, in a way that you can apply in your everyday life.

You won't find recommendations here for traditional meditation or practicing mantras. Not that anything is wrong with meditation and mantras; these are indeed powerful tools. Meditation, however, is just part of a process. A common mistake is trying to turn the process into the goal, instead of using it as a vehicle on the road to deeper awareness.

This journey is often filled with mental obstructions that can slow you down, at times even stop you from establishing a stronger spiritual connection. Working through these obstructions can build a solid bridge from our more psychological world to our more hidden spiritual territory.

I like this Japanese saying: "If you give a person a fish, you will satisfy his hunger for the day, but if you teach him how to fish, it will satisfy his hunger for life." In a similar way, I hope to equip you with many tools to help you overcome mental roadblocks.

At first I wanted to call this book *Practical Spirituality*. This title came to me after listening to people's complaints about how frustrating the effort was "to become more spiritual." The objections were often identical: Exposure to high quality material and eloquent ideas inspired them to contemplate change; but that initial excitement wore off once they asked the inevitable question, "So how exactly do I do this?" The problem with the title *Practical Spirituality* is that it implies the occurrence of impractical spirituality, which obviously does not exist.

The point of practicality is still an important one. I am not interested in teaching philosophical concepts that look beautiful on paper but are hard to practice and integrate. The purpose of this book is to show spirituality the way we can live it day by day—not in a monastery, or on top of a mountain, but right here amidst the chaos of our everyday lives.

I have never had a sole, earth-shattering spiritual experience that totally changed my life in an instant. My personal process was comprised of many deep, smaller scale realizations and spiritual experiences, which served to light many dark areas of my awareness. For me this has been a more gradual process of deeper learning, with transforming realizations that led to an improved feeling of balance, freedom, and inner peace. Throughout these pages, I will share some of my experiences with you.

You may encounter extraordinary spiritual experiences while exploring this territory. If you do, I want to hear about them. Please feel free to write to me.

Even if a miraculous event does not happen to you, once you "figure it out" on a deep level, you'll enjoy the same state of bliss usually felt after such remarkable experiences.

I often come across the term "seekers." Although I understand why this term is widely used, it still puzzles me. I used to ask myself, "How come so many people are constantly seeking? What exactly are they seeking and when will they finally find it?"

Those questions led me to the goal of this book: to help you identify what you ultimately seek, and then to help you transform from seeker to finder.

So why did I choose the title *Shortcut to Spirituality*? I began to look for more ways to connect deeply with the magical world of spirituality, and I believe I found a few shortcuts. A shortcut is a practical route to a destination, and I've already expressed my desire to teach spirituality in a practical way. Along with the principles and realizations that I will share with you, I will also guide you through different awareness exercises that will help you implement these ideas in your individual life right away.

Together we will consider the following fundamental questions:
- What exactly is spirituality?
- How does spirituality differ from religion?
- How can it be practiced daily?
- How can you overcome mental blocks that may interfere with increasing spiritual awareness?
- Who are you?
- What do you really want?
- What is your purpose in life?
- What is the meaning of life?

You will notice that this book has no chapters. Instead, it is divided into three parts. I wrote the book as a continuous flow of ideas from one part to another. Removing the need to follow certain structures can free your mind to find its unique pathway to an uncharted destination. Transforming our cubical, analytical, rational thinking into the unbounded, unrestricted area of spirituality requires a shift in how we view life. The lack of a traditional structure in the book is important as a way to begin to establish this fundamental shift.

I have included thoughts and ideas taken from the fields of cosmology, quantum physics, holography, biology, philosophy, and different religions. You will also find quotes from philosophers, poets, Holy Scriptures, and even movies, all to expand your mind and enable you to understand what lies beyond your present thoughts and perceptions.

You will not find a set program as part of the book because becoming more deeply spiritual does not happen in rigid steps. Transformation happens through each individual's realizations; and the deeper the realization, the deeper the change. Instead, you will find recommendations for different practices throughout the book, which can be useful to accelerate the process.

At this point, I'll summarize important messages that you will find in greater detail throughout this book.

1. *We cope excessively as individuals*. Unnecessary coping uses up too much energ.y, a commodity that is becoming rare for many people. This "energy crisis" may be the primary cause of many of the maladies people presently experience.

   For instance, in North America, visits to the doctor for depression are at their highest rate ever, second only to appointments related to high blood pressure. One reason for the increased rate of doctor visits may be the fact that more than ever before, people are willing to admit that they are depressed.

   But I also believe that the rise in depression is a direct result of the increased accumulation of stress. We have to move from just coping with stress to resolving the of fundamental issues that cause it in the first place. This will enable us to better handle the challenges we face, and will continue to face, in this new millennium.

2. *We overuse the analytical capacities of our mind.* Too much analysis compromises our innate creativity and intuition as well as the ability to connect on a deeper level. We don't want to let go of this ability completely, but we would like to learn to use this faculty in a more balanced way.

3. *We need to connect from within.* Galileo said, "You cannot teach a man anything, you can only help him to find it within himself." People need to make the time and effort to look below the surface and establish a deeper connection with themselves, even if it feels uncomfortable at first. It is only through this connection that we can fully manifest our spirituality. The answers to all our personal questions cannot be found outside of us, but rather lie within. Our true goal is to connect with this inner wisdom and manifest it in our lives.

4. *We need to significantly increase our conscious awareness and begin to see the complete world picture*, not just individual bits and pieces of it. We must learn to set aside personal agendas and begin to look at our planet as one territory and at its habitants as one big family. Then we can overcome the challenges of wars, terrorism, famine, racism, animosity, cruelty, prejudice, gender bias, and territorial conflicts. Peace on earth begins inside each person. We cannot accomplish it unless each of us achieves inner peace.

5. *Spirituality does not require coping mechanisms.* In fact, it offers solutions to the issues that call for coping in the first place. Spirituality carries the wisdom necessary to resolve the challenges we currently face, whether personal, social, or global. Given the time and focus, spirituality is the only way to deal with challenges effectively and, ultimately, to restore balance.

6. *Spirituality is attainable right now.* Nothing has to happen outside of you for a complete spiritual transformation to occur. Such metamorphosis can be quickly achieved through practical shortcuts.

You will find that a large part of this book deals with the contrast between the spiritual essence and the *ego*—the part in us that needs, wants, desires, and craves. This part is more concerned with the self and less with others. Being able to recognize and reduce our ego-based behavior is an absolute must for spiritual awakening.

By the end of this book, you will have a clear idea of how your ego works. You will also possess effective tools to significantly reduce its influence on your life. Some of the principles outlined in the book will be repeated over and over. It is not that they are difficult to understand; the goal is to integrate them deeper and enable them to be a natural part of your thought patterns and actions.

You can read this book in two ways. The first is what I call "reading for information," the less constructive option. Information alone is what keeps people in the seekers category. The second and more beneficial way is to absorb the information, and then take the time to practice the awareness exercises outlined in this book, noting how they affect your experience.

You'll recognize awareness exercises because they look like this:

> **Stop to reflect on the principles as you read, wrestle with them if you feel the need, and if you like them, ask yourself, "How can I apply them in my life?" Take your time. Treat this book as a spiritual fitness program rather than just external reading material, and you may soon join the "finders" club.**

Ralph Waldo Emerson once said, "We are always getting ready to live, but never living." I hope that you will use this book as a guide to living life more fully.

As you read and work through the exercises, you may experience personal realizations. You can record them in the "Realizations" section at the end of the book and refer to them from time to time. You can also note concepts that you want to understand better or that you need to explore. This will deepen the effectiveness of your study and help you to progress in quantum leaps.

Finally, if you are interested in practicing and promoting the principles taught in this book with like-minded individuals, please refer to the note at its end. You'll learn how to become part of a discussion group that I call "PeaceTogether."

Shall we begin?

Part 1

Preparation

The Teacher brought the new Student to the Principal. She inquired, "At which level should he start?"

The Principal examined the Student for a few moments and then asked, "Why did you come to this school?"

The Student replied, "To learn the art of happiness."

The Principal turned to the Teacher and said, "Level 1." He smiled, looking at the Student. "Now go to your classroom."

What Is Spirituality?

Merriam-Webster's Dictionary defines *spirituality* as "1. something that in ecclesiastical law belongs to the church or to a cleric as such, 2. clergy, 3. sensitivity or attachment to religious values, 4. the quality or state of being spiritual." *Spiritual* is defined as "relating to sacred matters, concerned with religious values, relating to supernatural beings or phenomena." The keywords we find in these definitions include sacred, supernatural, and, most often, religious references.

Later I'll expand on the difference between religion and spirituality, but to clarify now, this book is not about religion. The principles described here are not intended to promote any religious practice, but to enhance your perspective and understanding of religion's evolution and what it tries to accomplish.

Ordinarily, people use the word "spirituality" to mean sacred; beyond their daily, tangible experience; extraordinary; perhaps even miraculous. Although extraordinary, spirituality is also simple, a paradoxical concept that our analytical minds may have a problem comprehending.

Many patients who came to me for counseling said they were looking for spirituality, when they actually wanted to fill a void in their lives. The void was caused by circumstances beyond their control such as loss of a loved one, a crisis, a life-threatening disease, or unfulfilled needs. They were looking for deep answers in order to reconcile a part of their life that they couldn't accept or justify in their own minds. These people were faced with a first-class challenge.

But why spirituality? Many patients looked first for other strategies that would help fill their void. When nothing worked, they began to question the meaning of life, and this was when they turned to spirituality.

The famous Japanese director Akira Kurosawa filmed a beautiful Japanese movie called *Ikiru*, or "To Live," in black and white in 1952. The main character, played by Takashi Shimura, has drifted through life for over thirty years as a bureaucrat at Tokyo City Hall, when one day he finds out that he has cancer.

His initial shock is followed by the realization that for the past thirty years he hasn't really lived life. He has mostly pushed papers from one side of his desk to the other. He then begins a journey in which he tries to live life more fully. He tries going to parties, drinking, dancing, and hanging out with people. None of that really works for him. He then befriends a young woman from his office who decides that her job is too boring. She leaves her comfortable secretarial position to work in a toy factory.

After meeting with him a few times, she asks him what he really wants from her. He explains that he wants to be as happy as she is. The woman replies that it's simple. While she works in the factory producing toys, she imagines children playing with them and how happy they feel.

The man begins to understand what life really can mean. He dedicates what time he has left to help people in a suburban neighborhood who are caught in a web of bureaucracy, trying to get approval to build a playground for their children. He ultimately dies contented, knowing he figured it out.

Losing thirty years of his life no longer mattered. A few months of purposeful living compensated for the lost time.

Why wait for a terminal illness to drive us to look for spirituality? Why go through a crisis first? Why not find spirituality before crisis? Does this delay come from lack of awareness? Complacency? Wrong values or misplaced priorities?

Regardless of the cause, looking for spirituality involves an attitude that is not common to other practices. Initially it requires believing in something that cannot be proven, perhaps even defying scientific laws.

But is this right? Can't scientific principles allow room for spirituality? Not yet. Perhaps scientific discovery will never uncover all the secrets of the body, mind, and soul connection.

In science, what cannot be measured, observed, or calculated cannot be defined; and as a result the intangible is completely rejected or at least grossly ignored.

Fortunately, great scientists such as Albert Einstein, David Bohm, and Albert Schweitzer realized that spirituality starts where science ends, that conflict between the two is not necessary. They can coexist. The way I see it, science is only an attempt to understand how everything works, and spirituality is what makes it all come together.

Our educational system has focused exclusively on enhancing knowledge and mental competencies. The hallmark of such abilities is *IQ: Intelligence Quotient*. IQ primarily estimates the ability to apply analytical thinking, remember facts, and perform mathematical calculations.

> **Matter is the matrix of Spirit and Spirit is the higher state of Matter.**
>
> *Pierre Teilhard de Chardin*

In 1990 the term Emotional Quotient, or EQ, was introduced. Coined by Peter Salovey and John D. Mayer, this new measure of intelligence refers more to the soft skills. These include intra- and inter-personal skills (getting along with yourself and with others), both of which are indispensable to success and happiness.

Although *Emotional Quotient* is a relatively new term, the concept is not. The main task of most therapists involves teaching principles that will enhance a person's *EQ*. In contrast with IQ, which emphasizes mental abilities, EQ focuses on abilities drawn from our emotional realm. Unlike IQ, which is for the most part set at an early age, EQ can always be improved.

At this point I want to establish a new term: *Spiritual Quotient*, or *SQ*. Spiritual Quotient is more difficult to define because it is based on Spiritual Intelligence, a quite abstract concept.

Unlike EQ or IQ, SQ cannot be measured. The main difference between SQ and IQ or EQ is that the last two are in part genetic and in part learned (IQ has a very strong hereditary component and EQ is mostly learned), while SQ is entirely innate.

Spiritual Intelligence has always been there, completely, and it cannot be improved. In fact, it does not have to be measured or improved because it is already perfect!

SQ can be easily tapped into, and once practiced, it promises a life that is fulfilling regardless of any external conditions. That life will communicate, "I am fulfilled now, not later."

We cannot develop SQ. We can only enhance our understanding and awareness of it and expand our ability to practice it.

The Ultimate Shortcut

Since the main premise of the book is to find a shortcut to spirituality, I'll point out as we progress through it what I believe has to happen so you can significantly expand your spiritual experience.

Right now, I would like to give you a fair chance to "get it" before you read further. It may sound as if I am teasing you. Well, I am and I am not. What I am about to say is 100% true, but understanding it deeply could definitely pose a challenge. When I say "deeply," I mean realization beyond intellectual understanding. I mean achieving awareness so deep that you can feel it in every cell of your body.

> What humanity owes to personalities like Buddha, Moses, and Jesus ranks for me higher than all the achievements of the enquiring and constructive mind.
>
> *Albert Einstein*

I have said that Spiritual Intelligence is innate. This means that you are fully and completely spiritual already. This moment. You don't have to learn anything new. It's yours, and you can claim it right here, right now. You don't have to practice anything to manifest it.

All you have to do is clear your mind totally. Free it from everything: thoughts, analysis, mental concepts and perceptions, excuses, and conditions. Whatever is left, after you have cleared all that, is SPIRITUALITY.

I am not talking about a dead brain, but a calm mind. Your spirituality is staring at you this very moment. Can you remove the veil that obstructs this simple, yet profound clarity and realize it? Take a moment, an hour, a day or a week. Can you figure it out? Because once you do, you have figured out everything. EVERYTHING! You might as well close the book and give it to a friend. You won't need it anymore.

Take time to reflect on the shortcut of all shortcuts. It's challenging, isn't it? Chances are you will find this harder than it sounds. It's so simple, yet so difficult.

Why? The answer is—years of limiting mental programming. This programming is full of false ideas about what life is; about who we are and what we think we need to make us happy. The good news is that it's possible to transcend this programming. I wouldn't be writing this book if it weren't.

Are you still with me? For most people, this powerful shortcut statement requires more work. Even if you are not yet ready to take this step, please keep it in the back of your mind.

Finding spirituality is much like trying to open a combination lock. First you need to know the numbers and then the sequence. Finally the lock is open and freedom is yours. This freedom is total, freedom from the pain of the past, worrying about your future, the opinion of others, and all the limitations of your upbringing. Try this exercise:

> **Take a deep breath in and exhale slowly. Suspend all
> thinking while continuing to breathe slowly. Can you feel
> the freedom, even if only for a moment?**

The rest of the book will be dedicated to understanding what has to happen for you to permanently connect with this extraordinary reality. But if I had to summarize the process in one word, it would be *allowing*.

Spirituality is not about change. Change belongs to the psychological terrain. In a way, you will make the biggest change of all without altering a thing. Just by allowing yourself to connect deeper, by permitting the full dissolution of ideas and concepts that keep you where you are right now, by allowing yourself to broaden your view and really see, you can recognize what has always existed.

A moment ago you had an opportunity to ALLOW yourself to experience freedom. Did you?

Spirituality and Materialism

Materialism and its close relative commercialism are both in opposition to spirituality. According to Webster's Dictionary, materialism is "the doctrine that comfort, pleasure and wealth are the highest or only values or goals." Defining materialism as *doctrine* gives it policy, principle, or dogma—elevating it to life-governing status.

In the previous exercise you were asked to suspend thinking, while breathing slowly and deeply. This technique of clearing your mind from thoughts was meant to give you an experience of calm and freedom. Consumerism tends to fill the mind with distractions. How impossible it is to clear the mind when it is constantly focused on getting things. Consumerism relentlessly bombards us with messages in the form of advertising through every known media. Little wonder we have to work so hard to recognize our spirituality.

I want to ask you a question: *What is the hidden or indirect message advertisers send you?*

They tell you that you have to consume because you are not good enough, not attractive enough, not slim enough, not rich enough, or not smart enough. So much is available for you to buy, and you'd better buy! Your image depends on it. You have to consume because you need to prove that you are worthy, that you are successful, and that you fit in. Buy and it will make you feel good.

While all this subversion is happening, your spirit is smiling. It knows the truth. It is patiently waiting for you to wake up and smell the roses. It won't force you into awareness, though. It's your choice. What do YOU want to focus on?

Don't get me wrong; I don't believe in "all or nothing." You can still be a consumer if you want, to a certain extent. I too consume. I will never be a yogi in a cave on a mountain, which is quite appropriate for those who choose that life. I prefer to be spiritual here, in the city, with all its distractions; but I want to be able to transcend these distractions when I choose, not be a slave to them.

To be spiritual and to consume requires us to find a better balance between the two choices. We can create more balance by avoiding the many distractions that commercialism offers.

Consider what media—radio, TV, Internet, newspapers, magazines—invade your day with buying messages and the percentage of time you allot them. Could you give part of it

to connecting within? Remember our last awareness exercise? Take a few deep breaths in, exhale slowly and clear your mind. Reconnect yourself with inner freedom. How about repeating the exercise from time to time to strengthen your spiritual connection?

Once you achieve balance, you may find that you spend less money because you have fewer needs and are happy with what you have. You will also have more time available, which you can dedicate to sharing your bliss with others. Discover the worth of taking the time to better acquaint your known self with your lesser-known, deeper YOU, which is the source of spirituality.

No discussion of materialism is complete without mentioning television, not just a symbol of commercialism but also its devoted messenger. The problem with TV is not only the negative commercial messages of "not enoughness" through incessant promotion of consumerism, but also that viewing can remove you from life. Instead of living life, you watch it through the TV screen. You get caught up in the lives of screen stars and soap opera characters. What about your life? When will you fully live yours?

Yes, I also watch TV. I'm an ordinary person just like you. I'm not totally against TV. It's a convenient source of news, information, and even quality entertainment.

But we have to learn to create balance to achieve what I call *TruePeace*, the deep inner peace that arises from our spirituality.

If we use TV as an escape, then we need to learn what we are trying to escape from and resolve it. Only then can we achieve the desired state of inner balance.

Maurice Sendak put it well when he noted, "There must be more to life than having everything." You have to know this: You are enough! You already have it all. Everything you really need, in its purest form. What you have deep inside is the real deal.

Commercials are about packaging. You are good enough without the need for any packaging. You can be fulfilled even without the materialistic possessions Western society advocates that you "must own." Remove the veil, clean your glasses. Can you see it?

Are We Out of Balance?

We just considered the importance of creating balance. Some claim that our society is out of balance. In observing thousands of people who come to me suffering from debilitating conditions such as depression, anxiety, chronic fatigue, and chronic pain, I ask myself whether or not much of it is a result of a psychological and social imbalance.

I received the following message by e-mail from one of my patients. This is a clear message that we all should devote time to thinking about very seriously.

Something to Think About (author unknown)
The paradox of our time in history is that we have taller buildings,
    but shorter tempers;
wider freeways, but narrower viewpoints;
we spend more, but have less;
we buy more, but enjoy it less.
We have bigger houses and smaller families;
more conveniences, but less time;
we have more degrees, but less sense;
more knowledge, but less judgment;
more experts, but more problems;
more medicine, but less wellness.
We have multiplied our possessions, but reduced our values.
We talk too much, love too seldom, and hate too often. We've
    learned how to make a living, but not a life. We've added years
    to life, not life to years.
We've been all the way to the moon and back,
but have trouble crossing the street to meet the new neighbor.
We've conquered outer space, but not inner space. We've cleaned
    up the air, but polluted the soul.
We've split the atom, but not our prejudice;
We have higher incomes, but lower morals.
We've become long on quantity, but short on quality.
These are the times of tall men, and short character;
steep profits, and shallow relationships.

These are the times of world peace, but domestic warfare;
more leisure, but less fun;
more kinds of food, but less nutrition.
These are the days of two incomes, but more
       divorce;
of fancier houses, but broken homes.
It is a time when there is much in the show window
and nothing in the stockroom;
a time when technology can bring this letter to you, in a time
       when you can choose
either to make a difference,
or to just hit delete.

Presenting a problem without having a solution can be frustrating, but the challenges of our time may be best met within each individual. I believe that a *spiritual* solution is the only answer, or else resolving one problem may only create a new one in its place.

What Do Spiritual Experiences Feel Like?

A spiritual experience is not necessarily a lightning bolt striking you out of the blue. It is a special feeling that is different from simply feeling good. It's an elated state that doesn't originate from an accomplishment or a fulfillment of a need. Rather, this sublime feeling is associated with a deep realization caused by letting go of an old and useless concept. Making a deep connection with a person, an animal, or with nature may also evoke it.

When I ask my patients to describe a spiritual experience, they always start by saying, "Well, it's hard to put into words." They are right. It's like trying to explain a flower's scent. You could say it smells sweet, but for a person who has never smelled a flower, "sweet" would not capture the nature of the sensory experience.

Neither can spirituality be explained verbally, as it is beyond language. But you want to recognize the experience when you feel it. People usually describe it as a deep sense of love and connection;

feeling at one with everyone and with God; feeling deep peace, whole, limitless, boundless, and free.

Have you had similar feelings? To varying degrees, most people have connected with these uplifting states at certain times, but few explore them enough to allow a more meaningful impact on their lives.

Through patients' accounts and personal experiences, I have come to realize that when appreciated and better understood, the frequency and intensity of these spiritual events expand dramatically.

Pay attention as you continue to progress on this path. Earlier I suggested that you make notes. You can use the pages at the end of the book, or a separate journal, to record deep experiences. Later, reflect on them and notice what their messages to you are. Refer to them frequently to see how the depth and frequency of your personal spiritual experiences occur over time.

One of life's most powerful rules is what I call the Law of Focus #1: Whatever you focus on, expands. When we concentrate on a certain subject or a feeling, we attract circumstances that will enhance our experience in the realm we spotlight. Focus more on SPIRITUALITY and watch how your awareness of it expands.

Spirituality vs. Religion

At this point, I feel the need to make a clear distinction between spirituality and religion. Despite what many people believe, the two are not synonymous.

During a seminar I facilitated on spirituality, I was asked to define the difference between the two concepts. Out of nowhere I heard myself saying, "Religion equals Spirituality plus Politics."

> The divine test of a person's worth is not theology but life.
> *The Talmud*

While I was immediately aware that this was a gross generalization, I also believed that it might represent reality in a large portion of organized religion. Yes, spirituality does exist within organized religion but in many cases it is buried beneath layers of politics.

This comparison may sound shocking. Can we really say the words politics and religion in the same breath? Let's examine this idea for a moment.

What is the image we have of politicians? They are often seen as shrewd individuals who, at times, use manipulative behavior and tactics to promote themselves and their political parties. They will promise you a better life if you adhere to their vision and give them your support. At times religion makes similar promises.

On a theoretical and philosophical level, religion is far different from conventional, everyday politics. In practice many similarities exist. Organized religion has also used propaganda, promises, and manipulation to sell people on specific ideas including the promise of a good life and a better afterlife if you adhere to its particular rules.

Webster's Dictionary defines politics as "the art or science of government." By telling us how to view the world and how to live, is religion not attempting to govern us? And by imposing government, does religion not practice politics?

I sincerely respect religion as an important forum for bringing people together, as a source of hope and strength during times of crisis, and also as a good source for moral guidance in everyday life. It can also provide a lifestyle structure that may be important for many people.

However, on the most important level, religion has missed the main point. Religion's chief purpose should be to bring people to spirituality, and yet many of its attitudes achieve the opposite. Spirituality is the "religion" within YOU; it is not external.

The Arab writer Muhammad Nagulb said, "Religion is a multi-colored lantern. Everyone looks through a particular color, but the candle is always the same." Zen, Tao, Buddhism, Christianity, Judaism, Islam, and any other religion share the same core essence. That's because only one source illuminates all.

Unfortunately, spirituality became externalized for the purpose of religious groups' control. According to religion you are considered a good person only if you follow a certain path. Spirituality, on the other hand, is unconditional. Your personal path is within you, for you to recognize and honor. When people try to convince you otherwise, regard the effort as manipulation, which usually originates from lack of awareness.

For inner serenity and peaceful coexistence with others, we have to understand what gave rise to such religious structures. Religious intolerance splattered blood across history as it does over today's news.

Thousands of years ago, when people were more primitive, certain rules and rituals established order and directed people towards the practice of moral and social values. However, human beings were meant to transcend the need for outer control as we developed our understanding.

On a purely spiritual level, no precepts or values are important. Spirituality is the wellspring of all goodness. All we have to know is how to find the headwaters of spirituality within ourselves, then everything religion demands of us, and much more, will flow naturally.

I often tell my patients that therapy is regarded as a success when they no longer need the help of their therapist. Self-reliance, not dependence on outside resources, is the goal for maturity. Too often, religion makes us dependent on its principles. Even worse, we aren't supposed to question any of these principles. This fact alone has pushed many believers away from organized religion.

Millions of people were, and in some countries still are, persecuted and murdered in the name of religion. For what end? The answer will always be power and control. *Jihad*, the Muslim concept of holy war against enemies and unbelievers of Islam, is considered a religious duty. Its political implications are obvious, the consequences deadly. Religion has focused on the process for so long that it has almost forgotten what it intended to accomplish in the first place.

To me spirituality is the "religion of our being." Unfortunately, religion sometimes deals with restricting and disciplining us to produce an institution's results that have little to do with true spirituality.

A while ago I conducted a spiritual retreat outside the city. This was the last component in one of my workshops entitled "The Self-

Mastery Program." One of my patients, who was very involved in her Greek Orthodox church, called me a week before the workshop to say that although she had registered for the retreat, she would not be able to attend because she felt it would clash with her religion.

I promised her that nothing like that would happen, since I wouldn't teach religion. If anything, I would teach the same principles that any religious institution, faithful to true spirituality, would have taught her already. I encouraged her to keep an open mind and decide for herself.

During the workshop I shared with the participants my views including the above-mentioned formula: *religion = spirituality + politics.* No one disagreed with me on that.

A few weeks later, this woman approached me and said that our discussions during the workshop made her look at her church and many of its administrators in a very different light. It affected some of her relationships with church officials, but she did not mind, because the truth was more important than what people thought of her. She was able to look at her work in the church and differentiate between the important and the superficial. This view is one we all need to develop in order to discover what religion, to a great degree, has failed to teach us.

Much like commercialism, religion can make us feel inadequate and unworthy. After all, if we are still facing problems in our lives, perhaps it is because we are not good enough people in the eyes of God. Or if adversity hits us, perhaps it is because we are not trying hard enough to follow religious practices.

One of my patients told me that his pastor asked him how he was doing a long time after he had been severely injured. The man replied that the recovery process had been very slow. His pastor suggested that perhaps the delayed recovery was because he hadn't fully forgiven his ex-wife, who caused the injury in the first place. Upset, my patient concluded that the pastor just didn't understand what he was going through and was making him feel guilty. This felt unfair as he had done considerable inner work to be able to forgive his ex-wife and move on with his life.

If you are still not convinced, please read Anglican Bishop John Shelby Spong's book, *Why Christianity Must Change or Die*, published by Harper San Francisco, 1998. Bishop Spong's view is that, in order to return so many disillusioned individuals to the Church's faith, a radical shift has to occur. Look for this statement on pages 226, 227:

"The magical, personalistic, manipulative, supernatural, and sometimes vindictive power of these deities has been used historically not to enhance life but to bless the status quo, to increase priestly power, and to support those claims of state that have expanded the wealth and power of the ruling classes... Religious understanding is doomed to die, no matter how frantically or hysterically people seek to defend it. It will not survive. For countless numbers who live in the Christian world, it ceased long ago to be compelling."

The truth is that we do not need religion to develop spiritually. Religion is not the goal; it is just a tool. Religion is a human invention and spirituality is a universal, godly existence that is the core of life and not at its edge.

Let me ask you a question: *How does religion try to force us to stop being "sinners"*? Isn't it through promoting fear, shame, and guilt? I know this from personal experience, as well as from numerous patients whose fear and guilt, created by their own religions, made them feel miserable, ill, unhappy, inhibited, repressed, and at times almost insane.

Yes, mental illness can begin in religion. A disorder named Scrupulosity is a form of Obsessive-Compulsive Disorder. People experiencing this disorder are obsessed with sins, morality, and religion in general. Also, a phobia named peccatiphobia is associated with committing sins.

Fear, guilt, shame—is this what spirituality is all about? Obviously not. Such consequences only serve to remove people from spirituality. Does this make sense to you?

I believe that the big discrepancy between religion's offering and spiritual teachings' focus gave rise to the New Age movement. It's also the reason many people moved from traditional religions to Eastern practices such as Buddhism and Hinduism.

Clergy of all denominations would want you to believe that this is how things have always been and how they should remain, but we all know that even what seems to be a foolproof system can be challenged. Communists, as an example, thought that their power would exist forever. But they were wrong. It collapsed in all of Eastern Europe. The Berlin Wall was destroyed stone by stone by people from both sides of the border.

Many people are coming out and saying in response to religion's dogma, "We don't want to follow any rules blindly; we don't want to be intimidated into behaving one way or another." Bishop Spong calls them "Believers in Exile." Such believers in a Creator want to focus on practicing spiritual principles. They still want to be mentored, but not always the way organized religion does it.

One of my biggest contentions with organized religion is that it has not evolved and adapted at the pace of the rest of society. The way some religions treat women is a classic example. Women cannot be ordained as priests by the Catholic Church; they cannot become rabbis or even sit beside men in orthodox Jewish synagogues. Islam is no different.

This changed in some denominations like Lutheran and Anglican churches and Reformist Jewish Synagogues. Many women have pointed out to me that the percentage of woman volunteering for the different Catholic Church activities is very high. Why is assuming significant lay responsibility acceptable but becoming a priest is not?

The new millennium has just started, and almost every profession and institution has learned to accept and value women—medicine, law, sports, you name it. And yet most religious organizations remain stubborn on this glass ceiling. That to me is not spirituality.

Women were created equal and not as second-class human beings. Women tend to have a better ability to understand human feelings and conflicts. Most often, they become better able to relate and connect with people. Given the opportunity, women could provide excellent guidance in many areas of daily living as leaders for churches. In my opinion, if women ever decide to rebel by refraining from going to sermons, churches will be mostly empty. What will the Vatican do then?

Perhaps the major problem in facilitating such changes is the fear of change itself. Women have the potential to facilitate major changes not only with regard to religion, but also when it comes to the messages of "not enoughness." I also believe that women have a greater potential to bring peace to our world more so than men. Unlike men, who tend to gravitate more toward power and aggression, women seek ways to resolve conflicts in peaceful ways.

Margaret Mead, regarded as one of the most important anthropologists of all times, said, "Never doubt that a small group of thoughtful, committed citizens can change the world; indeed, it's the only thing that ever has."

> So God created man in his own image, in the image of God created he him; male and female created he them.
>
> *Genesis 1:27*

When women decide to put their proverbial foot down and adamantly refuse to be hampered by the distorted image and unreasonable expectations they are so often encouraged to adopt, we will then experience a significant global shift toward spirituality that will benefit everyone.

History has proven that whenever women fought for their rights, they eventually won. Why not in religious territory as well? This is their birthright, even according to the Bible!

Both men and women are created equally in God's image.

Sexism is only the tip of the iceberg. Sexuality inspires greater efforts at religious controls. For instance, *The Catechism of the Catholic Church* (Publications Services, Canadian Conference of Catholic Bishops, 1994) describes masturbation as an offense against chastity and, along with homosexuality, as a "disordered action." Fundamentalist church doctrines and rigid religious thinkers of all denominations are too often just as intolerant. These archaic attitudes cause people unnecessary shame and guilt.

Unfortunately, we can point to the private lives of priests and church leaders as a testament to what can happen when people are forced to repress their innate sexual desires. For instance, recently the Vatican acknowledged, although minimized, that priests and missionaries forced nuns into sex. A report written by Maura O'Donohue, a physician and a nun herself, is part of five separate reports dating back to 1994, written by senior members of women's religious orders citing many such cases that took place in 23 different countries including the United States, Europe, South America, India, and Southeast Asia.

I have done a great deal of work with patients about their sexual inhibitions because they considered their sexuality sinful or "dirty." Where do these messages come from? The church needs to recognize that sex is not dirty. Sex represents powerful creative energy that we need to learn to express in natural, healthy ways, free of inhibitions.

One of my patients told me that her husband was a Jesuit priest before they married. They fell in love many years ago and kept the relationship a secret, but when they decided to marry, he had to give up priesthood. Why would that be? Aren't priests supposed to help us navigate through life? How can they do that if they have no idea what it means to live with a mate and raise a family? Would you trust a financial planner who had no money and had invested none of his own?

CNN recently reported the result of a poll asking priests about the church requirement of celibacy. More than 50 percent confirmed that they would want to see celibacy dropped as a prerequisite for priesthood.

Religion has to reinvent itself, demonstrating awareness that people are interested in the truth and not just in empty promises. Fear and guilt should not be used in any denomination's religious practices.

I see the role of a religious figure such as a minister, rabbi, mullah, etc., not as a "religious guru," but more as a teacher, someone who can take you by the hand and gently lead you down the spiritual path, without rigid rules, intimidation, or using negative motivation. Preaching produces only temporary enthusiasm or motivation. People must question religious leaders who only preach and promise, and begin to look for genuine teachers instead.

If such leaders want to continue to play the role of spiritual mentors, they must genuinely teach their followers how to be in touch with who they really are, not what the church thinks they should be. This applies to any religion. If these leaders can teach people how to connect with deeper aspects of themselves, then their work is worthy.

> This is my simple religion. There is no need for temples, no need for complicated philosophy. Our own brain, our own heart is our temple; the philosophy is kindness.
>
> *Dalai Lama*

To teach connection with the spirituality within each of us, clergy of all faiths have to figure it out for themselves first. Like any teacher for any subject, a religious leader is more likely to guide you toward spiritual understanding if he demonstrates awareness of personal, deep spirituality and encourages positive instead of punitive religious practices.

I have no doubt that numerous priests and other religious teachers do a fine job serving their communities despite many limitations imposed by their own organizations. I also need to make very clear that I don't propose that you renounce your religion. Just become fully aware of the limitations within many organized religions so that you can deepen your spiritual understanding. This in turn may allow you to build a stronger personal foundation within your chosen religion.

Good and Bad

Religion often overuses good/bad terminology. In a discussion with a local priest I noticed that he kept mentioning the words good and bad when describing his own as well as people's general behavior and attitudes. When I pointed it out to him, he was quite surprised and admitted that he never paid attention to his use of those terms. The use of these judgmental constructs is often unconscious.

Kahlil Gibran said, "Good is to be one with yourself." That view seems like a more positive way to look at good and bad.

I will quote the Bible frequently throughout this book. Regardless of my opinion about the limiting aspects of religion, I consider

> There is nothing good or bad, but thinking makes it so.
>
> *Shakespeare*

the Bible and other religious guides as important sources of spiritual knowledge. When we examine them carefully, we find that some passages are saturated with spirituality. But you must know how to read them because, in my view, the Bible cannot always be taken literally. Biblical stories are not always accurate descriptions of what happened, but often serve as metaphors that help us to better understand an important spiritual message.

Going back now to the concept of good or bad, I quote Moses. "See, I have set before you this day life and good, and death and evil." (Deuteronomy 30:15)

Moses talks here about choice. Isn't it surprising, however, that Moses doesn't say, "Choose good and you will live; choose evil and you will die"? He says it in the reverse: Choose life and you will have good; choose death and you will have evil.

Moses equates life with what I call *Real Reality*, which is the spiritual reality, and death with superficial reality. When you associate to excess with your ego and its most extreme behavior, evil, you live an empty, dead existence.

This point is so important that Moses reemphasized the concept just a few verses later. "I have set before you, life and death, blessing and cursing: therefore, choose life that both you and your seed may live." (Deuteronomy 30:19)

Why are we given a choice between life and death? Naturally we will choose life. Moses did not say choose good, or choose blessing. He said, "Choose life!"

What kind of life, though? I believe that Moses did not just mean the physical aspect of life. Of course if you live, your seeds also live; that's too simple. I believe he referred to a spiritual kind of life. When you choose spiritual life, good and blessings naturally become a part of your life.

A similar idea appears in Romans 8:6. "For to be spiritually minded is life and peace."

I emphasize the Bible's point of view on the subject to strengthen my assertion that most religions miss the point even though it lies just under their noses. If we are to achieve spirituality, the pressure to follow certain religious laws and rituals and the use of intimidation to enforce them has to stop.

Instead of labeling us as good or bad, religion's focus should be on pure spirituality. When we are truly in touch with it, all the significant laws like the Ten Commandments will be carried out naturally.

Many of the religious rituals were useful thousands of years ago, like Jewish food-handling and consumption laws; but they have now become obsolete with modern sanitation. Aside from enforcing discipline and obedience, such rules may only serve to distract us from what is really important.

"Do it because we have done that for the last few thousand years" is not good enough anymore. Traditions are important but they aren't always sufficient to lead people deep enough to recognize their own spirituality. More and more people, even within the religious establishments, are realizing this truth.

Unfortunately, altering these religious organizations will be difficult because change often means losing the leading role they have played in society. However, power and control are the antithesis of spirituality.

Consider a very important question. *When you take away good and bad, what remains?*

You can get a clue to the answer from one of my favorite quotes, by Rumi. "Beyond ideas of wrong-doing and right-doing there is a field. I'll meet you there." This ineffable description is the foundation of spirituality.

Close your eyes and picture the field Rumi mentioned. What does it feel like? Please come back to this exercise often as you move along in the book and compare your experiences. I think you will find it quite interesting.

Religion: Past and Future

We must acknowledge the positive contribution religions have made. Judaism introduced monotheism beginning with Abraham and the special covenant between him and God. Judaism also introduced social values with emphasis on righteousness, altruism, and loving thy neighbor, through Moses and the Ten Commandments. Christianity, through Jesus, emphasized even more compellingly the concepts of love and forgiveness. Buddhism, through Buddha, promoted the concept of peace, which is a very fundamental principle in every religion. For example, the word Islam, in Arabic, is explained as surrender—surrendering to the will of God, but it was originally derived from the word "Asalam," which probably originated from "Shalom," the Hebrew word for peace.

> The truly religious man does not embrace religion; and he who embraces one has no religion.
>
> *Kahlil Gibran*

Sadly, we have changed since these concepts were first introduced. Much of our love has become egotistical. Some religious fundamentalists feel justified to kill in the name of God. Murder was not the original intent of spiritual leaders like Moses, Buddha, Jesus, and Mohammed, who many centuries ago promoted true spiritual teachings.

The word "religion" comes from the Latin word *religio*, which means scrupulousness. The etymology of the word points to the word "religare," which means to "bind together" and to "bind back." Both concepts are very important to understand. To bind together as in binding people together and to bind back or rebind, in my opinion, means rebinding with the core of who we really are.

I truly believe that one day, once more people fully connect with their spirituality, all religions will become one. *The Zohar*, The Book of Splendour, is the foundation of Jewish mystical Kabbalah. *The Zohar* states, "It is all one path." I sincerely believe that the true responsibility of religion is to help its followers walk that path. Why not stride it together?

To join together on one path, we need a nonreligious approach that is free of all the negative associations we may have absorbed about religion. The approach has to be very simple, purely spiritual, and free of dogma, rules, politics, and personal agendas. It requires less focus on the process and complete attention on the real essence of spirituality. I believe that every existing religion and tradition—including the small and less known ones such as Native American traditions, African tribal philosophies, Amazonian traditions, Hawaiian Shamanism, and many more—can contribute in its own way to such nonreligious religion.

Not that attempts haven't been made to achieve that. The Baha'i faith, as an example, undertook to unite all religious teaching without clergy and countless religious rules. However, even the Baha'i still has structure and its believers are required to recite certain daily prayers.

I was delighted to hear, recently, that a few hundred representatives of different faiths met during a special United Nations forum in New York called the "Millennium Peace Summit." Pleading to stop violence in the name of religion and promote tolerance was one of the main messages that came out of the summit. Great; that effort at unified spirituality is what we need in order to promote world peace.

But only a few days later, the Vatican through its Doctrine of the Faith office (the CDF), which not so long ago was named the Office of the Inquisition, issued a document (*Dominus Iesus*) announcing that not all religions, including other Christian denominations, are equal and that only the Roman Catholic Church is the proper church. One step forward, two steps back. Go figure.

Recently, a young woman came to see me for stress-related issues. She told me that about ten years ago, while she was still a minor, her parents joined the Jehovah's Witnesses organization and naturally, she was expected to follow their religious path. She didn't like her parents' newfound faith, for various reasons; and when she turned 18 she departed from Jehovah's Witnesses together with her siblings, who decided to follow her footsteps. Her parents were very upset and informed they would disconnect all ties with their children.

This divisive action is encouraged by this religious organization in certain circumstances. I asked a woman I know, also a Jehovah's Witnesses follower, about this belief. She explained that the rule is not to associate with apostates and that if it happened with her children she would do the same.

My patient experienced major stress as a result of negative dogma, but she realized that this attitude was exactly what she chose to run away from.

Where is spirituality in a religious rule that slashes family relationships? Why couldn't the children be respected for their individual beliefs and preferences?

Another patient, in his early twenties, told me that as a child, he had no motivation to do well in school because he kept hearing his parents preach about Armageddon and how the world the way we know it would soon come to an end. "What's the point of studying, if we were all going to die?" he asked himself.

Now, don't get me wrong. I have nothing against Jehovah's Witnesses. I have had long discussions with a few of their followers. I found their knowledge of the Bible to be quite remarkable, and many of their views about how we need to conduct our lives are noteworthy. The problem, in my opinion, lies with the way such principles are conveyed. Spreading negative messages about the destruction of the world as a way to convince people to join any religious structure needs to be avoided.

Recently I watched a TV program during which an Indian woman, an avid student of Hinduism, was asked what was the most important lesson she learned from Hinduism. She replied, "I learned that I am not a Hindu." What a great lesson! She realized that her essence transcended the concepts and beliefs of her own religion. Beautiful; my compliments to her teachers.

Just after India got its independence, Gandhi, known as Mahatma "Great Soul" Gandhi, was asked why he tried so hard to protect the Muslims in the country although he himself was Hindu. Gandhi's reply was similar in nature. "I am a Hindu

> The religion of the future will be a cosmic religion. It should transcend a personal God and avoid dogmas and theology. Covering both natural and spiritual, it should be based on a religious sense arising from the experience of all things, natural and spiritual in a meaningful way.
>
> *Albert Einstein*

and a Muslim and a Jew and a Christian. What's the difference?" he asked. "We are all children of God."

A great deal of wisdom and good intentions exists in different elements of all religions, taught and practiced by beautiful people. I have met many of them. Nevertheless, religion is fundamentally a belief system; and *spirituality is what is experienced when you fully let go of this very same belief system, without any need for a new one.* Does this make sense to you?

Heaven and Hell

A few months ago I noticed a message on a church's billboard that said, "A free trip to heaven—details inside." I had to laugh. "Is that it?" I asked myself. "Is that all religion has to offer, a trip to heaven?"

For me, gaining a reward only after I'm dead is a shallow promise. Can you imagine your mayor asking you for your vote by promising to improve health care in fifty years? Spirituality is the promise of a better life NOW, not after you die!

> I myself am heaven and hell.
> *Omar Khayyam*

This leads us directly to the question of heaven and hell. Christianity gets a lot of mileage from the concept of eternal reward or punishment. Unless you accept Jesus, you're headed straight to hell, regardless of how good you are. Does this make any sense to you? Other religions also stress the fact that adhering to religious rules will result in a better afterlife.

I certainly have a problem with such a concept. In a story, a warrior asked a Zen master to explain more about heaven and hell. The master looked at him and said, "I can do that, but first explain to me, what is the name of the general who is keeping such an ugly warrior like you in his army?"

The warrior was furious at the insult. He pulled out his sword and pointed it at the master's throat. "Apologize, old man, or you will die," he yelled.

The master quietly responded, "My dear friend, you have just opened the gates of hell."

The warrior quickly realized the message. Feeling embarrassed, he put his sword down and kneeled to ask for the master's forgiveness. The master smiled and whispered, "And now, my friend, you have opened the gates of heaven."

Whether hell and heaven exist after death is questionable. They are definitely not geographical territories. I once heard a rabbi describe hell as a state of shame. What kind of shame? The shame of committing bad deeds and not doing enough good ones while alive.

> All the way to heaven is heaven.
> St. Catherine of Siena

Regardless, I am more concerned with the real heaven and hell that exist in this lifetime. For me it is very simple. Hell is about extreme ego-based behavior, such as lust, greed, selfishness, hatred, and killing. Heaven is being spiritual right HERE, right NOW.

Sin is ego, nothing else. Soon I'll define spirituality for you, and good old ego will get a special treatment in this book.

Now I want you to close your eyes for a moment. Think about all the wars, killings, difficulties, and outrages you don't like about this world. Please take a moment and allow yourself to experience it.

How did it feel? Hellish, wasn't it?

Now take a deep, slow breath in and let all these thoughts go. Let yourself totally go. Clear your mind. Notice the rhythm of your breathing for a few moments. Doesn't that feel like heaven?

If you liked the second part of the exercise, feel free to practice it regularly.

So, Is There a God?

I don't consider myself religious, and by now I hope you understand why, but I do believe in the existence of a God. However, my idea of what or who God is differs from the version many people absorbed or developed. This is the place to tell you that, for the purpose of working with this book, you don't have to believe in God if you don't want to. I even have to qualify the entire issue of believing in God.

> If God did not exist, it would be necessary to invent Him.
>
> *Voltaire*

Belief can be misleading. Many people have a belief in God because they were taught to have it. Instead of a belief, you need to learn to KNOW God.

> Behold, the kingdom of God is within you.
>
> *Luke 17:21*

This inner knowing occurs only when you are more deeply immersed in spirituality. The realization of God will then come out of nowhere, naturally. It's quite amazing. The process of finding the real YOU is the same as finding God! This can be understood only when your true nature is fully realized. Your true nature is where you find the kingdom of God, but the only way to prove it is to experience it by yourself.

Cosmologists tell us that before the Big Bang (the big explosion that took place around 15 billion years ago and out of which the universe was created), matter and energy were one. They teach that all the forces as we know them today (gravity, electromagnetism, the strong nuclear force, and the weak nuclear force) were one combined force, called the Superforce.

Scientists postulate that what existed before the big bang was an incredible mass of energy condensed in one point, dubbed the "cosmic egg," out of which the universe was formed. We do not know scientifically how this cosmic egg came to be, only what happened microseconds after it "hatched." Outside of that cosmic egg was nothing, a sea of nothingness. Did this nothingness lay the cosmic egg? Was that nothing-ness God? Whatever gave birth to it was supremely intelligent.

Recently I read a message on a church's billboard: "God Commands—do you obey?" Do we want to imagine God as a general whom we have to be afraid of? Many people have negative associations with God. I know I did, but I have learned that God is not to be feared.

The opposite of fear is courage and confidence; but on a spiritual level, the opposite of fear is love. You cannot be frightened and experience true love at the same time. Surely it makes more sense to choose love of, rather than fear of, God.

God should be celebrated. As the sum total of all the beauty, intelligence, and love in the universe, what in God could scare us?

I've noticed that people feel much more comfortable with these ideas once they let go of childhood's religious concepts, which too often portray God as judgmental and vengeful. These characteristics are entirely human, and it seems rather naive to attribute mere human qualities to this supernatural, omnipotent being.

I recall a patient who didn't believe in the existence of God, but had no problems working with the spiritual practices I had taught her. Shortly after a conversation we had on the topic, she went to a resort in Arizona to relax and reflect, and when she came back I asked her how she felt while there. She described a deep sense of serenity and beauty and connection to nature. My response was: "That's God, for you." She had no problem accepting this concept of a Supreme Being.

> The eye with which I see God is the same eye with which God sees me.
>
> *Meister Eckhart*

God, in my opinion, is mostly passive in relationship with us. He is really about unlimited possibilities. All you need to do is to consider the universe to realize that.

These limitless possibilities are always available for us, much like unrestricted resources available in a large library. They are never forced onto us. What we choose to work on and how deep we want to go into the subject depends solely on us. The resources are available for us at all times.

We try to understand God by attempting to anthropomorphize Him. The early stories of the Bible reflect such an attempt as does the phrase "our Heavenly Father." God represents Intelligence with an infinite IQ, which we cannot possibly perceive. We can't even begin to understand what a person with an IQ of 500 will be like as no one has crossed the 250 level yet. God's Infinite Intelligence reflects all possible options from the beginning to the end of time. If a way were possible to observe the state of pre-creation through the eyes of the Supreme Intelligence, we would see all the possibilities from creation to perfection at the same time, before anything even started. This would be much like having an image of something you wanted to create before you even touched a chisel or a paintbrush.

When we connect with God we tap into this indescribable, tremendous intelligence and can then take positive action. God's main presence is to offer us tools and opportunities to grow, and the rest is up to us. At any moment of the day we are given all the right options to fully explore and manifest our spirituality, but the choice is always ours. It is our awareness that has to expand to be able to make the right choices.

I recall a story about a minister who was traveling somewhere in the Midwest when he suddenly noticed a beautiful property covered with trees, flowers, and green grass. He decided to pull over and knock on the door. The property's owner, a humble farmer, was happy to see the minister. "What a wonderful piece of land you have, my son. You should thank the Lord for giving you all that."

"I do," said the farmer, "I certainly do. But you should have seen the place when God had it all to himself."

Evolution vs. Creation: A New View

The everlasting debate between religion and science about our origin strikes me as very futile. The reason is that it is looked at as an either/or situation: We are either a result of a godly creation or a by-product of slow evolution. I believe that the truth is in a combination of the two. I would even go a step further and say that, aside from the arguments about the time frame—a few thousands years, according to religion, versus about 15 billion years, according to science—little difference exists between these two seemingly contradictory concepts.

"Creation-based" researchers and theologians want us to realize the astounding order and organization in the structure of the universe. Things fit too well for a simple set of circumstances to enable it all to exist. They point to a variety of parameters that are finely tuned to allow the universe to be the way it is now. They emphasize the fact that for just a couple of these parameters to come together, the odds were a million to one, let alone perfect synchrony.

For example, Creationists point out that the earth rotates in a perfect distance from the sun and in the right angle to enable life on our planet, claiming that this could not just be a simple coincidence. Such an amazing organization requires a Supreme Organizer to design it, rather than perfect alignment being a result of a big accident proceeded by a series of coincidences.

This makes much sense, because if you think about it, everything that humans ever created began with an idea, a thought, which was then pursued by certain actions to physically manifest the idea. Can we then assume that the creation of the universe was similar, that it started with a creative idea, which then manifested itself physically by unknown methods?

Those scientists who suggest evolution as the basis of the development of the universe do not disagree with the order, organization, or symmetry and with how things fit; but they attribute it to an evolutionary process. The universe has evolved to the level of what we see around us at the present time. Life was formed because the conditions were right, not the other way around.

Especially when it comes to our planet and its habitants, scientists, based on Darwin's concept of Natural Selection, propose a theory of adaptation and survival that guided nature to develop the way it has.

A scientist's biggest challenge is to work with the principle that matter can be neither created nor destroyed, just transformed; that something cannot come out of nothing. When it comes to the creation of the universe, what was the origin of the cosmic egg out of which the universe was created? When you can finally discover that source, then the question would be what was the source of that source, and so on to infinity.

The alternative option also poses a big challenge: Whatever it was, the source existed forever. It was not a product of creation.

Neither Creationism nor Evolutionism can be explained using the knowledge and tools we currently possess. Scientists believe they figured out how human beings evolved from a primitive microbe (the oldest microbes found so far living in salt crystals are 250 million years old), but they still can't explain how we turned from nonlife to life. Science cannot explain where microbes came from. As the great physicist Max Planck said, "Whence come I and whither go I? That is the great unfathomable question, the same for every one of us. Science has no answer to it."

Those who profess that we were created by God point to different loopholes in scientific theories and findings. For instance, they claim that, if it's true that humans originally evolved from fish into amphibians, then reptiles, birds, mammals, and finally into their present form, we should have found fossils that prove intermediate forms. We've found fossils of each one of these forms but no trace of in-between stages.

Recently scientists confirmed through experimentation a theory originally proposed by the physicist Peter Higgs that a subatomic particle called "boson" is what gives matter its mass. Dubbed the "Holy Grail of modern physics," this particle sheds some light on how matter was formed. But scientists face the same old question: how did boson come to be? This particle brings scientists closer to understanding how it all began but not where it originated.

That may remain a mystery. So is spirituality—one big mystery. It is not as important to crack this mystery as it is vital to experience this magical world, a world that starts where familiarity ends.

InteliTapping

In my opinion, what scientists call evolution is a distinct process of constantly tapping into the Ultimate Intelligence. To characterize this concept, I named this process *InteliTapping*.

InteliTapping allows everything in nature to draw from the Ultimate Intelligence the wisdom it requires to survive and evolve. This permitted the astounding development of the universe as we observe it today. Tapping into this Infinite Wisdom is an internal act, since this wisdom is fully embodied in us and in all of nature.

You'll notice that I use these terms alternately to convey the same meaning: Ultimate Intelligence, Universal Intelligence, Supreme Intelligence, Divine Intelligence, Spiritual Intelligence, Infinite Wisdom, and God. All refer to the Source, the Intelligence that started it all. Whatever name you use for the Source, feel free to substitute it for these terms in your mind if that aids your understanding.

Let's examine my idea that evolution is a process of continually drawing on the Source. We may think that our physical world came out of nothing, but it would be more accurate to assume that it came from a no-thing. The Universal Intelligence is a no-thing and yet it is everything. This non-physical, indescribable Intelligence created the physical world and continuously allows all living things to draw from its power and infinite knowledge base for growth.

When we look at the wonderful world of animals and their survival skills, we can see powerful application of the Divine Intelligence. For instance, when we observe how animals use colors to hide and adapt to their environment, it would be too simplistic to assume that this is a product of evolution. Scientists claim that within a span of a million years everything is possible, but I believe that these adaptation techniques require tremendous wisdom. How could different animals including snakes, spiders, and even fish go about manufacturing poison for survival purposes? How did they "think" of it, and even more remarkable, how were they able to produce it in the first place?

I believe that InteliTapping may replace the concept of the *survival of the fittest* with *survival of the smartest*. Many species survived not because they were so strong, but because they were able to make the necessary changes successfully to adjust to their environment through the process of InteliTapping. For instance, the nautilus survived over 500 million years mainly because it was smart. From being a bottom feeder it gradually learned how to float, and later even developed the ability to move forward by using jet propulsion power. How did it develop this sophisticated mechanism?

You may have heard about butterflies and various fish creating eye-like spots to confuse predators. Where did this amazing awareness of predators, plus a way to confuse them, originate? How do some types of stonefish produce fake algae to fool predators? How did the parrotfish come up with the idea and the ability to produce a transparent mucus-like cover at night to keep bigger fish from smelling them while they are asleep? How did it create the right chemistry to produce that protective substance? Sharks have reflector plates behind their eyeballs to improve sight by allowing more light into the eyes. Where did this knowledge in optics come from? Scallops may have up to 200 eyes for fast identification of danger; how did they do it?

I recently saw a documentary on the Discovery Channel about mussels in the streams of Missouri. Unlike the scallops, mussels don't have any eyes. These mussels developed exact replicas of lures that attract bass fish. When the bass tries to catch the lure, the mussel sprays its eggs, which then penetrate the bass's gills and feed off its blood, until they are ready to grow on their own. Think about it for a moment: Not having the ability to see, how did the "blind" mussels observe what the bass fish were after, and how were they able to design and create a small fish-like form that would lure the bass to come at them?

I won't go into the countless intricate details of the phenomenal human body, which includes trillions of smart cells and thousands of complex biochemical processes occurring each and every second, let alone the ability to think and be self aware. It's miraculous. I strongly believe that all of nature's potential to develop further is based on the ability to better use the Ultimate Intelligence we all comprise. Nature constantly draws from this Intelligence for the purpose of preservation and balance.

Creationists may use the above examples as proof that evolution can't account for these marvels, that only an intelligent creator—God—could have produced that progression. But if this were exactly the case, then why didn't God, the absolute Intelligence, create animals perfectly to begin with, without the need to evolve?

For example, the human brain was originally very basic. Called the reptilian brain, it consisted mainly of the brain stem and it was built to support strong survival instincts. After many years the mammalian brain, which among other things was geared to develop emotions, emerged. It took a few million years for the neo-cortex, or the thinking brain, to develop. This brain is capable of many of our day-to-day functions such as performing mathematical calculation and reasoning.

Experts agree that these three brain areas are not always coordinated. In fact, in times of stress they activate in the order of their creation. First the reptilian brain reacts, then the mammalian, followed by the neo-cortex. In other words, the brain responds to stressors first from the instinct region, then from emotion, and finally from reason.

Did you ever get mad at someone only to ask yourself the next day why you had to become so angry in the first place? The reason for that question was that the neo-cortex kicked in hours after the mammalian brain did. If the brain was directly designed and created by God, in His Infinite Wisdom He would have done a more effective job.

Because the brain developed only as humans' needs evolved, I believe that like all of nature, development happened through the process of InteliTapping. This phenomenon can more clearly explain on the one hand the development of the most complex and sophisticated organ in the planet, and on the other a somewhat uncoordinated and to a certain extent ineffective brain.

Every new perception of knowledge is always based either directly or indirectly on older knowledge. InteliTapping allows us to connect with the oldest, yet most complete source of knowledge.

We think that technology is great and that some of the inventions—for instance the light bulb, cars, airplanes, radar, and computers—are miraculous. But one way or another, all inventions are a result of InteliTapping. What drives us to InteliTap deeper begins with the basic need for preservation and overcoming challenges that may threaten our survival, but it also encompasses our curiosity and our innate desire to progress.

Somehow the Divine Intelligence will always make available the resources to maintain balance. Everything that happens in nature, every little organism, is important to maintain such balance. Every such organism InteliTaps not just to survive, but also to contribute indirectly to the overall state of balance in nature.

For the longest time researchers have unsuccessfully tried to find ways to overcome viruses, a cause of many diseases. I recall, not too long ago, a debate about the usefulness of viruses in nature. Hopefully, with further research and proper InteliTapping, scientists will be able to find solutions to disease conditions caused by deadly viruses.

In the meantime, researchers have found positive uses for certain viruses in treating cancer. For instance, just recently researchers at the University of Calgary in Canada implanted reovirus in mice to destroy brain tumours, usually resistant to most available treatments. Further studies also proved successful results with other forms of cancer such as breast, prostate, and pancreatic cancer. Human trials are planned for the near future.

So many puzzles remain that we still don't know how to understand or resolve. However, as we continue to learn how to InteliTap, not just indirectly, but also consciously and directly, more will be revealed about nature and ourselves in general.

According to the famous Stephen Hawking (*The Universe in a Nutshell*, Bantam Books, 2001), by the year 2600, taking the current rate of growth of population, the planet will be so overpopulated that people will be standing shoulder to shoulder and electricity use will make earth glow red-hot. How will we solve this challenge?

I guess answers will take a lot of InteliTapping. I would like to believe in a positive solution, rather than a pessimistic assumption that the population will decrease only as a result of some massive extinction like a nuclear disaster. We may still have 600 years to go, but we have to start thinking seriously now about these tremendous challenges ahead. Such solutions reveal themselves as we learn to understand more about nature and ourselves.

Intel Inside

As I key these words into my notebook computer, I notice a big label near the screen. It says, "Intel Inside, MMX Pentium Processor." This Pentium processor is an intelligent device that drives the entire computer. As an extension of the Infinite Intelligence, your spirit drives your mind/body system.

Look at any mechanical system and you get to the same source: What drives the car? The engine, of course. And what drives the engine? Fuel, which comes from crude oil. Oil comes from nature, which is the physical manifestation of the Universal Intelligence. On a different level, you, as the operator of the car, are driven by the brain that is driven by the mind that is driven by Universal Intelligence.

All intelligence is one. The spirit is the highest manifestation of this intelligence in us. Do you understand the power you have? You are driven by a five zillion megahertz Pentium, so to speak. Your processor is meant to be used for great things right now where you are. Allow this tremendous intelligence to pour out and see what miracles you can create.

During a discussion with my daughter, she told me that I had to "get a life."

"I have a life," my reply quickly followed.

"In that case," she said matter of factly, "get a better one."

We tend to stay within the comfort level of the ego and believe that's the life we need or have to live. But a much more than "comfortable life" is possible just beyond, one that offers a very different existence. A life propelled by Spiritual Intelligence offers a life that is filled with peace, love, joy, warmth, connectedness, helping, and sharing. This life is available to everyone, but we have to choose it to be able to experience it.

The Universe Model

We are a part of a huge universe. Currently over a hundred billion galaxies each contain billions of stars and planets. The Milky Way,

for instance, contains about two hundred billion s
able, isn't it?

At the present time, the universe is still rapidly ex
tists estimate that the universe will continue to expar
point it will begin to cool off and eventually die of "h
model is called "the open universe." Another the
closed universe" asserts that at some point gravitati
slow down and begin to reverse its rate of expansion
the condition that existed during the Big Bang. T
called the "big crunch," assumes that at some point, the Big Bang
may reoccur leading to the rebirth of the universe.

This brings interesting questions to mind: To where does the
universe expand? How much nothingness is out there? And what is
the difference, if any, between the space within the universe and the
space outside of the universe? It's all a mystery, so far at least, to our
finite minds.

Everything that happens to the universe on a macro level also
happens in the universe on a micro level. We are the reflection of the
universe and the process of human evolution may be very similar to
the evolution of the universe. The hypothesis of a "recycling"
universe can be found in every part of nature.

Let's see how the micro-macro theory enhances the understanding of the process the human race goes through. I believe that
everything we experience has three levels or dimensions to it: physical, psychological, and spiritual.

On a physical level, our micro-cyclical process is very clear. After
birth, the body expands until around midlife, then it begins a
shrinking process until it dies. The mind goes through a somewhat
similar process. It starts out as a clean slate—totally empty. Through
most of life, it develops, reaches a peak, and at some point, begins to
slow down. At the end, the mind as we know it dies.

The spirit, in contrast, is constant. Only our relationship with it
changes. For most people this relationship expands as they age.

The body and the mind constantly evolve. I'm not sure exactly
how and to what extent, but I'm quite certain that a few thousand

v, humans will look and operate much differently.
w we shall develop physically, but human form will
f our ever more sedentary lifestyle
me more and more spiritually aware, the way we
es will change dramatically. Will change ever end? I
As all of the human race achieves the highest level of
will become on a par with the Ultimate Intelligence.
just start over as a cosmic egg and wait for the next
ll over again

In Hinduism this eternal cycle of birth, death, and rebirth is called Samsara. Some even add suffering to the formula: birth, suffering, death and rebirth. Breaking free from this cycle is called Nirvana.

I believe that the evolution of the physical, mental, and spiritual aspects of human beings and of all nature will meet at the highest level and then re-integrate with its source, the Ultimate Intelligence—God. This may take a few trillion years, hopefully less.

For the Supreme Intelligence that exists beyond time and space, a few million years makes no difference; but for us mortals, it matters. We have to make every possible effort to live our life here to the fullest and contribute the best we can for the betterment of humanity.

Our Three Levels of Existence

Here is the complete model of the three levels I mentioned earlier:

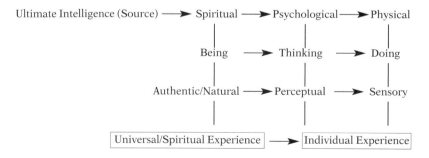

Do We Really Have Choice?

The question of free will versus a life that is predestined has forever preoccupied believers and philosophers alike. Believers struggle with the question somewhat more.

Ultimately, everyone wants to believe that he has choice; otherwise what's the point in motivating yourself to do anything? As in many other spiritually related topics, no one really knows the answer to that question.

Here is how I reconciled the paradox for myself. Imagine you want to paint a picture of nature. You may begin by visualizing the sunset, the ocean, the waves, and the sky. Once a clear picture forms in your mind, you have a few ways to bring this idea into a finished product. You can take your time or you can work intensively until you are done. You can start with the sky or you may choose to begin with the ocean.

I believe that the ideal picture of utopia was set right from the start, which means that the world and its habitants are evolving in a predestined manner. However, much flexibility is built into how the progression will happen, in what sequence, and how long it will take. We are equipped with the brushes and the paints necessary to produce this final picture, but how we use them is our choice. I believe that we do have the flexibility to change the course of events in many ways.

> **Pray as if everything depended on God, but live as if everything depended on you.**
>
> *Author Unknown*

Another metaphor I sometimes use is that we may be given specific ingredients to prepare a dish, but how we cook it and the amount of seasonings we add is up to us. This goes back to what I said earlier: The Supreme Intelligence has all we require; whether and how much we choose to tap into it is totally up to us.

My 15-year-old daughter came to me one day and explained that believing in fate helped her to reduce stress. A couple of weeks later she admitted that this attitude made her lazy at times, so she didn't think it was a good idea to believe in it.

I explained my view to her. In this context of choice versus destiny, I choose to treat my future as if it is 100 percent up to me, but in retrospect I regard what happened as if it was predestined to be. This may sound contradictory, but on a spiritual level it makes perfect sense.

Let's take as an example planning an event. I start working on all the details to make the event happen as if it is totally up to me, and of course it is. If for the sake of this example, the event did not materialize, I would say, "It was not meant to be, and there is a reason it happened that way."

I would then do two things. First, I would ask myself what I could learn about the event and the process that led to it. Then I would completely let go of any emotional overtones related to the experience. This way I avoid accumulating any emotional "garbage."

To make this work, two infallible principles have to be built in: When you have the choice, do the best that you can. When your choice plays out, look at the result to review the learning process you experienced, and then completely let it go.

Another example to demonstrate how free will works employs a treasure hunt reality game. In the game I will hide a treasure of some sort. I will then create a series of milestones, where one will lead to the other. The participants in the game will have to discover these milestones in order to progress until they find the treasure.

Spirituality is like that. It is hidden (ironically, deep within us) and the milestones are pre-arranged for us. But we still have to look for the signs and move from station to station to reach the prize.

The belief in next lives, which I will discuss later, presupposes that as we learn important spiritual lessons this time around, our next life will enable us to expand these lessons to an even greater degree. Next time around, we will choose more challenging experiences to go through, to learn the needed spiritual lessons. The ultimate purpose is for everyone inhabiting our universe to become completely spiritually aware.

This notion may more completely reconcile the debate between choice and destiny. On some level we always choose our paths in

life. Even not choosing is a choice with consequences. Some of the choice is made throughout
life and some on a much higher plane before we
come to this world.

> We choose our
> joys and sorrows
> long before we
> experience them.
>
> *Khalil Gibran*

My Personal Experience with Religion

Having been raised in the tradition of Judaism, I did not always see
God the way I do today. I have always been proud of my heritage,
but I must admit that I had some issues with Judaism. For many
years it was a burden for me. I expected to be judged based on
whether I attended synagogue and said my prayers, fasted during
Yom Kippur (the Day of Atonement), or kept all or most of the 613
rules that a Jew is expected to follow.

The fact that my life and happiness depended, at least in part, on
obeying the rules and customs of my religion did not sit well with
me. In my adult years, I avoided observing many of the traditions. I
could understand why secular individuals totally removed themselves from religion. And yet without it, something was missing
from my life.

Around the time I started to explore spirituality, my father passed
away. The pain of his death drove me back to Judaism. I wanted to
show respect for my father, and I went to synagogue to say special
prayers. The members of the synagogue turned out to be a valuable
source of support and comfort in my grief. This is, no doubt, one of
the many positive sides of religion.

Deep grief encouraged me to explore the connection between
spirituality and religion with more intensity and urgency. The rabbi
in the synagogue I attended was a very wise man who reinforced the
notion that although preferred, one need not observe all the rules
and regulations to be a good Jew. This was a relief.

Through continuous work I finally realized that I didn't have to
follow any unreasonable rules and that I didn't have to feel guilty or
fearful about it. This was an epiphany. I realized that such an omni-

scient God would not judge me and that I should not judge myself either. Rules may be fine for the purpose of self-discipline, but we should never forget what the real goal is, which is to completely manifest our spirituality.

I also changed how I referred to God in terms of sex. For thousands of years God has been referred to as a masculine figure. When we look carefully, we find that through genetics as well as social conditioning, masculinity represents power, order, control, strength, and survival. Female energy is more about creativity, intuition, caring, sensitivity, forgiveness, and empathy. God is a perfect mix of both.

For the last five thousand years we had the need to connect with God's masculine side. I believe that we are at a time when we have to connect more with God's feminine energy to be able to transcend our physically oriented reality, which is today still significantly more masculine in nature.

At present, we are more in need of a maternal figure. Nurturing, loving, generosity, and understanding are some of the qualities we search for.

The Bible refers to God exclusively as masculine. As a result, religion became very sexist. Some theologians believe that Jesus made references to the female aspects of God, but these references were modified later on in order to fit with the views of those who translated and edited the Scriptures and who were all men.

In Native American traditions, women represent the source of creation. As an Ojibwa saying goes, "Woman is forever eternal. Man comes from woman and to woman he returns."

Arriving at the conclusion that God is not an old man sitting on a throne somewhere up in the sky, deciding to punish someone because he or she was not following certain religious rules, was indeed an enormous revelation for me. I then realized how much burden religion could put on people who, to a great degree, were brainwashed and as a result unable to exercise healthier choices.

God is not a punishing entity. She does not have to be. Through the creation of the ego, the mechanism for self-punishment is built in. Retribution is not initiated by God but by our beliefs. The Qur'an says: "Surely, God wrongs not men, but themselves men wrong." We have a conscience, which serves as a built-in punishment and reward system. God does not even have to interfere. She gave you the tools; the rest is up to you.

Focusing too much on ego-based agendas simply blocks us from being able to InteliTap into the innate wisdom inside; we are then removed from God and everything She represents. That's severe punishment. By the same token, when we focus on soul-based activities, we unlock the door to the Unlimited Intelligence that carries resources and answers for any challenge we may ever face. That's the ultimate reward.

For me God is the Supreme Intelligence who makes everything—in nature, in our planet, and in the rest of the universe—tick accurately, harmoniously, just like the best Swiss watch, even if it does not always feel that way to us.

Poor God. Of the entire universe, only humans give Him problems, but it's all God's choice. This is the price for giving us free will. All God really wants from you is to figure it out. Do that and you have fulfilled your purpose. When you, I, and everyone else do this, we will then reach the peak of our spiritual evolution. This is how, I believe, God wants it to be.

What do we have to figure out? First and foremost who we really are. Secondly, our connection with others as well as with nature. This is the ultimate picture of our existence.

I went from believing in God, to disbelieving in Him, to later realizing that God does exist, but in a very different way compared with what I first thought. When I realized that I was not under God's microscope every second of the day, at least not the way religion wanted me to believe, all my problems with religion were completely dissolved. I could see my religion naked. I realized that religion failed in effectively promoting what is always at our core: pure spirituality. I was transformed right then and there.

You can call it God, or you can call it the Universe or Nature; it's all the same power, the same Intelligence. As I realized what God wasn't, I realized for the first time what She was: a tremendous source of wisdom, creativity, and love that lives in us and in every living thing. We don't need to look anywhere else—God is inside and all around us. We can experience Her by embracing our spirituality, which lies within each of us waiting to be found. God is real and you can fully experience Her in your heart, but only if you choose to.

Harold Kushner, in his book *When Bad Things Happen to Good People* (paperback edition by Avon Books, New York), reached a similar conclusion. Kushner makes a distinction between an act of nature and an act of God. God does not make people die. God endows people with strength to deal with tough situations.

God helps people to connect deep inside, to connect with Him. This is, in my opinion, what "binding back" really means. This connection existed before we were born and separated as we grew up. Our purpose is to rebind with the Source. Don't you prefer this kind of God, a God who is in us as opposed to one who is totally external?

If you are an atheist, you probably don't believe in the idea of God at all. That's okay. Your spirituality is still available within you. For me it is the connection with your true essence, your real substance that is important. Meher Baba said, "The finding of God is the coming to one's own self." As I indicated before, when you find yourself, you find God. What a deal!

You may ask at this point, "So how do I find myself?" Have patience, as I will dedicate a big part of the book to the answer for this important question.

A Man-Made Crisis

About 80 percent of my patients are women. Is this because women have more emotional problems? Or perhaps because they are more open about such issues?

I truly believe that the reason women live longer than men, an average of eight years longer in North America, is because of their openness and how they deal with their feelings. As a result, women handle stress better.

Men are much more repressed. The message that men receive in childhood is that crying is not manly, and they are encouraged to suppress anything that feels like weakness. Girls get similar messages, but the communication is much stronger with boys, sometimes accompanied by ridicule or even punishment.

Studies show that men are less likely to recognize and seek help for depression.

A few years ago I went with my family to a movie called *Stepmom* with Julia Roberts and Susan Sarandon. I expected a comedy, but the movie had some sensitive scenes and I found myself quite teary. Caught unprepared, I had to run to the washroom to get tissue paper. On the way there I met a woman I know, who was also rushing to the washroom for the very same reason. A few months later, we met at a party and laughed about it. Another woman who happened to overhear the conversation approached me and said, "I have never heard of men who cry, unless someone close to them died, let alone admitting it in public."

That's the expectation men carry, and it is not a healthy one, especially when it comes to the spiritual journey. Neither is it a healthy requirement in male relationships with women and children they love. All of society suffers from unreasonable demands that males repress emotions, yet pressure is imposed through social conditioning from infancy. How reasonable is that?

I discovered that getting in touch with my spirituality made me a much more sensitive person. But in a typical male fashion, I first saw sensitivity as an appalling weakness. I tried to do "inner work" to overcome it. In time I accepted the fact that nothing is wrong with embracing sensitivities, even if it involves crying, for males or females. In fact, this type of crying comes from a very warm and beautiful place inside and only serves to enhance our spiritual qualities as human beings.

I am not through with men yet. And women, if you share your life with a man, encourage him to read at least this section of the book.

A few years ago I gave a lecture to members of a Christian congregation. At the end, a woman in the audience asked me what I would suggest to women so that they could finally achieve equality with men.

Without even thinking came my answer, "Why would you want to come down to a man's level?" As all the women in the audience applauded, I realized that men are in for the greatest crisis ever. Men are gradually losing their role as the sole provider and protector of the family unit. Women have become more independent and know how to take care of themselves. They have undertaken a part of the traditional male role.

Where does that leave men? It leaves them with one big identity crisis. I can already see the early signs of it in some of my male patients, but within ten years it will become significantly more critical.

The good news is that crisis is always an opportunity for growth, especially spiritual growth. I hope that more men will begin to wake up and realize what will happen if they don't change, if they don't balance their lives rather than try to defend their artificial world of power and control.

Obviously not all men are bound by these restrictive customs. Every so often I meet men who have come to realize that feelings are important and that spirituality is not frivolous. This encourages me, but it is definitely not enough. Men need to put much more focus into this realm.

I believe that eventually, through the evolutionary process, men and women will be equal, but first I foresee women growing to a level that will give them the control even in areas that were previously male dominated. We started with one extreme and the pendulum will soon swing to the other side, though hopefully not to the same level of extremity; and then gradually balance will be established. This will result in manifesting our wholeness that, like God, is a perfect blend of masculinity and femininity. Boys will still be boys and girls will still be girls but they will be balanced in responsibility, rewards, and social expectations.

At this point of evolution, this idea may be difficult to accept for many people, but I strongly believe that balance is bound to happen. The only question that remains unanswered in my mind is how long it will take to complete.

And my advice to women? Let me quote Mary Wollstonecraft, an Anglo-Irish feminist and author from the 18th century: "I do not wish women to have power over men, but over themselves." My extensive work with women has proven to me that they are on the right track.

Now it's men's turn.

What Exactly Is Spirituality?

I have talked about the difference between spirituality and religion and I even presented to you the ultimate shortcut to spirituality, but I haven't yet established what spirituality really is. So let's explore that now.

Let me start with my first definition: Spirituality is living life to its FULLEST. Sound simple enough?

But what does it mean to live life to the fullest? Since life basically consists of moments, spirituality is living life moment by moment.

The problem is that we can only do that when we become who we really are, and who we really are is spiritual. Sound like a Catch-22? Let's further clarify it.

Here is what has been stated so far:
1. Living a spiritual life is living life to the fullest.
2. Living life to its fullest is living life moment by moment.
3. To be able to do that, we need to become who we really are.
4. Who we really are is purely spiritual.

These assumptions raise further questions that are quite intriguing:
1. What does it mean to be fully spiritual?
2. What does it mean to live life moment by moment?
3. What is that "spiritual self" all about? Where does it come from and how can we fully manifest it?
4. Who are we anyway?

> The aim of life is to live, and to live means to be aware, joyously, drunkenly, serenely, divinely aware.
>
> *Henry Miller*

Living life to the fullest and living life moment by moment are somewhat abstract concepts. Let me, therefore, give you a second definition that is more tangible and that I hinted at when I discussed the "Ultimate Shortcut." Here it is: Spirituality is DEEP AWARENESS without mental processing. What is deep awareness? Let's do an exercise that will promote further understanding.

How We See Things

I want you to do a short experiment. Take a sheet of tissue paper and spend three minutes exploring it. Don't put it off, please do it now! Trust me on this. We have to move from knowledge to deeper understanding. We don't want to just know about spirituality, but to experience it. Okay, now back to studying the tissue paper. Three minutes only.

How was the experience? What did you think? How did you feel? Were you bored? Did you explore the paper from all angles? Were you wondering why I asked you to do this exercise? Did you often check your watch? Did your mind drift to other areas and if it did, were those topics or experiences related to the subject?

And here is the most important question: Did you explore the tissue paper with your mind or with your senses? For instance, did you notice if the material was white, odourless, light, and soft? Did you confirm your visual impressions by rubbing it between your fingers, even smelling it? These are all forms of sensory awareness.

Mental processing would constitute a thought you had while looking at the tissue. "I need to buy another box." "This is boring, I have to kill three minutes, what's the time now, who cares about a stupid piece of paper?" Spirituality is deep awareness without mental processing, remember that? I don't know if the tissue example is meaningful for you, but I hope you understand what I want to emphasize here.

The general model of human experience is in a sense similar to what any computer does. The computer model looks like this:

Input ⟶ Processing ⟶ Output

And here is the human equivalent:

LIFE (Occurrences)—Input (5 Senses) ⟶ Processing (Mind) ⟶ Concept (Subjective Experience) ⟶ Output (Reaction) ⟶ Perceived Life (Subjective Reality)

All kinds of things happen in life. People don't believe you or are not nice to you for no apparent reason; you get stuck in the slowest line in the store; your car breaks down in the middle of a highway and so forth. Normally, life includes many positive experiences as well.

You take all this data in through your senses: sight, smell, sound, taste, and touch. This sensory-based information is fed into the processing part of the mind, which examines the information and compares it to your beliefs, expectations, past experiences, and values.

This results in an internal experience, which in turn creates a specific reaction. Such reactions create our perceived life or subjective reality.

Here is an example: Suppose a friend promised to help you move some furniture. He cancels on you at the last minute. You remember how you helped him move his stuff last year. "How dare he?" you ask. "He didn't even give me any reasonable excuse." Angered by his rejection, you decide never to talk to your friend again.

I know this is an extreme example but can you see how this works? How you process ongoing events determines your experience and reactions to them. Ultimately, your reactions determine your outcomes in life. You make the choice.

For instance, had you responded more sympathetically to the situation and given your friend a second chance, your friendship could have continued. Who knows, your friend would have probably helped you the next time you needed him.

Let's Examine the Spiritual Process

The equivalent formula in the spiritual arena starts the same, but it avoids the processing component and consequently the chain reaction that such processing creates.

$$LIFE \longrightarrow Senses \longrightarrow Awareness \longrightarrow Real\ Reality$$
$$(sensory\text{-}based\ experience)$$

Your friend tells you he can't help you although he had promised to do so. You take the information in, perhaps through a conversation over the phone, and if you do no processing, you will feel no reaction. You are faced with a fact: your friend is not available, and so you call someone else instead. No bad feelings, no loss of friendships, and also, no loss of time and energy trying to interpret and analyze the situation. Instead of dwelling on the problem, you are free to figure out a new solution. Quite different from the first scenario, isn't it?

> If the doors of perception were cleansed, everything would appear to man as it is—infinite.
>
> *William Blake*

Your concepts about life are nothing but a thought process, not life itself. Perceived life does not equal real life! Think about it for a moment. What type of lenses do your senses wear? When you take them off you can see life just the way it is. Away goes subjective reality and with it the unnecessary suffering that our perceptions cause. You can now enjoy true freedom that can be found only in Real Reality.

Living in the Deep Moment

Can we really free ourselves from the mental processing that so deeply pervades every aspect of our lives? Maybe not, but we can dramatically reduce it.

When you process, in most cases you really don't live in the moment. You live in the mind, and herein lies the biggest problem of mental processing. When you live in your mind you can either focus on the past or on the future. Your friend said he couldn't help you—that's a fact. As soon as you started to process it, you were dwelling on the past ("Why did he do it?") and on the future ("I don't want to be his friend anymore").

A Buddhist tale tells about a teacher and his student who were just about to cross the river when they noticed a naked woman trying unsuccessfully to do the same. The master asked the student to help him carry the woman across. The student assisted but was surprised. How could his master touch a woman, let alone a naked one?

After a few hours of trying to come to terms with it, the student could not hold back any longer. "How could you hold a naked woman?" he asked.

The master smiled and said, "I left the woman on the riverbank two hours ago; you are still carrying her with you."

You can choose either to live in the moment (the present) or in the mind (past or future). Do you know what the clinical condition of someone who lives mostly in the past is called? Depression. And what is the clinical condition associated with dwelling too much on the future? Anxiety.

Can you now understand how people get themselves in trouble? "My boyfriend left me" is a fact. "My boyfriend left me and I can't live without him" is processing that can lead to depression. If you're really good at it, you may even add, "and I will never find somebody else." Now you have anxiety too. Your boyfriend left you. PERIOD! Less processing, fewer bad feelings. No processing, no bad feelings.

Can we not feel sad about a friend who left us, or get angry at a boss who criticized us, or become frustrated because we lost money on the Stock Exchange? Of course we can, and most times we really need to. It is the prolonged lingering, the constant processing, at times to a level of obsession, which we need to learn to avoid.

But wait a minute. Will this not lead to apathy, insensitivity, or indifference? Not at all. That is called repression. Living in the moment is quite the opposite. When you live in the moment you take things as they are and do the best you can with it.

This is really important to understand: The journey to spirituality stops at the moment. As soon as you fully connect with it, you have arrived!

What is also called a present? A gift. Can you see why we call living in the moment the "present?" It is a true gift of life.

I prefer to talk about the "deep moment" as opposed to just "moment." Because people take moments for granted, they very often treat such moments superficially. Going deep into the moment allows you to move from the analyzing aspect to a deeper level of the experience.

> Let us not look back in anger or forward in fear but around in awareness.
>
> *James Thurber*

Woody Allen once said: "Most of my life I don't enjoy so much, and the rest I don't enjoy at all." I would hope that after so many years of psycho-analysis Woody would finally understand that living too much in the mind can cause much unhappi-ness; and if not, that's fine, too, since in the mean-time he has produced many good movies.

The Deep Moment Is Really a Miracle

Take the tissue paper in your hands again and feel it. This paper is a real miracle. Think about how it came to be: from the seed of a tree sprouting in the ground, through years of maturing, withstanding heat, cold, winds, and other weather-related conditions. The tree is then cut and processed in the mill, turned into paper, and refined into a tissue paper that normally you would use for a second, then throw in the garbage without a minimal sign of appreciation or gratitude. Now pretend that you are a three-year-old child exploring a tissue for the first time. Notice how the experience changes.

All creation is indeed a miracle but we take a lot of it for granted. We have become too complacent, too busy, to notice the little things in life. Life has become so rushed, with so many distractions, how can we possibly enjoy it?

The moment connects you with creation and with life, and is, therefore, a total miracle. Not only that, but the moment contains many delights. It is jam-packed with energy, beauty, serenity, and harmony. It is energizing, calming, and invigorating. It enables us to connect with our true essence and experience bliss and joy. We need to feel it and explore its beauty and depth. But we can do it only with a mind that is clear of preconceived notions—just like a child. The deep moment IS spiritual and when you connect with it YOU manifest your spirituality, instantly.

Have you ever had an experience, perhaps playing a game, creating something, or being engaged in a hobby, in which you were so absorbed that you "lost yourself in the moment" and forgot everything else in the world? That's living in the deep moment.

Yes, you can still keep your watch, but don't let it run your life. And yes, you can look at old pictures and reminisce, or plan what you're going to do next Christmas. But when you allow the mind to wander too often to the territories of Past and Future, you miss out on life. Just remember to come back to the here and now, fully, with little or no processing. PERIOD!

We sometimes call living in the deep moment "living in the now." I refer to NOW as No Other Way, and there isn't. The alternative option is an artificial life that is filled with suffering, denial, and disappointment. It is a life filled with questions that solve nothing. Why did it happen? Why me? Why didn't I? How could she do that? Living in the moment is the answer to all these questions.

During a discussion with a young patient who did not like high school and was on the verge of quitting, she stated that she did not enjoy school and she would rather "live in the moment, instead." What she really meant by that was that she didn't want to do uncomfortable tasks, such as homework, and was trying to avoid responsibility.

That is not what living in the deep moment means. True living in the moment treats every moment equally and doesn't accept only "preferred" ones. All moments are equal, whether they give us pleasure and enjoyment, or require us to do important things that may be temporarily unpleasant or uncomfortable.

Lovemaking is a very good example of what living in the moment means. I remember a man working as an executive in a fast-paced financial corporation who complained about his sexual dysfunction. He explained that while in the office, he was constantly thinking about his wife, but when he was in bed with her he very often worried about his business deals.

To engage in sex, you have to get naked—physically, of course, but also mentally. You need to forget everything else and be fully absorbed in the act itself. Time ceases. This is a totally sensual experience. If you try to think about how you are performing, analyze what you are doing, wonder what time it is, or worry about business deals, you've lost it.

Similarly, when you want to experience any moment deeply, your mind has to get naked. That's the "stop processing" principle I have been emphasizing. When your mind is clear, you can enjoy whatever it is that the moment has to offer and you can realize its depth and beauty.

When you get to the end of your life and you reflect, I can promise you that you will never regret not working more hours, making more money, or watching more TV. If anything, you will regret missing out on life. You will miss not spending enough time with your children, parents, and friends. You might regret being too serious, too uptight, holding on to grudges, and not slowing down to enjoy the little things in life.

To turn hindsight into foresight, start doing those things you know you might regret not doing when you grow older.

This is a powerful exercise we all need to practice regularly. Why don't you take a short break to practice this exercise right now? You can write down the results at the end of the book. Examine your life. If you know one thing without a shadow of a doubt that you should be doing right now, or else you may regret missing it, what would it be? Can you do it?

Slowing Down to Accomplish More

Studies indicated that the reason French people have fewer heart attacks compared to Americans relates to their consumption of wine. It is believed that the ingredient responsible for the benefit is resveratrol, which acts as an antioxidant. Although I can see the correlation, I do not believe that wine is the only reason for the cardiovascular benefits.

I personally realized that the French people take their time more than we do. Here is one example. On a recent visit to Paris I needed a new battery for my camera. As I reached the counter of a nearby photo store, the clerk handed an envelope to another customer, who opened the envelope and started looking at his photos. While he was occupied, I asked the clerk if I could get the battery I needed. She explained that she was still busy with the first gentleman and asked me to wait.

That may explain why the French people don't suffer from cardio-vascular disease as much as Americans although French are considered the biggest consumers of fat, more than any other country in the world. They simply take their time and avoid, whenever possible, doing more than one task at a time. I encountered that difference many times while in France.

Interestingly, I also noticed that on an average basis, French people smoke more and exercise less. This phenomenon, dubbed "The French Paradox," cannot be explained just by the amount of wine they drink. I looked more carefully into it, and found out that other Europeans such as Italians also consume similar levels of wine, but they still do not have France's low mortality rate associated with coronary heart disease. The answer, in my opinion, has to do with the difference in stress levels. French people may, in fact, experience lower levels of stress because they take their time to do things, they take breaks (a couple of hours for a lunch break is traditional), and they don't do a million things at once, as we sometimes tend to do.

"Slow" is the language of living in the moment. Think about drinking a cup of tea, coffee, or wine, strolling on the beach, even making love. You can enjoy such activities most, only by slowing down.

This is one of the problems with our speed-obsessed Western society and its pursuit of success. The cost of doing things too fast has too often compromised quality. To live life fully, you have to become intimate with the moment, to live each moment with great passion. This can happen only when you delve deeper into your present experience and when you meet the present naked, without any predetermined ideas and expectations about the experience.

If I Had My Life To Live Over

I would make more mistakes next time.
I'd relax.
I'd like to limber up. I would be sillier than I have been this trip.
I would take fewer things seriously. I would take more chances.
I would climb more mountains and swim more rivers.
I would eat more ice cream and less beans.
I would perhaps have more actual troubles, but
I'd have fewer imaginary ones.
You see I'm one of those people
who live sensibly and sanely,
hour after hour, day after day.
Oh, I've had my moments, and if
I had it to do over again,
I'd have more of them. In fact,
I'd try to have nothing else.
Just moments, one after another,
instead of living so many years ahead of each day.
I've been one of those persons
who never goes anywhere without
a thermometer, a hot-water bottle,
a raincoat and a parachute.
If it had to do it again,
I would travel lighter than I have.
If I had my life to live over,

I would start barefoot earlier in the spring
and stay that way later in the fall.
I would go to more dances.
I would ride more merry-go-rounds.
I would pick more daisies.
—*Nadine Stair, 85 years old, Louisville, Kentucky*

Please remember that the past and the future happen in your mind. Only the PRESENT really exists.

Let me ask you this: Can your appetite be satisfied with a meal that you had yesterday, or a meal you plan to have tomorrow? Of course not. In a similar way, you can enjoy and draw true satisfaction only from connecting with the here and now. Remembering some past experiences as well as future thinking can also be experienced in the moment as long as they are not overly processed or don't become a form of distraction from what needs to be experienced now.

One day I became more aware of my own rushed mentality. It dawned on me that I was rushing through an activity to complete it quickly so that I could start rushing through the next task. I realized that I needed to make the process enjoyable and not just the achievement of a goal. For instance, during the morning hours I looked forward to the noontime break, and in the afternoon I thought about going home. At the end of the day I thought about the weekend and so on and so forth.

When was this vicious cycle ever going to end? At death? I decided to break the cycle by starting to focus more on what I was doing, and avoid running future scenarios in my mind. This shift of consciousness enabled me to get the full benefit from my present experiences.

Naturally, we don't want to ignore the future. Since our present actions affect our future directly, we want to have future awareness. A broad difference exists between constantly living in the future

> The moment one gives close attention to anything, even a blade of grass, it becomes a mysterious, awesome, indescribable, magnificent world unto itself.
>
> *Henry Miller*

and taking time to plan for the future. The latter can also be an "in the moment" activity when kept in balance.

Slowing down enables you to accomplish more of the important things in life, because it allows you to connect with the deep moment, thereby accelerating your spiritual pursuit.

Mind-ful-ness

The term *mindfulness* is widely used to describe the process of connecting with the moment. I must admit that I'm not fond of this term because it creates for me a picture of a "full mind." Aren't our minds full enough already? Do we need to fill them up with more? I prefer the terms "living in the deep moment" or "becoming fully aware"—both mean the same thing. When you become deeply aware of what is happening just the way it is, the mind at that moment is actually empty of any data and is experiencing a pure state of being. This is a process of disengaging from the racing mind and re-connecting with Real Reality.

Let's learn some practical methods to accomplish that.

A Small Test

Close your eyes and take a few moments to relax as you breathe very slowly. Now start counting with each exhalation as follows: Breathe in slowly, breathe out, and count one. Breathe in again, breathe out and count two and so forth. If you get distracted by a thought and lose count, start the counting all over again. Try that for a few minutes.

Were you able to concentrate or did your mind wander? If it did, at what count, and where did your mind go? Can you see how easy it is for the mind to wander?

I recommend that you repeat this exercise from time to time to improve your ability to control and focus your own mind.

As you progress, you will notice that you can sustain your concentration for longer.

Now that I have mentioned breathing, we have to go into this subject in greater depth.

Breathing for Balance

We have to breathe in order to live. However, most people breathe very shallowly. You can live eating hamburgers and hot dogs, but this kind of poor quality nutrition will eventually catch up with you. The same goes for poor breathing. Breathing is the barometer of the entire mind-body system. Ongoing stress, anxiety, and illness will result in poor breathing. Conversely, you can improve the quality of your system by improving the quality of your breathing.

Take a deep breath in and then exhale. If you are like most people, you probably used your chest to get air in and then get rid of it even faster. Yes, you got enough air to survive, but definitely not enough oxygen to allow the body all that it needs.

Breathing techniques are one of the first things I teach my patients. I can probably write a book about "breathing stories" my patients have told me after they practiced it for a while. Only recently, a patient told me that her son was not doing so well in a national athletic competition. She noticed that he was holding his breath and seemed nervous, so she told him to do some deep breathing before continuing his routines. He listened to her and ended up winning the competition. I would like to teach you more about this wonderful mechanism that can dramatically improve your physical and emotional well-being.

I associate the process of breathing with three major components. The first one is *mechanics*.

Breathe in, using your diaphragm, straight from the center of your belly. Put one hand on your chest, where nothing much should move. Put your other hand on your belly.

Breathe in and imagine filling your abdomen with air. Hold it in for a few seconds. Then very slowly exhale. Rest for a few seconds and then repeat. No one should be able to see or hear it; it needs to be very gentle and effortless. Ideally, you should do one cycle of inhale, hold, exhale, and wait (before starting the next cycle) for about 10 seconds. Make the exhalation longer than the inhalation.

This diaphragmatic breathing translates to about six cycles per minute, to begin with. Gradually you will be able to do five, four, even three cycles per minute. Try that for a couple of minutes and find out how it feels.

How did it go? If it felt strange and somewhat unnatural, it probably means that you have become accustomed to stressful-type breathing, which is fast and shallow. You have some work to do!

Don't worry, though, it will become easier with practice. Most people feel calmer and more relaxed after a few minutes of deep breathing. You can also practice the breathing a few times in front of the mirror to make sure that your breathing is deep, by noticing that your shoulders do not move up and down, a movement that indicates shallower breathing. All movement has to be in the abdomen, moving out while inhaling, and in while exhaling.

I cannot emphasize enough how beneficial it can be to practice deep breathing throughout the day. Its effect on the nervous system is remarkable.

One of the assessments I do with my patients is called Heart Rate Variability. This assessment helps to monitor the activities of the sympathetic and parasympathetic branches of the autonomic nervous system, which regulates important body systems such as respiration, endocrine, cardiovascular, digestive, and immune. When asked to think of stressful situations, the negative changes are immediately visible on the graph as emotions directly affect the autonomic nervous system. But when deep breathing follows such emotional upset, the positive effect on the graph is unbelievable, and the person practicing it usually feels it as a comfortable sense of relaxation and calm.

In addition to its calming effect on the mind and body, deep breathing can balance the autonomic nervous system. That improves the function of many subsystems in the body. Not bad for a technique that is free, effortless, and that our bodies come already equipped with.

After you have practiced the breathing mechanics for a while, you can move to the next level. The second component I attach to breathing is *concentration*.

A point comes in the training where the effect of the breathing grows even higher. This happens when you can stop thinking and concentrate solely on the breathing, as if nothing else exists. Disengaging the analytical mind and being in the deep moment by fully connecting with your breathing is what does it. Ideally, this happens naturally, without a great effort to make it happen.

> **Go back to your breathing now. This time, as you breathe deeply, pay complete attention to your breathing. Focus on either the flow of air, or your belly going in and out or, better yet, the overall feeling of breathing deeply. If you get distracted while doing it, just gently resume concentration on your breathing as soon as you notice the distraction. Try that now and see how it feels.**

With practice, this will become more natural. Whenever you can, just take a few deep breaths in and exhale slowly. This can take place while you are driving (eyes opened and focused on the road, please), reading, watching TV, etc. However, three to five times a day, set aside a few minutes to stop everything and concentrate solely on your breathing. If you can extend the time to five or ten minutes for each session, that would be even better, but start with what is most comfortable, which is the only way it will work for you.

You can do the above-mentioned breathing technique with your eyes closed to induce relaxation, or with your eyes opened to emphasize focus and alertness. This will be very energizing for you. It's

> Breathing in, I
>   calm my body.
> Breathing out, I
>   smile.
> Dwelling in the
>   present moment,
> I know this is a
>   wonderful
>   moment.
>   *Thich Nhat Nanh*

like taking a mini vacation and your mind and body will thank you for it.

By the way, the more you don't have time to do it, the more you need to do it!

Interestingly, in many traditions the word for breathing, spirit, and life force is identical. Examples include Latin (*spiritus*), Hindu (*prana*), and Chinese (*chi*). As well, the Hebrew word for soul is *Neshama* and for breathing it is *Neshima*. The Hebrew word for spirit is *Ruah*, which also means wind.

Please remember this: You cannot breathe deeply and be tense at the same time! Deep breathing immediately works on the brain to bring about release and relaxation, and you don't have to believe in that for it to work. That's the way the system is wired.

Breathing builds an instant bridge from the mind to the deep moment. It enables the gentle disengagement from your thought process, bringing your attention into your senses. First you connect with the feeling of breathing, and then you can shift your awareness to your senses. Let me explain this with a series of very powerful awareness exercises.

F   E   E   L

Please read this paragraph first, then close your eyes and practice the exercise described: start by breathing deeply and slowly for a few moments. Then, I would like you to return to normal breathing but keep concentrating on it for a while with your eyes closed. As you do, notice how your body feels on the chair, the bed, or wherever you are. Do that for ten to twenty seconds, and then notice how your clothes feel on your skin, for the same period of time. Next, notice the feeling of your feet in the shoes if they are on, the shoes touching the floor if you are sitting, the touch of jewelery or your watch on your skin. Feel the air's temperature, notice sensations in your body. The order is not important. After you have done that, become aware of your breathing again and then open your eyes. Please take a few minutes to complete the exercise now.

Did this exercise feel strange to do? Was your mind racing or were you able to concentrate? Did you analyze your experience, or did you just immerse yourself in it, forgetting everything else?

The difference between a pure experience and an experience that has been tainted by a thinking process is demonstrated in the following examples. Notice the difference between the facts and the analysis or commentary on the facts:.

Moment: The temperature is warm.

Mind: It's so warm in this room. I am boiling.

Moment: I am sitting on a slant.

Mind: This chair is so uncomfortable.

Are you getting a feel for the difference between the two? If you were able to follow the exercise while avoiding excessive mental processing, you must have felt calm. If you have difficulties feeling that, you simply need more practice because this important exercise represents a pure deep moment experience.

This is when your true essence comes to the surface. It will never force itself. It just waits for a gentle invitation. Open the door for it and experience the true bliss of your authentic self.

This exercise is very effective in creating deeper experiences. Do it three times a day and watch how much calmer you become.

The Drama of Your Life

For the most part, we live life as a drama. Imagine yourself an actor in a play. Say you play a beggar. You go backstage to prepare, where you dress yourself as a beggar and pick an old hat for collecting the coins. Your scene is coming now. You go on stage and give your best performance ever. The audience cheers enthusiastically and the show is over.

But wait, what's going on here? Instead of going backstage to change clothes, you go outside to a corner of a busy street, lay the hat on the pavement, and start begging pedestrians for money.

What happened? Did you forget who you were outside the theater? Go home, put the costume

> All the world is a stage, and all the men and women merely players.
>
> *Shakespeare*

aside, have dinner, enjoy the evening. Why are you still living your role on stage?

You would never do that, right? I have news for you. To some degree you are doing it. You live most of your life in some sort of role in some sort of drama. You may play the role of a mother/father, sister/brother, friend, rescuer, problem solver, fixer, or peacemaker, to name few. You have invested so much in your drama that by now you believe this is how life should be.

This kind of drama determines your priorities and wastes a lot of your energy. When you play a role, you need to find other actors, a stage, and an audience. Others don't realize they're part of your drama, so they must be manipulated into playing their parts or supporting your role as spectators. To assume another identity, you must camouflage your true self, even think yourself into the character you decide to feign.

In Real Reality, which hides underneath the drama, no roles or players lurk. Instead, moment after moment unfolds, wanting you to capture it fully and then let it go. Such moments give you constant opportunities to be the best that you can be, to experience life to its fullest, with all of your obligations and commitments.

You can still be a mother, father, or a sibling. You can still rescue, please, and fix. But you act from choice and not because you have to do it as part of your conditioning. When you choose your part in interactions with other people, your attitude is more positive. When you neither manipulate others into taking part in false dramas nor allow yourself to be manoeuvred into playing tragedy or comedy, you live a genuine experience.

I use the acronym *L.I.F.E.* to describe how we are supposed to relate to life: *Let It Flow Effortlessly*. Too much thinking can block the energy of life, causing stress, tension, pain, and dis-ease. It's like trying to block the flow of a river, which would not only be futile, but also very tiring.

When you allow the energy of the moment to flow through you and you flow through it, you can prevent or significantly reduce unwanted symptoms. Without flow, stagnation sets in; no rejuvenation takes place and decay spreads on all levels. You have to understand, expose, and then let go of the drama you are acting in order to connect with your spirituality. Otherwise, you will continue to live in the drama's reality instead of in Real Reality.

By now you are probably getting the idea that living in the present, fully, is more than just a concept; it's a blueprint for a healthy, fulfilled, and balanced life. And even if you cannot do it all the time, part time is an improvement. Some is better than none. Once you realize how living in the moment can enhance your life and deepen your spiritual awareness, this way of living will expand and become more natural for you.

How long does it take to achieve spiritual transformation? It can take a split second or a thousand lifetimes. It all depends on how open you are, how much you allow yourself to let go, and how much time and attention you give to the exercises and principles described in this book.

A movie I watched when I was younger called *The Karate Kid* can demonstrate the serenity of choosing to be real. I remember being fascinated by one of the main characters in the movie, Mr. Miagi, a retired martial artist. I could articulate what fascinated me about him only years later. He portrayed a true role model of spirituality. Totally engaged in the moment, attending to the needs of the moment as they arose. He was a humble, respectful man who reacted very little and understood it all. Nothing upset him and he was afraid of nothing. He fully embraced everything he encountered without any resistance. When we live this way, regardless of what we experience, life does not seem to be a struggle anymore.

L I S T E N

Some people hear but they don't listen. Repeat the FEEL exercise now, with a small addition.

> **Close your eyes and take a few deep breaths in, exhale**
> **slowly, concentrate on your breathing for a few moments.**
> **Feel your surroundings through touch and sensations. Then**
> **turn on your hearing channel. Notice sounds, perhaps the**
> **humming of a fluorescent light or the air-conditioning, the**

birds chirping if you are outside, whatever sound is near you. Spend a minute or two on expanding your hearing, then go back to full awareness of your breathing and open your eyes.

Usually, this experience expands the calmness even further. You may have also noticed sounds that you were not paying attention to before the exercise. Recall your reactions to these sounds and decide if you were in the moment or into mind use as you experienced them.

Moment: I hear the cars driving by outside.

Mind: I hate the traffic; it's so noisy.

Moment: I can notice the rattling sound of the air conditioner.

Mind: This monotone noise is going to drive me crazy!

One of the most powerful and useful ways to practice "listening in the moment" is when you communicate with people. Unfortunately, most people don't really communicate. They just take turns talking. When you communicate with others, do you quickly process in your mind what the other person is saying only to formulate a quick response, sometimes even cutting the other person off halfway through his sentence?

"Why is he telling me all this, I don't care what he did last weekend," you think. "He thinks he knows it all; I am not stupid." Processing, processing, processing.

Next time you communicate with someone, just listen. Pay attention to the words and avoid internal commentary. The reason God gave us two ears and only one mouth is because we have to listen at least twice as much as we talk. If you can listen without processing, you will understand much more. Hearing enables us to notice the "speaking" and good listening enables understanding the meaning.

Listening in the moment is not easy to do if you aren't used to it. With practice, not only will you find that you're learning much more about the person you communicate with, but people will probably start praising you for being considerate, understanding, and a good listener. Guaranteed!

S   E   E

Some people look, but they don't see. Let's practice deep awareness using the most important sense in the system: vision.

I want you to repeat the feel/listen exercise, but this time with your eyes open.

> **After taking a few deep breaths in and slowly exhaling, notice your breathing for a while. Get briefly in touch with sensations (FEEL) and sounds (LISTEN). Then, start looking around. Just become aware of objects, colors, and shapes, avoiding all mental processing. Continue for two or three minutes, then pay attention to your breathing again for a few seconds and come back to reading the book.**

I remember one of my patients doing this exercise for the first time. I watched her as she noticed the pictures, books, objects, and colors in my office. But when her gaze reached the bookshelf, she quickly skipped it and continued to notice other things. When I asked her about it, she told me she could not stand looking at the unorganized pile of papers on the shelf. Being the perfectionist that she was, it irritated her to look at a mess. I explained to her that this was exactly the purpose of the exercise: to experience things without processing, without attaching our beliefs and expectations to anything, as we normally do.

If you do tend to drift or react during these exercises, don't let that discourage you. Simply recognize that you drifted or processed and acknowledge it without judgment; become aware of your breathing for a few seconds, and resume the exercise. I promise that if you practice a few times a day, you will learn how to disengage from the processing mind that tends to constantly react, even over-react, to experiences in your day-to-day life.

Moment: I can see a pile of books and paperwork on the desk.

Mind: What a mess. He really should organize it.

Moment: It's cloudy today.

Mind: It's such a depressing day.

When you live in the moment, you can see, hear, and feel many things you did not realize exist, even notice things you might otherwise find "irritating" without resorting to the distorting filters of the mind. This is a radical change in how we conduct ourselves, how we think, and how we relate to life in general.

The faster you make this shift, the faster you can enjoy a state of freedom without the limitations and bondage of the mind. It's said that the mind could make heaven out of hell and hell out heaven. Stop processing and taste heaven.

Three Especially Powerful Tricks

1. When you're stuck in your thinking and want to connect with the deep moment, get in touch with an object, a sound, or a sensation around you. This can very quickly orient you to the present.

    Have you noticed that the mind is very much like a merry-go-round? It just keeps going around and around, often until you get nauseated. So here is what to do: Next time when you catch yourself in the roller coaster of your mind, re-orient yourself by using your kinesthetic sense. For instance, touch the table, feel it for a moment. Feel the texture, the temperature, and so on. You are back in the now.

    Sometimes when my children talk to me while my mind is still preoccupied with whatever I was doing before, I notice something about them, their eyes or a garment they are wearing. This is enough to fully orient myself to them, which allows me to fully pay attention to what they are saying.

2. One of our "living in the mind" problems is that we never take a break between activities. That's why the day sometimes seems like one long drag. Taking time to do deep breathing and to connect with the senses is an excellent way to separate activities. For instance, when you wake up in the morning, just before you rush to the bathroom, notice something in the bedroom—maybe the way your blanket is sitting on the bed or the way the sheets feel. Use any one or more of the senses for just a few seconds. As

you go into the kitchen, touch the table or the fridge and fully notice it. When you get into the car, notice the temperature of the steering wheel, and so on.

Try that for a week and see how you feel by the end of it. I am certain you will feel less tired, less stressed, and much calmer.

3. Try to become aware of details regularly in your environment that were always there and that you have taken for granted, or perhaps have never noticed before. I remember practicing this while taking walks in the neighborhood, and I was stunned at the richness of details and the beauty that I had been blind to for so long. I was so inspired that I wrote the following poem:

They Were Always There
For many years the trees were right in front of me,
But I saw the houses.

For many years the flowers were all around me,
But I noticed the cars.

For many years the birds were singing everywhere,
But I listened to the radio and the TV.

Now I look at the trees and the flowers and the birds
And I ask: where was I all this time?
Because the trees and the flowers and the birds
Were really always there, waiting for me to notice them,
and say hello.

Myself, Me, and I

Earlier I said that spirituality is living life to its fullest, and since life is nothing but a string of moments, manifesting spirituality means living life moment by moment. I asserted that we can only live fully when we become who we really are and who we really are is fundamentally spiritual. I also established that spirituality is awareness without processing.

At this point I am sure you have a pretty good idea about the importance of living in the deep moment and that the way to do that is to significantly reduce excessive mental processing. We've already practiced awareness exercises that can help accomplish that. Later I will teach you more techniques and approaches to enable you to further reduce your processing. At this point, however, it is important to explore who you really are.

Just saying that fundamentally you are spiritual is not enough. The very fact that we have to explore it means that some uncertainty or misunderstanding surrounds this subject. What does this misunderstanding reflect? Does it mean that more than one of us is inside? Or perhaps that we have made a mistake about who we perceive ourselves to be? Both these statements are apparently correct. No, we don't have split personalities; something else is going on.

We refer to ourselves in three major ways: Myself, Me, and I. I attribute each reference to a different aspect of our being. Without understanding the distinctions, we get confused and make fundamental mistakes in how we relate to our selves. Let's look at a few examples of how we usually use these three points of self-reference.

1. "I hate myself." Think about this for a moment. Who hates whom here? A person, "I," hates his or her own self. Which self is the "I" hating, and what is the difference between the "I" person and the "self" part of the person?

2. "I am lost." What does this really mean? That you cannot find YOU? Who is lost and who is still looking?

3. "You are full of yourself." Full of what self? If you are full of the self, haven't you become the self? So what's left of you?

   Am I confusing you? Not to worry, it will be clearer shortly. But first, a few more examples:

4. "I just want to be me." Who is the me that you want to be? And what is it that you don't want to be that makes you want to be that "me"?

5. "I made a fool of myself." Who exactly is that important self that you made a fool of?

6. "I want to be by myself." We usually say this to tell others that we want to be alone. But look at the language. Which self exactly would you like to be by?

7. "I was beside myself." Who was beside whom?

These mistakes are not grammatical or linguistic. All these statements convey common, acceptable meaning. But on a deeper level they are quite confusing, and the only reason for that is because we are not clear about these three points of reference: Myself, Me, and I.

When I first began to play with the above statements, I thought they were quite entertaining. But as I looked very carefully at these three references I came up with an explanation that solves the confusion.

"Myself" represents the ego. When we use the term ego, we refer to that part of ourselves that is mostly concerned with our personal interest. The ego is the part that wants to look good, feel important, and be fulfilled. It is the part that wants to avoid mistakes, never fail, and never feel bored or lonely. It is also the part that sometimes drives us into self-destructive behavior such as drug abuse, alcoholism, stealing, lying and so forth.

"Me" represents the soul. The soul is the part of us that is all good, which cares about others and wants to better the world. It's a part that harbors no hatred or resentment. On the contrary, it is exceedingly forgiving and loving and wants to give and share everything we have with other people.

By the way, if you feel discomfort when reading this paragraph, know that the ego is creating that uneasiness. The ego is so preoccupied with its own little agendas that it fails to see the bigger picture.

"I" represents the spirit. Unlike the way we usually use the reference "I," it really should represent our spirit. This is the wise, creative, all knowing, intuitive, calm, core essence of who we are. It represents God in us.

So what does it really mean when you say, "I am mad at myself"? Is the spirit mad at the ego? No! The spirit cannot get mad at anyone or anything. It is one self that is mad at another self or "myself is mad at my other self."

"I just want to be me" literally means that you want to be your soul more than to be the ego. We all have that deep yearning, don't we?

When you ask your partner, "Do you love me?" you cannot possibly mean to ask if he or she loves your ego. Who can love that self-centered part anyway? You obviously mean your soul, don't you?

This may also explain how we sometimes fall in and out of love. When you first meet somebody whom you want to impress, you bring the best of you out. The best is always the soul. In the meantime, the ego is pushed down. After all, who in their right mind would show their ego when they want to attract someone they love?

So, you get married or live together for a while and guess who begins to creep up? Good old ego. A few years later your partner may be asking, "Where is the person I fell in love with?"

That person isn't gone. But throughout the years the ego pushed the soul down and took over to a large degree. Now some of the negative aspects of the self show more often and it isn't that difficult to fall out of love. When this happens to one or even both partners, it may lead to an unfulfilling relationship or even a break-up.

To be accurate, we should say, "Myself does not like my other self," and "Myself lost part of itself." But be careful; say it out loud and some nosy psychiatrist may recommend putting all of you in a straightjacket. As long as you understand the true meaning of all that, you will be fine.

One exception exists: the way you use "I am." This cannot be compromised and I will shortly explain why that is.

The following two verses are taken from the song "Lost Mind" by Percy Mayfield, from Diana Krall's *Love Scenes* CD:

If you could be so kind
to help me find my mind
I'd like to thank you in advance
Know this before you start
My soul's been torn apart
I lost my mind in a wild romance

My future is my past
Its memory will last
I'll live to love the days gone by
Each day this comes and goes is like
the one before
My mind is lost till the day I die

What a mess! This person feels she has lost her mind forever. She has a torn soul and lives entirely in the past believing that this state will stay forever. We also know that she lost it in a romance. Wow! Ego at its best. The prescription would either be Prozac or a good lesson in spirituality. What I am trying to demonstrate here is that our language usually reveals how we feel inside. When it comes to how we feel about who we are, many people feel quite confused. Let's continue to demystify the confusion.

More Common Self-Reference Mistakes

A friend of mine told me that she was working so hard that she had to take a break to be able to get back to herself. Which self did she mean? She was surprised at my question for a few long moments and then mumbled something about not being able to be productive until she was able to break away for a vacation. Unfortunately, she was not looking to get back to her true essence, which was always there. She didn't need to go to the other side of the globe to find it. What she was looking for was the "comfort zone" self. Perhaps it was better than the "out of control" self, but still very compromised.

I was listening to a song on the radio ("Little Sumthin'" by Kayle) and I picked up the following pearl: "I'll give you my love if you make me feel complete." Can external love make you feel complete? Of course not. The ego cannot make you complete because it will never be complete. The ego is fragmented, spilt, incongruent, and very confused. Ego is the opposite of completeness. It only knows how to cause separation, entanglements, and division. To be complete, you have to be spiritual. Only the spirit is whole, perfect, and totally self-contained.

The Soul-Spirit Connection

People view the soul and spirit in all kinds of ways. Many refer to them as one. I see them as two different aspects of us. For me, the spirit is that core essence of our being. It never changes and will always stay the essence of our existence. It was forever perfect. The soul is the aspect of the spirit that is manifested in a physical being and serves as a mediator between the spirit and the ego. Since the gap between these two is so huge, both need someone as a referee. Being the "sophisticated" creatures that we are, we humans have developed a very complex ego, and the soul is there to make sure that we do not lose touch with our spiritual side.

The soul is always trying to bring the person to the level of the spirit. This is what fulfilling one's purpose in life is all about.

If you consider the belief in reincarnation, you may understand this concept better. The soul is affected by the way the ego behaves. The soul's goal is to become as complete as it was before it separated from the spirit as part of its mission on earth. As long as the soul has not completed its mission, it keeps coming back to this world. Once it has completed its purpose, the soul reconnects with its spirit, which is always connected to God. When ego is transcended, the global spiritual evolutionary process is completed.

And then what? I would speculate that the entire process would start all over again.

What do we mean when we say, "I need to do some soul searching"? If you think about it in terms of what I have explained so far, the process takes place when the individual unsuccessfully exhausts all ego-based tactics as it attempts to feel truly happy and deeply fulfilled.

The process of soul searching is supposed to allow the person to find meaningful answers and solutions to a crisis or the confusion that developed prior to a crisis. Ideally, we need to do the soul searching constantly, not just when emergencies hit us. The problem is that many people who are "searching for themselves" are doing it within the realm of the ego.

> Every crisis is spiritual crisis.
>
> *Carl Jung*

More on Ego—Soul—Spirit

Going back to our three points of self-reference, we can determine the following self-identifications.

I = higher self (Spirit)

Me = intermediate self (Soul)

Myself = lower self (Ego)

Here's how Webster's Dictionary defines the same terms.

Spirit: "An animating or vital principle held to give life to a physical organism" and "A supernatural being or essence."

Both definitions fit the bill. The spirit is considered the Intelligence that makes every living organism tick. This "I" is an extension of the big "I," God.

Soul is defined by the dictionary as "Immaterial essence of an individual life, essential nature."

The soul is the source of the innate human good nature. It has the shape and essence of the spirit adjusted to operate "on the ground" while residing in a physical body. The spirit is there, all knowing but not showing itself unless approached directly, whereas the soul is a little bit pushier. It is trying to guide the individual into becoming a better human being. When it "fails" in fulfilling the mission it feels tortured and torn.

Some people confuse the soul with the superego, a term coined by Freud, which refers to the critical aspect that will put you down if you did not act in a way it deems moral or proper. The superego wants to make sure that you follow moralistic and idealistic rules. Although the soul also wants you to do good, it does not have a self-punishing, guilt-fear mechanism like the superego.

The soul gives you guidance if you care to listen. It gives you warm feedback when you follow its direction. You can say that the superego is a cheap imitation of what the soul truly strives for.

Here is an important rule to remember: If an inner voice has negative emotions associated with it, it is always ego-based.

Ego is defined in the dictionary as "The self, especially as contrasted with another self or the world."

Freud made the distinction between ego, id (the part in us that is pleasure seeking, constantly looking for gratification), and superego (a part which is critical of the ego, and tries to avoid the impulses of the id). In my opinion all three are parts of the same ego.

One of the biggest problems with the ego is that it has stolen the use of the "I" for its own purpose. It wants us to believe that it is who we are. Since the spirit does not voice itself directly, the ego can take advantage and lead you to believe that it is the all-knowing aspect of you. The ego asserts, "I am smart" and "I am good looking" and "I am in control." The spirit has no use for such statements. It just *is*.

Please take a moment to close your eyes. After taking a few deep breaths in, say to yourself very slowly,

> **And God said to Moses: "I AM THAT I AM.**
> *Exodus 3:14*

"I AM."

How did you feel? Was it a feeling of expansion and boundlessness, or did you feel constricted and limited?

What Would You Choose?

Ego-related behavior is usually based on fear. The ego feels lonely, separated, and isolated. It constantly runs "what if" scenarios. It feels that it deserves everything. It needs constant stimulation, satisfaction, and reassurance. Compare it with the soul/spirit that represents warmth, care, true love, joy, and peace. They need no action to feel satisfied. The choice is not so hard. However, the practice may be.

In Timothy 1:7 we read, "For God hath not given us the spirit of fear; but of power, and of love, and of sound mind." To experience all God intended, you have to separate yourself more and more from your ego and connect deeper and deeper with your soul/spirit.

A woman I counseled was going through very rough times. As a result of a chronic health condition, she lost her source of income and became financially strapped. She was consumed with fears about her future. Gradually, as she progressed with her spiritual pursuit, she was able to connect with her purpose. She didn't like what she found because it meant giving up the more lavish life she enjoyed before she became ill.

I asked her if she would prefer to have a soap opera type of life because, if she wanted it, she could re-create her previous lifestyle. The alternative choice would be joy, inner fulfillment, and peace.

Letting go of the idea of having a comfortable life was not easy for her, to say the least, but she knew she would ultimately choose true freedom. Instead of being frustrated with what she lost, she was able to connect more deeply with her true essence and to accept the challenges she faced. Most importantly, she accepted her purpose and was able to contribute from her natural talents to many people she came in contact with.

Who Are You Really?

When I ask people the question "Who are you?" I'm usually greeted with silence. People are not sure; in fact, some have never even stopped to think about it. Can you imagine living all your life without knowing who you really are? People may have some idea about who they are, but it is usually vague and quite often inaccurate.

I want you to write at the end of the book (List 1) who you think you are. Write everything that comes to mind. Please do this before you proceed. After reading part 2 of the book, use List 2 to update your understanding of who you are and when you finish reading the book you will have the opportunity to use List 3 to conclude your ideas and feelings on the subject. I recommend that if you can't complete the list now, please suspend reading until you can.

Once people recover from the initial surprise of the question they respond with all kinds of definitions, most of which are based on their character or abilities. "I am Anna, I am a teacher, I am a mother, I am good-natured, I am artistic, I am a driven individual, I like helping others," and so on. Is this similar to what you have just written?

> The greatest thing
> in the world is to
> know how to be
> one's own self.
>
> *Montaigne*

Let me ask you a question: Would you agree that *who you are* is a collection of your experiences, memories, thoughts, feelings, and beliefs? Most people tend to agree with that.

Let's examine this deeper. Are we our experiences and memories or are these only events that we have encountered, no more? Are we our thoughts?

If you answered yes, then let me ask you this: Can we change a thought? Of course we can. So who then is changing the thought? Is there someone "bigger" than the thoughts who can change them if he or she wishes to? The thought cannot change itself, the same way a book cannot turn its own pages, or a car start its own engine.

Such thoughts can only be changed by someone or something else, correct? So who inside can do it? You may say: "I do. I can change my thought." So in that case you are not your thoughts, are you?

Are you your feelings? As with thoughts, you can say that you have feelings but not that you are them. And what about beliefs? Are you your belief system? Many assume that they are, but we need to use the same rationale: we can change or update a belief or an attitude. It may be hard to do, but it can be done. You may have beliefs and attitudes but you are not them, wouldn't you agree?

In that case who is this person who is having thoughts, memories, feelings, and beliefs? You may say it's the PERSONALITY. But is this who we are, the personality? Many psychologists would agree with that, so suppose again, we are each just a personality. Were you not there as a baby before you developed a personality? Who then, is the entity who has the personality?

You may answer again, "I do." In that case, who are you? We are back to square one, but at least we know, at this point, who we are not. We are not totally thoughts, feelings, or personalities.

The word "person" comes from the Latin word "persona," which means a mask. Indeed, people wear all kinds of masks that enable them to play the dramas I talked about earlier. But even if you wear a thousand different masks, a "you" is still the one wearing them. You are not your masks. You may think that you are and even act as if you are, but you are not! A face must exist behind the mask. When you take off all the masks, someone exists who was present before you put on all these masks.

What is the difference between the masks we wear, the roles we play, and the *CoreSelf*? We present many selves including the self that we would like others to think we are, the self we actually think we are, the self we are afraid we are, and then, of course, the core essence that we really are. When you take off the masks, you find the true face of who you are.

Let's look at an example to demonstrate how this works. Larry is a successful architect. He lives a wonderful life in New York with his wife and two kids. One day he decides to go to Paris to seek inspiration for his next project. After a couple of weeks in Paris, he decides to extend his trip and go to Rome. He has not had the opportunity to tell his wife that he is now in Rome, because of the time difference. That morning he puts on shorts and a T-shirt and goes for a jog, when suddenly a car hits him. Larry sustains a head injury. He is in a coma for three weeks.

Meanwhile, his family looks for him in Paris. He cannot be found. Larry wakes up after three weeks and cannot remember anything. Diagnosed with post-traumatic amnesia, and without identification papers or a hotel room key (let's assume it's lost on impact) on him, nobody, himself included, knows anything about who he is.

After being discharged and with local help, he gets a small place to live in. He learns Italian, adopts the name Angelo, and finds a job as a waiter in a local restaurant. Several years go by and Angelo has built a new life in Rome. Things change when one day, a good friend who came to visit Rome from New York happens to dine in the restaurant where Angelo is working. He recognizes Larry instantly.

In their discussion, Angelo learns that he is not Angelo; that, in fact, he is Larry, an architect from New York, and that he is married with two children. Angelo/Larry is convinced to go to New York, hoping to rediscover his true identity. Though he still cannot remember his past, he believes the story because he knows he has lost his memory as a result of an accident. He now has to start exploring his past to be able to re-establish his life as Larry.

In a way, we too are like Larry. We are also suffering from a type of amnesia. We thought we were Angelo and we can only remember ourselves as Angelo, but deep down we have always known that something was missing, something we'd lost touch with. We have to get in touch with the essence of who we are to be able to live life fully.

In his famous statement, Descartes declared, "I think, therefore, I am." From a spiritual perspective, the more appropriate statement would be, I think, therefore I THINK I am. Who we think we are is nothing but a bunch of thoughts! Who we really are is beyond thought.

Just do some deep breathing and clear your mind. Who is present?

I would like to ask you a question related to Larry. Even if he changed his identity a hundred times, wouldn't some aspect of him never change, but always exist? What was the one constant that was in both Larry and Angelo? What is the identity built on? What do we call it?

This is much like the engine that drives a car. You can put it under any hood, but it is still the same engine.

You can look at the spirit as a universal engine. The spirit is indeed the Divine Intelligence that drives us all. That's the engine each and every one of us is equipped with, and we want to improve our awareness and understanding of it so that we can make better use of it in our lives. The one thing that prevents us from doing that is our ego. So let's explore who the ego is, how it was formed, and what we can do to control it better.

Ego

When asked by patients if I believe in evil forces, I tell them that I don't believe in such a thing. However, I do believe in ego gone out of control. If we look at Adolf Hitler, who was responsible for the deaths of over 40 million people (civilian and military), we can clearly see an egomaniac who cared about nothing except himself and his plan to conquer the world.

Evil surfaces when a person is completely disconnected from his or her soul. Understanding the dynamics of the ego, how it came to be, what its purpose in the system is, and how it operates is very important for spiritual transformation.

I sincerely believe that we are, at this point in history, at a level where we will never again allow people like Hitler to exist. In fact, we are now desperately looking for leaders who represent the opposite.

Ego and spirit are like light and darkness. When you switch the light on in a dark room, darkness disappears. Likewise, you must tap into and embrace your spirituality (light) in order to reduce the control of your ego (darkness) on your life.

Notice I said reduce, not eliminate, mainly because eliminating ego's control altogether is very difficult to do and we have to be realistic. Also, if you choose to live in modern society as opposed to living a more secluded life, a little bit of ego is allowed and is even essential, until more people catch up with this kind of progress. Such level of ego allows day-to-day interaction between individuals. For instance, when someone abuses your rights, you need to protest it.

> Surely, we are not human beings having a spiritual experience, but spiritual beings having a human experience.
>
> *Pierre Teilhard de Chardin*

If we look in the Bible, we first encounter the ego in the story about the Garden of Eden, when Adam and Eve tasted the forbidden fruit. This creation story clearly depicts the difference between ego and spirit.

The Garden of Eden was designed as a true paradise. No knowledge was required to live a life that was totally blissful. But God had placed the "Tree of Knowledge of Good and Bad" in the garden. Adam and Eve were not supposed to eat from the fruits of this tree. Clearly, this tree represents the ego: good and bad, neediness and temptations. Mental processing versus living life to the fullest.

But here is an intriguing alternative. I believe that Adam and Eve must have had the seeds of ego in them; otherwise, they would have never felt tempted to try the forbidden fruit in the first place. Tricky on God's part, wasn't it? Adam and Eve were willing to sacrifice a life of pure contentment just so that they could see what the tree had to offer. That is the true nature of the ego: it can get you so absorbed with selfish pursuits that you may lose sight of what's truly important.

Why did God put the tree there in the first place? Why even give Adam and Eve the option to know about Evil? Perhaps God wanted them to have this knowledge anyway. Maybe He even deliberately intended to kick them out of Paradise, like children are encouraged toward self-responsibility away from home. For what purpose? So that they can find a way to return for healthy purposes, based on their own will. That's how they would learn to exercise free choice.

We can look at the story as a metaphor for what happens when we separate from our spirituality. Basically, we lose our own paradise. Interestingly, the knowledge Adam and Eve acquired after tasting the forbidden fruit was shame and fear. That's Ego at its most real. Bliss is gone, now big problems begin. Religion has enforced these ego-based patterns ever since.

The Penguin Dictionary of Psychology lists no fewer than 36 ego-based terms. Essentially, psychology is all about the EGO.

I have worked with ego-based problems for most of my career. My biggest realization has been that psychology cannot resolve such ego-related problems entirely. It can, perhaps, make life more comfortable by improving coping skills and removing extremities from our behavior.

The only option for real resolution comes from connecting with our spiritual essence. Notably, the word *psyche* means first of all *soul*, and not *mind* as most people would think. We will expand the understanding of the ego even further in part two of the book.

The Role of the Mind

All of our experiences are felt through the mind and its physical counterpart the brain. Furthermore, the mind's reflective, contemplative, and analytical modes are indeed very important. To access our spirituality, we try to minimize the part of the mind that is preoccupied with overanalyzing and trying hard to outsmart life. Mind you—oops—right at this moment, you're trying to figure out how to use the principles I'm discussing in order to increase your spiritual awareness, correct?

The mind is a multidimensional wonder. How you use it is what really counts. The goal of spiritual transformation is, in essence, to use the mind to transcend the mind. Mind over mind, if you will. This transcendence leads to a full spiritual experience that still uses the mind but in a very different way.

The necessity of crossing the mind barrier to arrive at a spiritual state is well established in Zen Buddhism. Zen masters used to reply to the "deep" questions of their students by making irrelevant statements. A question like "What does enlightenment feel like?" would be answered, "Like the straw floating in a river." They also used Koans, paradoxical questions and conundrums, to drive the students beyond the analytical aspect of the mind, where they could attain enlightenment.

One of the classical Koans was the following: "What is the sound of one hand clapping?" When the student tried to answer the question logically, no matter how intelligent or insightful the answer, the master would send the student for further contemplation. When enlightenment was experienced, no answer was necessary.

Part 2

Transformation

The Principal called the Student to his office. "So what have you learned about happiness?" he asked.

"I have learned that to be happy I need to know myself better."

"And what have you learned about yourself so far?"

The Student thought for a few seconds and then proudly recited, "I have learned that I am the sun and the moon, the ocean and the wind."

"Good," said the Principal. "Now go back to class."

The Ego's Evolution

From a general evolutionary point of view, the ego has developed side by side with our emotional evolution. In our more primitive stages, the basic emotions that existed were fear and anger, directly related to physical survival. Finding food, escaping from or fighting predators, procreating, and protecting one's family and belongings were the primary concerns.

However, as human beings evolved, emotions have become increasingly complex. For instance, where once we experienced only fear of danger or physical harm, we can now feel fear of rejection, fear of change, fear of failure, fear of commitment, and fear of success, to name a few.

The more we have developed emotionally, the more we have come to rely on the ego, not for its original purpose of physical survival, but instead for its emotional protective mechanism. Protection or defense mechanisms are ego-based patterns that are created to protect from feelings that the person is not comfortable experiencing directly, such as shame, conflict, anxiety, anger, hurt, inadequacy, and insecurity. Such protective mechanisms may have been important for us to be able to cope better at one stage, but the price that we pay for using the ego in this way is very high. The cost is called "unhappiness."

From Spirituality to Unhappiness

Here are the stages we go through after birth, to arrive at discomfort, unhappiness, and disease:

Spirituality (pure state of being) ⟶ hurt ⟶ ego is developed ⟶ fear ⟶ protection mechanisms ⟶ denial ⟶ distraction/avoidance ⟶ artificial/superficial life ⟶ tension/problems/unnecessary suffering ⟶ unhappiness ⟶ physical and/or psychological disorders ⟶ more unhappiness

Children are naturally spontaneous, playful, carefree, uninhibited, and joyful—all soul-originated conditions. Unfortunately, as we grow up and experience hurt and fear, protection mechanisms prevent us from fully enjoying these beautiful states. One of the problems is that we are more aware of the difficulties on or closer to the surface (typically the last few components of the process described above), and less about what is happening deep inside. Let's explore this even further.

> May the outward and the inward of man be at one.
>
> *Plato*

The Inner Worlds We Live In

We live in two separate worlds. The outside world is manifested in our interaction with others, our daily experiences, our life at home and work. But beneath that exterior lies a world we try to avoid. It is a world where demons and dragons live. A world that may be filled with anger, sadness, hurt, fear, shame, guilt, disappointment, and dissatisfaction. At least that's how we sometimes perceive it to be.

Nobody really likes this world. It's a bleak place of enforced, not natural, darkness. From time to time it sends us reminders of its presence: depression, anxiety, outbursts of anger, feelings of loneliness, addictions, obsessions, and despair. But we refuse to acknowledge it because we are afraid to look inside. We are often afraid even to admit that it exists. But if we are really honest, we know it is indeed there.

It is the ego that mediates these two contrasting worlds. In therapy, the ultimate goal is to confront and reconcile the deeper world that developed as a result of rejection, neglect, intimidation, criticism, ridicule, abuse, and abandonment in childhood.

One of my patients was experiencing excessive anger. As we went deeper into her feelings, she began to get in touch with sadness. At first she was very surprised. "I never knew there was sadness in me," she said and quickly moved on to dismiss it. But as the feelings lingered, she broke into tears and gradually a protective pattern emerged. For over forty years she repressed feelings of sadness because her father treated her as a boy he always wanted to have and never did. He also told her that "Sadness is a sign of weakness." She covered the feelings of sadness with anger. The anger gave her a false feeling of power, masking the weakness and vulnerability she had locked away deep inside.

As all the motivation behind her limiting behavior around other people became clear to her, a release of anger followed by a sense of liberation set in. She was then free to do the work she had always avoided—facing and gradually resolving many of the repressed feelings she still carried.

I worked briefly with another woman who drove herself into burnout by overwhelming herself with activities. She arrived at a point where she couldn't function anymore and she called me for help. In the session I helped her connect with deeper levels of her "busy mentality" so that she could figure out once and for all what she was running from. She sent me the following note after the session:

"...re over-achiever I think this is all related...not smart enough, not good enough, therefore keep working harder, faster, crazier, just keep moving harder to hit a moving target. If I'm so fast, maybe people won't notice how worthless I am?! I am putting the exclamation mark because this is not just a question but also a realization."

I recommended that she begin a healing process to resolve her insecurities. Such insecurities reside in our deeper world and cause us, at times, to avoid situations or certain people. They also prompt us to do things for the wrong reasons.

Surprise, Surprise!

As we continue to resolve the difficulties of the inner world, almost out of nowhere, a third world emerges: the spiritual world. Below the pain, it lies silent and still, just waiting to be found.

We become more spiritual in two ways. The most common one is to cultivate spiritual practices. For instance, people who practice meditation try to bypass both worlds and get straight to the deeper third world. Although the good feeling of calm that comes after meditation helps in better dealing with the everyday challenges, the inner world may still continue to overshadow life to a great degree. For instance, these people may still be overly needy, insecure, resentful, or envious.

The second way to become more spiritual is to clear that inner world and reduce the role of the ego. This can be done through emotional awareness and resolution of repressed material, which is the main objective of effective psychotherapy. Less ego equals more spirit.

> It is not that we have a soul, we are a soul.
> *Amelia E. Barr*

The best way to become more spiritual is to combine both approaches. This is where I see the fastest results in people with whom I have worked in my practice.

In the beginning of the therapeutic process one of my patients made every possible effort to avoid going inward to face her "dark world." Finally she agreed to do it. After working for a while she connected with the deeper world, a beautiful world she didn't know even existed. The following are her reflections as she wrote them in her diary.

> That which is truly beautiful rests before our eyes
> That which is truly joyful, lies within our hearts
> That which is truly peaceful rests within our souls
> That which I long to touch, is the essence of our being
> I immerse myself in the emotions that my eyes behold
> I feel the depth of love that an open heart can receive
> I relinquish my soul from all boundaries and feel peace
> I move closer to the eternal light of love and closer to the
>   essence of
> The who, that I am

Connecting with this part of who we are is one of the most amazing things that can happen to anyone. But even after we do, we still have to continue clearing our darker world of difficulties. That may take some time, but with the newfound experience it is much easier to do. As we clear more and more, the light of our spirit can shine through, allowing us finally to live life to its fullest.

The Ego's Conspiracy

To reduce the role of the ego, we have to understand its motives, agendas, and way of thinking. We need to recognize its purpose in our lives and what needs to happen so that we can live with less manifestation of it.

Imagine the following scenario. A little child is constantly criticized by his father. The father has very high expectations of the child. He reprimands him when he doesn't meet those standards and doesn't praise the child when he does well. As a result the child feels constant pressure, frustration, fear, and even guilt and rejection. Most of all, he feels hurt as he longs for his dad's approval. No child knows how to deal with that kind of pain.

What does the child do? He looks for help—anything to make the pain go away. And whom does he turn to? Uncle Ego. "Don't be afraid," it tells the little child reassuringly, "I'll take care of it for you."

The ego takes the pain, pushes it deep down, and puts a protective layer on top to avoid any direct contact. This emotional material is taken out of conscious memory. After all, if you don't remember it, it isn't there, right?

Not really. But it does the trick for the short term. The child learns gradually to stop feeling and along with that becomes less caring. The ego has just gained more control of the system, and the more control the ego has, the less control you have. The more unresolved feelings, the more repression. Now many layers of protection cover the pain. Great, isn't it? No, no, no!

The price of avoidance is horrendous. Not only is ego in full control and calling the shots, but it also drives you, now the grown-up child, to compensating behaviors. Addictions would be one example of how we compensate. "Let's work real hard, let's please everybody, let's be perfect," it says. STRESS, STRESS, and more STRESS.

And what happens to real joy? It becomes buried under all of the protective layers. You cannot cover up only the negative feelings. The same happens to the positive ones. But you don't know that. More accurately, you have forgotten it.

You may ask, "What's the point? I don't care, I simply don't care." You should! Caring is important. Caring is the soul's most important characteristic. Caring leads to kindness, giving, sharing, supporting, and generosity. We need a world of people who care to be able to transform it.

But do you care too much?

That's also ego based. Perhaps you do everything for everybody because you want the approval of everybody. In that case you pay a personal price by neglecting your own health. "People pleasers" are one of the highest stress groups, especially among women.

Approval, recognition, I don't care, I care too much. These states provide no balance. The impetuous ego has no time for balance. It's too busy with agendas that make no real sense.

Any therapist will tell you that the greatest challenge in therapy is to work through denial. Denial is a form of defense mechanism used to avoid contact with challenging feelings. Denial helps to push away what cannot be dealt with consciously. So when a patient is asked to get in touch with, or just to verify that he is withholding, certain feelings, he may deny that he even has them.

This denial is not the same as lying. It may be that the feelings are blocked from consciousness. Many individuals lose their ability to feel because they use denial as a coping technique.

In my experience, a closed heart is a hurting heart. The trick is to pay attention to external symptoms and allow them to lead you into repressed emotions so that you can begin to release them.

Recently I worked with a woman who admitted she was severely abused when she was younger but insisted that she had resolved everything around that situation. When I gently probed into it, she said that she preferred not to recall that time in her life because it would make her cry and she hated crying.

Her reluctance meant to me that she had not resolved this issue, at least not completely. If you've really let go of the past, it doesn't just mean you don't think about it anymore. It means that the negative emotions surrounding it are resolved and that you would have no problem revisiting it, if you wish to do so.

Letting go is always letting the EGO go!

Life in the Bubble

The way ego hides our inner world is by creating a bubble, an illusion that everything is fine, and that it, the ego, is working hard to make things better. But once you recognize what life in the bubble looks like, you can see the price that is paid for allowing the ego to take care of business.

In the bubble you may:
- Need to overprotect yourself.
- Need to manipulate others.
- Do things for the wrong reasons.
- Have to be perfect.
- Want everything to go your way.
- Seek other people's approval.
- Have to please others.
- Need always to be in full control.
- Have to appear smart, attractive, and successful.
- Do a lot of pretending.

Isolated within our illusions, we mistakenly believe that this is how life is supposed to be. We fall victim to the conspiracy of the ego: "I will take care of you but from now on, I will tell you what to do."

When one of my patients decided to get rid of her negative patterns, especially fears she experienced, she finally reconnected with her CoreSelf. She became spontaneous, natural, uninhibited, and very caring. This woman became a magnet drawing other people to her. She attracted people from all walks of life, naturally and without intending to do so. She described how people just wanted to be around her, unable to explain why.

I explained to her that she had become a person who lives in real life and not in the bubble. When people came in contact with her, they sensed her genuineness. Indirectly, she enabled people to get in touch with the similar wonderful place within themselves without understanding what had really happened.

We don't always know that we live in a bubble and, even if we do recognize the illusions ego creates, we don't always know how to pop them. Seeing through our personal illusions is not an easy job to do.

Popping the Bubble

In order to pop the bubble, you first have to realize that living an illusion is false. This pseudo shelter drastically limits your experience. It's like using newspaper to protect yourself from a heavy rain. To pop the bubble you have to understand that a life is possible beyond the ego, life that is natural and truly magnificent. To live this life you must commit to exploring who you really are and to striving continuously for living in the deep moment. This commitment requires you to surrender yourself to the NOW. Living in the present's reality totally contradicts life in the bubble where the motto is pretense, imitation, and make-believe.

Continuous existence in the bubble is almost always the result of a lack of awareness. We squander our lives in an illusionary world.

This kind of unawareness is depicted in the movie *The Truman Show* (Paramount Pictures, directed by Peter Weir). Jim Carrey plays a character, Truman, who appears to live a normal life. But Truman's world is nothing but the setting of a TV show, controlled by its producer Cristof (played by Ed Harris), in which Truman is an unwitting pawn. Everyone, including his wife, is an actor, and the whole town is nothing but a giant studio. Everything around him is a fabrication, and the only one who doesn't know it is Truman himself. He has come to accept his life because he does not know any better, but he cannot escape an uneasy feeling that something is missing, that something is not quite right. A series of events lead him to realize that things aren't as they seem. He is able to overcome the many obstacles created by Cristof, who is trying hard to keep him in the show.

Truman's awareness grows to a degree that enables him to see the truth and to face his own fears. He can then reclaim his freedom.

Like Truman, we have to become more acutely cognizant of our egos' agendas, symbolized by Cristof in *The Truman Show*. As we finally challenge our perceived reality, we can then exercise our real freedom and move toward living our truth.

Some time ago I went to Mexico to scuba dive. I was certified a year earlier, but had little opportunity to practice. I was told during the certification course that in order to maximize the air in the tank, and consequently the time I could stay underwater, I should stay calm and breathe slowly and evenly.

I had no problems doing that during classes. But in my first few dives in Mexico, I was always one of the first in the group to finish the air in the tank. I couldn't understand why, as I was calm and breathing correctly. I decided to ask the dive master, who guided the group during the dives, about my problem.

"You just move too much," he said, laughing.

I examined myself during the following dive and realized he was right. I was moving too fast and too much. I decided to imagine myself being a fish, swimming slowly, and I significantly limited my movement as a result.

About forty minutes later, most of the divers were ascending. To my amazement I still had plenty of air left. I realized that I had stopped focusing on my efforts to control my buoyancy and totally surrendered myself to the ocean. Instead of being a foreign object in the ocean, I became an integral part of it. I even noticed that my enjoyment rose dramatically. The attention shifted from "doing it" to "flowing with it."

Why am I telling you this? To make the point that when you surrender to spiritual reality, you can "swim" in it effortlessly and better enjoy your life. In contrast, life in the bubble requires a lot of work, usually expending much energy for very limited results. Now more about the ego.

Games Ego Plays

Ego is the master of deception and disguise. It uses false reasoning to make you believe not only that IT is important, but that it is actually who you are. Remember the unconscious agreement you made with the ego? "I will do what you (ego) want; just make sure I don't feel pain."

Another common technique the ego uses is distraction. See if you recognize any of these tactics: Let's do something else. Let's work more hours, go see a movie, open a chocolate box— anything, so that you don't have to think of what's really bothering you. Done for the purpose of distraction, these activities can lead to excessive stress, disappointment, burnout, and addiction. Smoking, drinking, drugs, and even overeating are also considered distraction techniques, a way to numb the deeper feelings. However, unlike the less harmful distractions mentioned earlier, these can be quite destructive.

More often than not, despondency, unhappiness, and even physical pain are the symptoms of repressed issues. We can distract ourselves from painful emotions, we can try to mask them with more bearable feelings; we can minimize them, try to rationalize them or deny that they even exist. We can keep them caged up inside, but emotions find a way to surface and affect our lives until we gather our courage to deal with them and resolve them permanently.

A woman I recently worked with was treated for a number of years for her panic attacks. By the time she came to see me, she had about ten smaller scale attacks and at least three heavy duty ones every day. We worked together for a few weeks and managed to bring down the panic attacks to a manageable level.

Since we couldn't completely resolve the panic attacks, I estimated that she harbored repressed material that hadn't surfaced yet. We went through her history and resolved more issues, which resulted in further improvement, but still not in total clearance of her panic.

I was ready to recommend a break in therapy to give her more time to solidify the changes when she called me in great panic, saying she had nightmares about being molested as a child. After a few weeks of incredulous discussion, we gradually resolved the trauma of the abuse. Her panic attacks improved by 95 percent. She is now almost free of them, and I estimate that it will not take too long for her to be totally free of a condition that debilitated her for years. We don't always know what we keep inside, but our external symptoms many times serve as a clear indication that it is time to go within and let go.

We must also pay close attention to the never-ending patterns that the ego runs through the mind. "What if" scenarios are one example, which tend to generate excessive worry and anxiety. Dwelling on regrets, on what you lack, on what you missed out on, and things you could have done can create states of frustration, disappointment, even depression. Whenever you catch your ego wasting time and energy by reviewing such scenarios, insist on connecting with the deep moment. This will defuse these patterns, which are nothing but mental processes as compared with the deep moment, which connects you right away with Real Reality.

> **You can use the Appendix at the end of the book to make a list of the games your ego plays with you. As you keep compiling the list, also notice the frequency with which these patterns repeat themselves.**

This type of accurate awareness will gradually allow you to reduce the frequency as well as the intensity of these games, which will no doubt result in better self-control and a much calmer life.

Ego vs. Spirit

The difference between ego and spirit is the difference between fake and real. If somebody offered you a million dollars in Monopoly money or a hundred dollars in hard cash, which would you take?

The EGO feels insecure and fragile. It is critical and judgmental and likes to indulge in the pleasures of the body. It uses some sort of a twisted rationale to convince you that it knows what is best for you, and uses guilt and fear to motivate you. The ego is bothered by little things in life and gets stressed out very quickly. It creates negative cycles by causing many of our problems and then it fights to fix them. What a bind!

The ego needs to know everything. It is never fully satisfied. It always wants more. It has agendas, impulses, cravings, and needs. These words can warn you when the ego is active: "I must, I have to, I need, I should, I want." It is always calculating, always worrying and trying to outsmart life. Give yourself a break! You have to stop the madness. Neurosis is pure ego!

Your CoreSelf is peaceful and joyful. It demands nothing and is willing to give everything. It has no needs or expectations. It is pure, balanced, and very comfortable within itself. It is creative and always intuitive, eager to share, love, and do good, unconditionally. You have all of that inside right now!

Unlike your CoreSelf, ego is saturated with desires. Have you noticed that when you fulfill one desire a new one comes in its stead? It really never ends. You can easily spend a lifetime upgrading your desires and trying to fulfill them. The spirit's desire, if you will, is only to get your attention so that you can remember who you really are, and to recognize your innate ability to contribute to the common good of people.

Ego is very big on trust and control. It constantly focuses outwardly thus creating feelings of insecurity, betrayal, hopelessness, and vulnerability. A major principle in Buddhism is that if you want to stop suffering you have to stop desiring. Since the ego's preoccupation with desire is almost unstoppable, we need to switch from materialistic propensities to desiring to live life to its fullest. The one desire we may leave ourselves is to experience all the moments in life to their greatest depth.

Strangely, we have an ego that never is fully content, and at the same time we also have a spirit that is already fully satisfied. Once we open the tap, so to speak, spirituality can pour into our darker sides and allow us to feel complete.

More Comparison

From the following comparison you can easily see why we want to significantly reduce the effect of ego in our life and deepen our spiritual connection.

EGO	SPIRITUAL
superficial	deep
conditional love	unconditional love
isolated	connected
disturbed	calm
insecure	secure
quantity	quality
impatient	patient
moody	balanced
fear	faith
suspicious/skeptical	trusting
time bound	timeless
knowledge	wisdom
manipulation	integrity
taking	giving
money	abundance
pride	humility
conflicted	peaceful
split	whole
lacking	complete
ephemeral	enduring
selfish	generous
discord	harmony
greedy	generous
prejudiced	tolerant
judgmental	accepting
giving up	enduring
temporary	eternal
confusion	clarity
numb	enlightened

The ego looks for peace—the spirit rests in it
The ego looks for love—the spirit gives it freely
The ego is in constant search for happiness—the spirit is
    absorbed in joy

The ego looks for control—the spirit is totally free

The ego looks for longevity—the spirit is immortal

The ego accumulates information—the spirit is Supreme Wisdom

The ego is limited by space and time—the spirit is boundless

The ego is only a player in a show—the spirit is life itself

The ego is false—the spirit is real

The ego wants more and more—the spirit has it all!

The Ego's Biggest Fear

The ego knows things that you don't. Since it controls everything from quite deep inside, it knows what really hides underneath it all. As a result, it will try anything to detour you from going deeper. As soon as you sit quietly and try to go deeper, it will throw a temper tantrum, creating a state of anxiety, or alternately, get you in touch with sadness. It will remind you of your insecurities, anything imaginable.

> One can take a photograph of a candle, but it will not emit light.
>
> *Maharaja*
> *Nisargadatta*

Are you getting the picture? I know I am personifying the ego here, but that is the best way to expose its agendas. Besides, don't you feel, at times, that the ego has a mind of its own, which is not always in sync with your best interests?

Imagine you've heard of a treasure chest buried in a cave somewhere on top of a mountain. You cross rivers, go through forests, climb hills, and finally reach the cave, only to realize that a dragon guards the cave. What do you do? You can't fight the dragon, so you wait until it falls asleep. Then you slowly pass it, to go inside the cave and get your treasure. Once you have it, your job is done. And so is the dragon's. It has no purpose staying because it has nothing to protect anymore and so it disappears.

The ego's worst fear is that you will discover YOUR treasure. That would mean that its role in the system is over—hence the resistance and trickery to prevent you from getting into spiritual territory. The ego will try to intimidate you. "Do you really want to challenge me? Do you want to feel the pain I've been protecting you from?"

What you would want to say in return? "I am okay with that."

The ego is not going to accept defeat so easily. "Are you sure you want to get in touch with your skeletons?" it asks. "Don't you remember our deal?"

You answer, "It's about time I face them. They are MY skeletons. I am going to deal with them once and for all. Repression stops right here."

As you stand up for yourself and face the truth, and as you encounter difficult emotions as a result, know one thing: You can overcome them. I will show you how! Don't be afraid. Take the first step by proclaiming, "No more pretending, no more covering up. It's time to be me!"

Let me tell you something very important. When you become you, fully and completely, life becomes very easy. You won't have to pretend anymore, you won't have to be so conscious about what others think of you; you won't have to prove yourself, nor constantly look for approval from others. You will just live life as it is presented to you.

But before you can fully become who you truly are, you have to continue to take back the power you originally gave your ego. Although that may sound quite difficult to do, it is accomplishable.

A Quick Anatomy of the Ego

The two prime goals of the ego are approval and security. The ego will go to extreme measures to accomplish these goals. A good exercise right now would be to take a few minutes and think what these two concepts mean to you.

Generally speaking, the ego will give up a lot in order to obtain the approval of others. It is quite comical that we seek approval from people who are also seeking approval themselves. Even more than approval, we strive to feel secure. However, security contrived in this way is mostly artificial, as is all of ego-based behavior.

The ego also has a few secondary goals. They include comfort, power, and control. The real problem with the ego is that it has to create all kinds of convoluted strategies to accomplish its desired states. Gradually you must disconnect your association with it to be able to realize what you are missing out on.

Ego Makes You Tired

We live in a society that is fatigued. Why are people so tired? I believe that with the constant promotion of materialism in Western society and the rise in stress associated with acquiring, our vitality is used to keep up with the energy-consuming ego. A lot of our energy is locked up serving the ego's background activities, especially suppression and repression.

We need to free up that energy. Compare this situation to a merchant who realizes that he has no money because all of his fortune is tied up with merchandise. He has to free up inventory by selling some of his merchandise to be able to cash in.

A while ago I came up with my favorite definition of the *EGO: Energy Going nOwhere.* In other words, it is energy put to waste.

I want you to understand fully what repression is like.

Imagine that you are in a pool playing with a ball. Say someone comes to the pool area and you don't want her to know that you are playing with a ball, so you push it under the water and you keep it there. But your friend stays longer, so you continue to hold the ball under the water.

How does your arm feel by now? Tired, doesn't it? It takes too much effort to keep the ball under the water. As you push downward without relief, pain sets in. The arm, shoulders, neck and back, they are all in pain.

Now let me ask you a question: what if you had to push two balls under the water at the same time? How about ten, a hundred, a thousand balls? Where is all your energy going? You're focusing more on keeping the balls underwater than enjoying the pool or your friend! It has been said that repressed material can take up to 75 percent of your overall energy. The ego's daily coping games may take 15 to 20 percent more. What's left for you then?

Intelligent Energy

The ego focuses on what we don't have. It seldom appreciates, and may not even recognize, what we do have.

Understand that when we feel that we lack something inside, it doesn't really mean that we don't have it. What it actually means is that we still have not found the way to satisfy that need internally. Yet the know-how for internal satisfaction is built in as part of our Spiritual Intelligence. This intelligence works with the raw energy we possess inside and shapes it into many forms.

Every mental and emotional state is a product of shaping one's energy a certain way, much like clay in the hands of an artist. The clay has the potential to be formed in any shape and the artist decides what form the clay will take.

Let's take a person who needs constant reassurance as an example. As a result of internal need, this person creates all kinds of relationships to attract the reassurances he requires. He exhausts his energies, sometimes even his acquaintances, as he uses relation-ships to feed his desire for reassurance.

However, feeling reassured is a state that is built in as part of Spiritual Intelligence. When a person goes deep enough he will be able to create it internally and will consequently free himself of the need to get it constantly from others.

The same goes for the other needs mentioned earlier: control, comfort, power, and security. Each need can be satisfied best by reaching deep within yourself to create it. Accepting and working with this idea will make it much easier for you to reduce the dependency on your ego and free you up to enjoy life more fully. You also reduce your dependency on other people, removing burdens on relationships.

Reducing the Influence of the Ego

The reason I put intense focus on the ego is because you need to know how the ego affects your life so you can finally reclaim the power it has taken away from you. At this point, I want to mention a few attitudes that can be of great help in accomplishing that.

- Express yourself freely.
- Ask for what you want when it's reasonable.
- Treat others with deep respect.
- Choose peace instead of conflict.
- Stop all or nothing thinking.
- Stop striving for perfection.
- Stop trying to please everyone.
- Remember that we are all equal.
- Speak the truth.
- Remember that everybody makes mistakes.
- Stop thinking in good and bad terms.
- Remember that the only control is self-control; you cannot control others.
- Trust yourself.
- Stop putting yourself and others down.
- Face any problem, conflict, or difficult emotions head on.

Some of these attitudes may be difficult for you to adopt. However, with continued awareness and practice you will be able to disengage from ego-based behavior. This will allow you to operate from a soul-based level. In the meantime, remember to connect with the moment, breathe deeply, and get in touch with the senses while reducing mental processing as much as you can. How do you feel?

The Jigsaw Puzzle of Evolution

From a human perspective, we can look at evolution as the evolution of the mind. We have become more sophisticated, more knowledgeable, and more complex. I believe that the next phase of human evolution will occur within the spiritual realm.

The ultimate picture of worldwide peace and harmony is actually more like a puzzle in which every person represents a distinct piece. As long as we act from our ego, this puzzle cannot be completed. The parts simply won't fit. In order for them to fit you have to be who you really are, transcending the ego. You have to be fully YOU.

> You must be part of the change you want to see in the world.
>
> *Gandhi*

Peace is an attitude that must be demonstrated within every individual in each society, not just negotiated by governments. Whatever a treaty may state, rebellious individuals can destroy its intent. Harmony must be lived, not legislated.

Accomplishing this stage in evolution may take a long time. In the meantime, how do we make it work? One person at a time.

What Are You?

Earlier I alluded to the fact that in reality we are spiritual beings. However, to be perfectly accurate, we now have to differentiate between who we are and what we are. We usually refer to who we are in psychological terms: ideas, thoughts, attitudes, beliefs, memories. This is the realm of personality and identity. What we are is that special nonmaterial magic called spirit.

To better understand what this nonmaterial is made of, I will take an example from the physical world, water. Water has a strong resemblance to the spirit. Water comprises the majority of the physical world. More than 75 percent of the surface of the earth is covered by water. All living organisms consist of 50 to 90 percent water. Water flows and changes form just as the spirit does.

What is water? What do we know about it? Much like the spirit, it is tasteless and odorless. It is soft but has the capability to penetrate hard rock. Water is mostly transparent. It can take many forms: ice, rain, crystals, snow, steam, fog, clouds, rivers and oceans. But let me ask you this: Can we say that water is an ocean? Can we say that water is ice, or rain, or morning dew? No, for these are just some of the forms that water can take.

The spirit is much like that. It can take many forms. You can find spirit in a human being, a tree, an animal, or a flower.

What is water? Water is H_2O. That's the basic structure. Water is a substance made of two molecules of hydrogen and one molecule of oxygen. No matter what form water takes, it will always be H_2O.

> In the depth of winter, I finally learned that there was within me an invincible summer.
>
> *Albert Camus*

The spirit is also composed of two very basic elements. Any guesses as to what they are? You may be a bit surprised with the answer, especially if you lived in the sixties. But before I get into that, I want you to put the book down and connect with the deep moment. Now please do the exercise, so that you can discover what the first molecule of the spirit is.

> Just push all the thoughts and ideas and questions aside. Get in touch with your breath. Get in touch with the senses. No mental processing. When the thinking mind is fully set aside, the spirit is revealed.

So what did you feel? Usually the feeling is relaxation and calm. If you felt that way that's great, and if not, your mind was still preoccupied. This feeling of calmness actually comes from a much deeper sensation. Which one is it? Peace. Repeat the above exercise, giving it more time. Can you feel the peace?

What about the second molecule?

> Think about someone whom you care about—your child, parent, even a pet. Connect with him or her while clearing your mind of any other thoughts and notice how you feel.

This feeling has to do with our relationship with other living beings. What do we call this deep feeling? You guessed it: love. The major qualities of the spirit, therefore, include peace and love.

Remember when I said that those living in the sixties would be surprised? I refer to the conceptual icons of the sixties, Love and Peace. Sound cliché? Maybe, but the idea is true. The hippies understood this concept but they made one cardinal mistake. They were looking for the manifestation of these principles externally. Free sex and doing drugs were just two examples. This was merely an emulation of the "real thing." Drugs are a poor substitute for feeling good about oneself and uncontrollable sex rarely offers warmth, closeness, or love.

In my opinion, that's why the hippies gradually disappeared as a movement. They simply missed the point. When I was younger, I could never say those two words, peace and love, together without giggling. It sounded too cliché. Life is certainly full of surprises, isn't it?

How can we see what we are made of? Microscopes allow us to see the atomic level of material; telescopes allow us to see billions of light years into space to figure out what material galaxies are made of. But we cannot see what our spiritual beings are made of, because we cannot perceive it or sense it and no language can describe it. To understand it we have to deeply connect with it. Then, we can experience it and fully appreciate how magnificent it is.

This is not a far-fetched concept. If we use science to investigate the subject of dark matter, we find out that it occupies a very big chunk of the universe. Perhaps as much as 90 percent of the matter in the universe is dark matter. Yet we cannot see it or even measure it, because it does not emit any light or electromagnetic radiation. We can only assume it is there by observations of other aspects of the universe. For instance, the speed at which galaxies rotate can be accomplished only if significantly more matter exists than what can be observed. This dark energy is such a strong force that it is constantly pushing the universe forward and accelerating its expansion.

> But the fruit of the Spirit is love, joy, peace, patience, kindness, goodness, faithfulness.
>
> *Galatians 5:22*

Dark energy is subtle but powerful. So is spirituality, which is the real driving force in nature. Both are totally invisible. We cannot measure either in any scientific way, but when we tune into our spirituality, we can realize its ability to transform our lives.

Science accepts the effect of dark energy as proof of its existence. The wonderful effect of spirituality in everyday life confirms this deepest part of our being.

The Third Definition of Spirituality

So here is the third and shortest definition of spirituality: PEACE. Short, simple, and powerful, isn't it? Sir Winston Churchill once said that only the simple things work.

As opposed to the complexities and intricacies of the ego, the spirit is so simple and all knowing. It already includes the blueprint for what everyone is looking for. I said earlier that spirituality is peace and love. However, peace is the highest order. Love emerges from peace. When you come from a base of total peace, everything you create is done with abounding love.

I would like to share with you a personal revelation I had. Right after I started using the water metaphor as a way to explain the nature of the spirit, I found myself in the car one day pondering the spirit equals peace plus love formula in my mind. I suddenly had an unexpected interruption. My surname, "Gottfried," just kept popping into my head, no matter how hard I tried to distract myself to shut this voice off. As the name kept echoing in my mind, I decided that this was probably happening for a reason, and before long something dawned on me.

My surname is divided into two words originating from German (my father was of Jewish–Austrian descent): "Gott," which means God, and "fried(e)" (pronounced "freed"), German for peace. Everything came together. God, the source of all spirituality, is peace. My name also confirmed my purpose in life: to help people connect with their inner peace. Interestingly, "friede" is also the root of the German word "zufrieden" which means pleased and fulfilled. So here you have it. Experiencing spirituality will bring you true peace and you will feel naturally fulfilled.

Isaiah 45:7 says, "I form the light and create darkness, I make peace and create evil, I the Lord do all these things." Evil is considered the opposite of peace. Evil is ego. To more deeply connect with peace, we need to be less ego. Ego is our false sense of self and everything that is false ends up creating trouble.

One of my patients told me that when his father passed away, he went to his priest and asked him why his 57-year-old father, who was a good person and had complete faith in God, had to die so young. The priest could not give him an answer except to say that God's ways are mysterious. My patient decided to remove himself from religion right there and then.

This example demonstrates a problem with religion and points to one of the major differences between religion and spirituality. Religion professes that if you do good deeds you will be rewarded accordingly. But when so-called "good people" continue to go through tribulation despite being faithful followers, they become conflicted, disillusioned, and at times desert their faith. Spirituality, on the other hand, does not make such promises. All it says is that if you practice it, you will enjoy complete peace. You may still go through hard times, but you will be able to overcome adversities by connecting deeply with peace.

> **There is no way to peace; peace is the way!**
>
> *A.J. Muste*

For many years I focused on helping patients transform their lives through working with their values, beliefs, attitudes, behaviors, and habits. I later discovered that when I taught individuals how to connect with their deep sense of inner peace we were able to dramatically shorten the process. For some people, this spiritual connection clicked in fast; for others more work had to be done before they could connect with peace. Regardless, when this was accomplished many patterns they had struggled with for years diminished, at times even disappeared.

When Do You Feel Peace?

Review your daily experiences and notice when you feel peace. Is it during any specific activity, or perhaps during meditation? Are you with someone or by yourself? Is this at work or at home? In addition, pay attention when the experience of peace is terminated. Is it when the activity is over? Also notice how frequently you feel it. It would be a good idea to start raising your "peace awareness."

Here is another important exercise to which I would like you to dedicate time for further exploration:

What needs to happen in you or in your life that will bring complete peace? Please make a list. Use the appendix at the back of the book for this purpose. This list will represent your conditions for peace.

I am sure that many of the criteria described in your list are reasonable. On the other hand, you are capable of connecting with peace now, without the fulfillment of any of the items on your list. That's what spiritual practice is really all about—letting go of the conditions. External situations can provide only superficial and temporary peace. True peace always comes from deep inside. That is why we call it inner peace and not outer peace.

When you were much younger you had inner peace but you may have lost touch with it at some point. Children usually lose it when they experience abuse or neglect. It also happens when they are exposed to negativity or extremely high expectations, and when they have to take adult-type responsibility long before they are ready for it.

When did you lose touch with your inner peace, either in full or in part? The good news is that you can reconnect with it anytime. But you will have to let go of some of the beliefs you acquired as a result of the circumstances that caused you to disconnect from peace in the first place. Such beliefs include thoughts like the following:

Life is too difficult. You cannot trust people. You shouldn't express your feelings. You need to worry about everything in order to be prepared for the worst. Other people's approval is very important. You have to be perfect. You are not good enough. You shouldn't disappoint other people.

As you identify such attitudes that destroy your peace, add them to the list of limiting patterns you would like to transform at the end of the book.

Experiencing PEACE

I want you to try the following exercise.

> Close your eyes and become aware of your breathing. Begin
> to clear your mind of thoughts and ideas. Follow your
> breathing to go deeper within. Next, I would like you to go to
> a time when you felt totally peaceful and carefree. Perhaps
> when you were a child, or when you were on vacation, or
> any other experience that connects you with feeling free of
> worry, tension, and stress. Once you are in touch with the
> feeling of peace, allow it to flow through you, fully. If the
> feeling were a color, what would it be? Take that color
> and imagine painting your present life with it. Paint all the
> challenging circumstances with your personal shade of
> "peace paint."

How does it feel? From now on, you can connect with peace by
remembering your individual peace color whenever you want, and
it will always bring lightness into any "heavy" situations. You can
also imagine painting your future with this color. How does it feel
doing that? The more frequently you connect with the feeling, the
deeper the connection becomes.

Calling the Ego's Bluff

The ego constantly promises that one day you will be happy. Work
more, get a promotion, buy a bigger house, just do all these long
lists of things and you will be happy.

> Peace is the fairest
> form of happiness.
>
> *William Ellery*
> *Channing*

These promises are nothing but a big bluff.
Even if you accomplished them, you wouldn't
necessarily be fulfilled. Do you know why? Because
the ego cannot give you true happiness. It may give
you comfort or temporary satisfaction, but never
true fulfillment. It is bluffing you and if you've just about had it with
the games ego plays, you have to call ego's bluff.

So this is how you call its bluff. You tell the ego, "I have had it with your promises for happiness. I want to be happy now. Can you do it?"

"Just wait a little longer," the ego may reply. "We just need to do a few more things and it'll happen."

Procrastination is a well-known ego-based delay tactic. Insist, "No! I want happiness now or forget it."

Now the ego is feeling the heat. Its bluff is called. The ego has to show its cards. Unwilling to expose itself, the ego goes for its last resort. "You don't really want to connect with the pain, do you? Trust me, let's go back to the arrangement we had before. It's taken you this far, why change now?"

This is a critical juncture in your quest. You might feel tempted to accept the ego's proposal. You'll need guts to say no, guts to mean it, and guts to pursue it. But I want you to know this: You have what it takes. Will you do it?

Tell the ego that you're okay. Tell it that you want to face your past, that you are not afraid of the pain. You are willing to release your repression.

Let me tell you something very important. Deep inside, you are still viewing your problems through the eyes of a child. But you are not a child anymore. You can handle difficulties. You can face the truth.

This is a big shift with the highest reward possible: finding YOURSELF. Make it all right to feel vulnerable. You are stronger than all of your fears and insecurities. Vulnerability is only a perception, whereas your inner strength, which comes from your core, is real. You know what it is that you have to face. Now is the time to muster up all the courage that you have and do it. Go for it!

The Biggest Blocks to Spirituality

As we continue to reduce the role of the ego, I would like to talk about more specific ego-based patterns that create big roadblocks on the way to the Promised Land. I have learned one important thing through my work with patients as well as with myself. If you want to make big changes in your life, you have to make big changes in your thinking.

We are going to look now at those thinking patterns that come between you and total peace. Your goal will be to identify them in your life and then gradually let them go.

The biggest block to full and complete peace is comparison. This mental pattern is one of the ego's major preoccupations. I think that people underestimate how much they compare on all levels. This is almost an ongoing, 24 hours a day process that can cause enormous amounts of stress.

I recently worked with an individual who was a manager in an import/export company. After we talked about this thinking pattern he decided to pay close attention and record every bit of comparison he did both consciously and unconsciously. He was shocked at the number of entries on his list and as a result decided to reduce this type of futile mental involvement dramatically. This profound awareness immediately reduced his stress at work, which he had battled for many years.

The most classical comparison is comparing yourself to others. "How come she has ____ and I don't? Why did he get a raise and I didn't? She has prettier hair. She is taller, he is smarter, they are happier, they have a bigger house, their children are more polite." Painful comparison goes on and on and on. Sure, some people preoccupy themselves more with such useless comparisons and others, less.

I guide parents away from ever comparing their children to other kids. Children feel defeated and frustrated when they are compared. The child begins to form the idea that he is not good enough and should be like others. This sets a pattern that creates endless self-criticism, being down on oneself, which can then cause more challenging conditions later on in life.

Also, this is how rebellious behavior grows more intense, especially during teenage years. Many parents in my practice complain about how their child has become so resistant and rebellious and they can't figure out why. I explain that when parental expectations are too high, when they set unrealistic goals, and when they compare their children and their performance to others, rebellion results.

A child wants to be himself. A child wants to know that he or she is respected and accepted for who they are, not just when they perform or achieve certain accomplishments.

I remember watching an interview on TV with the lightweight boxing champion Oscar de la Hoya, a four-time world champion, also nicknamed The Golden Boy. What caught my attention was de la Hoya saying he did not care so much about winning championships. What he cared about was getting his father, who was also his coach, to tell him that he fought well.

> **Comparison is the death of true self-contentment.**
>
> *John Powell*

Apparently his father had never said that to him and de la Hoya looked quite disappointed as he talked about the lack of approval from his dad.

It is never too late to rectify such patterns of behavior, but at times it may require a long healing time. Sometimes, the parent we want so much approval from is unable to give it. The parent can also be deceased by the time we connect with our deeper feelings. Either way, we have to resolve this within ourselves. I will talk much more about how to do it in the section dealing with difficult emotions.

We don't just compare ourselves to others. We also compare our current condition to situations in the past. If we have more now than what we had then, we feel good. But if the opposite case is our reality, we tend to feel bad.

When something is taken from us—a possession, our health, or a loved one—we get depressed because we compare what we had in the past to what we have now or to what we miss in the present. When working with people who were injured, for instance in a motor vehicle accident, this comparison becomes a source of immense frustration. The problem is that when the injured individual keeps comparing his present health condition to how it was before, he is living in the past and not in the present. This will always hinder recovery.

Such comparison is normal; most people would react the same at first, under similar circumstances. But as I already mentioned, it is dwelling on the past that causes the problems.

We all have certain standards that we try to live up to. If these standards are reasonable, they tend to motivate us and help us to develop and grow. If they are unrealistic, they can cause us much anguish. The problem with many such standards is that our parents or other important people in our lives set them, and they may not even be suitable for us. If a specific standard is causing you much stress, it is probably time to let it go.

Some of what I call "reference comparison" is fine. This means that we may look at a role model or an expert in order to find out what we have to learn to improve in certain areas. Such comparison would be acceptable and usually beneficial. The trick is to avoid over-processing such as, "I will never be like him. Why can't I get it right like she does?" This type of comparison would fall under the category of self-criticism.

> Cherish your yesterdays; dream your tomorrows; but live your today!
>
> *Author Unknown*

We also compare our present situations to the future. This is called worrying. When we worry that our position, situation, status, or even health may change for the worse, we create unnecessary anxiety. We do the same if we are afraid of negative consequences of certain actions we contemplate.

As discussed earlier, when you live in the past or future, you live in the mind. You can choose to stay in the present and do the most you can with what you have. You can't make the past better. You can only affect the present. That in turn will positively affect the future.

In fact, you can't even let go of the past. All you can do is resolve the repressed feelings you carry from the past.

Judgment

Judgment, criticism, and cynicism all fall under the same category. When we engage in such behaviors we really press the ego's accelerator to the maximum.

Judgment is nothing but a comparison process. When we judge, we compare other people's behavior, values, and beliefs to ours or to how we think they should be. When a person judges or criticizes someone else, it is as if he is saying, "I know better than you," and even worse, "I am better than you." When someone thinks that they are better than others, they assert that they are superior while acting out the flaw of judgment.

I was fortunate enough to go through a transformation many years ago when I decided to stop judging people and comparing myself to others. I realized I had been judging and comparing frequently without even being aware of it. I developed tremendous respect for people, even if the thought that they could do better crossed my mind. I just let that thought pass, without acting on it. Gradually, these thoughts became more and more scarce. You can't imagine how freeing that is, unless you are already doing the same.

Prejudice is perhaps the worst way of judging. When we judge people by their cultural background, the color of their skin, or their race, we claim, even if unconsciously, to be superior to them. We have seen the devastating results of such prejudice when hundreds of years ago, different European countries invaded other territories such as South America, Asia, and Africa.

When you stop judging, you allow yourself to see the good in people and you respect people with all of their weaknesses as well as strengths. Fundamentally, people want to connect with each other, to be accepted as they are, and to feel good about themselves. If you can give people such a safe feeling of connection and warmth, you have done something really important. To achieve that, judgment must be completely suspended.

Later on, you will see that comparison and judgment also work against one of the most important spiritual truths.

Attachments

We get attached to people, possessions, even to our jobs. In Eastern philosophies, attachments are one of the biggest no-no's, and rightfully so. The ego says, "My car, my computer, my child, my wife, my money. I have this and I have that, and I won't give it away." Naturally, an attachment to a car is not the same as an attachment to a spouse. Nevertheless, we are programmed to accumulate, collect, and hang on to things.

> He who binds to
> himself a joy
> Doth the winged
> life destroy;
> But he who kisses
> the joy as it flies
> Lives in Eternity's
> sunrise.
>
> *William Blake*

There is nothing wrong with possessions. It is the attachment to them that we need to avoid. The biggest problem with attachment and its more extreme form, possessiveness, is that if for any reason this attachment is broken, it can dramatically affect your mental and emotional state. When you are free of attachments (which is not the same as being free of possessions), changes in belongings do not affect you.

As human beings, it is quite normal to form attachments, but we need to learn to reduce them if we want to attain a high level of spiritual awareness. You cannot get attached to the moment, and the moment is really all that you have! Think about it for a moment.

Here is a question that tends to confuse many people: Is attachment to a good state or feeling acceptable? After all, don't we want to feel good?

Any attachment, even to good feelings, should be avoided. Such attachment can also cause pain and suffering. Isn't that what happens when something that we consider irreplaceable is taken from us and causes us pain for a long time? Isn't that also the root of all addictions, trying to hang on to a certain state or feeling? No attachments—no problems.

I'm not telling you that we should not feel good. Again, trying to hold on to the feeling's origin, when the moment is already dealing you the next card, may cause unnecessary pain.

Do you know what the real test of happiness is? If an important possession were taken away from you, would that take away your happiness? If it would, was your happiness real?

If you feel more confused by what I'm saying than ever, consider that happiness and joy are not synonymous. Happiness is typically an ego-based state. We feel happy when things go the way we want them to. The spiritual counterpart of happiness is joy, and joy is not attached to anything. Joy comes either from a creative expression or from deeply connecting with people and with nature.

A few weeks ago while driving, I noticed the most amazing sunset. The sky was first covered with stripes of orange which then turned red. Normally, I would have gone back home to pick up my camera, but I was on my way to meet someone and I could not go back home. Initially, I felt some disappointment but I quickly let that go and enjoyed the colors until they disappeared, and then I let that go too. With acceptance and letting go, it did not feel as if I had missed anything.

That night I had a dream that was similar to my sunset experience, except that a few minutes after I let go, the sun arrived again, ready to create another amazing sunset. I was not too surprised at what the dream was trying to tell me. It signaled from deep within that we are constantly given second chances; but to attract them we have to accept the moment, then let go, and await the next one.

This issue of attachment becomes much harder to deal with when we experience extremely difficult feelings, for instance, after the loss of a loved one. Therefore, I will discuss this issue separately.

Blaming

Blaming is a unique ego-based technique that tries very hard to brush off any personal responsibility. Thoughts or statements that reveal shifting of responsibility include, "She made me do it. It's all because of him. I am like that because of my parents."

The ego does not like making mistakes or even admitting to making them. It is generally not comfortable taking responsibility. Blaming is easier.

But blaming is the opposite of living in the deep moment, where everything that happens is accepted as is, without pointing a finger in any direction. Living in the deep moment without clinging to it avoids all the feelings that usually accompany blame, including hurt, anger, and jealousy.

Taking responsibility does not equal self-blame. It means that you accept responsibility for your actions and work on making corrections, learning from the situation, and then letting go of the negative feelings associated with what happened.

A very close relative of blaming is complaining. I think sometimes that our society has turned into one big complaining machine. I meet so many people who complain of just about everything—their work environments, their families, the government, you name it.

So what is complaining? It is a combination of comparison, judging, criticism, and sometimes even blaming.

Here is my favorite complaint technique. Many times my patients complain about the weather. I take them over to the window and point out that it's cloudy or snowing or raining. I explain to them, "Nothing is bad, or ugly, or depressing about any weather condition. The negative feeling is only created in our thinking."

Isn't it funny that we talk so much about the weather and yet there is absolutely nothing we can do to change it? All you can do is adjust to it. Any other action, including complaining, is wasted effort that floods you with negativity. If it rains, take an umbrella. If it's cold, dress warmer. If it's sunny, put the sunscreen on. PERIOD.

Whether you're dealing with weather conditions or more significant life situations, you can choose not to complain. Instead, it would be more practical to accept and adapt.

Learning to put these big PERIODS directly after we connect with our senses prevents unnecessary mental processing and enables a deeper connection with the moment I call them **Spiritual Periods**.

Impatience

The biggest deterrent to dramatic progress in spiritual territory is usually impatience. It's said that in life you need a cup of understanding, a bucket of love, and an ocean of patience. Many times I have encountered people who missed out on opportunities to break limiting habits because their impatience kept them from persisting with the necessary practice.

Impatience is also a comparison process. Suppose you are waiting in line at a grocery store and the line is moving very slowly. You notice the line to the right and the one to your left are moving faster and you become impatient. The reason is that you made a comparison and expected your line to move as fast. Impatience can only be experienced in the mind. In the moment, nothing is too slow or too fast, it just IS.

Have you noticed how impatient our society has become? With so much road rage and more cases of air rage, where exactly do you think are we heading with that? Recently, I had lunch in the food court of a nearby mall. At the next table, a mother and her son, about 8 years old, were drinking juice. About five minutes later, the father came back with a tray full of food. The child asked his dad what took him so long, to which the father responded, "The girl was very slow, almost as slow as you are." This was a very clear example of how we, as parents, reinforce impatience in our children.

> Adopt the pace of nature: Its secret is patience.
>
> *Ralph Waldo Emerson*

You may get the impression that I was born one of those slow paced, peaceful individuals who takes his time in whatever he does. The opposite is true. Impatience used to be one of my biggest challenges, and although I haven't entirely overcome it, I have curbed a lot of it. Whether I'm standing in line, sitting in traffic, or just waiting for someone, I do my breathing and I become deeply aware of everything around me. The passing of time then becomes a non-issue.

I came to believe that I was given impatience as a gift in order to learn not only to appreciate the important things in life, but also to motivate me to look for shortcuts in my work. So just for good measure I hold on to a little bit of it, until the time comes when I recognize that even that reminder is not necessary anymore.

Sometimes I do an interesting exercise to reinforce patience. I do it when I feel a little impatient in circumstances like waiting in a particularly long line in a grocery store. From time to time I give my turn to the person behind me, especially if they have a cart full of groceries. People have great difficulties believing it when I offer them my turn, so I explain to them that I'm practicing patience. Most of them agree with me on the importance of patience, thank me for my gesture, and jump ahead. Some of them think that I am nuts, but as soon as I do it, I feel truly empowered and my impatience completely disappears.

Try it and see for yourself. I promise you will find this exercise quite powerful and entertaining too.

Identification

When we identify with someone or something, we become that association. When you identify with a group, you begin to act and think like the rest of the group. Many cults, for instance, force this type of identification on all of their members. If the leader of that cult is an extremely ego-based individual, as most of them are, you will become the same if you are a follower.

Many patients ask me how to identify a cult when encountered. The gauge is very simple. If the cult leader claims that only one way exists, his or her way, and will not allow any flexibility or free flow of ideas, you have a cult on your hands. Not too long ago, a cult leader in Uganda (the Movement for the Restoration of the Ten Commandments of God) was responsible for the death of more than 500 of his followers by committing fire suicide. It is suspected that he himself ran away because his body was never found.

If you ever encounter groups that enforce any kind of one-way thinking, run while you can. Groups that encourage individual thinking, choice, and flexibility represent the opposite.

We also identify with roles: "I am a teacher," "I am a therapist." People usually ask shortly after meeting, "What do you do?" and we answer: "I am a truck driver" or "I am a doctor." We tend to identify completely with what we do.

Are we our roles? Of course not, but when we identify with these roles, we lose touch with our true essence. We can also identify with a behavior or a trait. "I am lazy," "I am selfish," or "I am smart" are examples of such identification.

Even more devastating can be the identification with emotions. For example, identifying with anger makes you feel even angrier.

How do we articulate it? "I am angry." This identification with your emotion makes as much sense as saying "I am plaid." When you say, "I am angry," you're completely identifying with the state of anger. Can you see the danger in that?

Or how about identifying with your problems? "I am a basket case." I used to be annoyed when people said that, and I would immediately correct them. "You are not a basket case, you are just experiencing certain challenges," I would say. Now I choose to stay calm, but I also take the opportunity to explain the concept of identification. Most people say something like, "I've never thought about it." From that moment on, they usually do.

Do you see how people can make themselves miserable by the thoughts they preserve and the words they use to express them? So, you may ask, what's the right way to say it? You can say, "I DO teaching," "I DO therapy," "I FEEL angry." Or you can have fun with it and say, "My ego is getting angry." By changing the words in your mind, you break the identification with the role or the behavior.

I always like to have fun with these definitions. Sometimes, when I am asked what I do for a living, I answer that I'm involved in the block removal business, and most people then think that I am in construction. Some of my other job descriptions include "I do internal design," and "I am in sales." When asked what I sell I usually reply: "I sell change." In my more serious moments I answer, "I do counseling."

Defensive Reactions

The ego is very reactive. What really happens when we react? A defensive reaction is a way to defend our perceived weaknesses and sensitivities.

Not a lot of difference exists between an offensive and a defensive reaction. Offensiveness is in fact part of defensiveness and both are part of our protection mechanisms.

Recently one of my patients told me about her high level of stress caused by peer interaction in her office. When I asked what sensitivity she protected through her defensive reactions, she thought for a while and then said, "I hate it when people are talking down to me; I have always been like that." I explained to her that for someone to put her down, she has to cooperate with that person. This collaboration is done on an unconscious level. Later on she revealed that her reaction was originally created by her mother, who constantly put her down.

The higher the self-esteem, the less reactive you get. We react when a soft spot in us is somehow touched, but we are not always aware that this is the real reason. We will usually come up with some sort of an excuse instead. We might say, "How dare he talk to me like that; I'm going to give him a piece of my mind." What we're really saying deeper inside is, "I am quite sensitive to criticism, and when I am criticized, it somehow reminds me of how my mother used to criticize me." When you're aware of your reactions and where they truly come from, you can begin to better control your behavior.

When I find myself in a defensive mode, I usually go inside as soon as I become aware of it, completely let go of the external trigger, and then trace its real source. Going inward enables me to fix something that will avoid a reaction the next time around.

One of my patients told me she was improving with her stress management skills and cited an example to prove it. "When I get stuck in traffic," she said, "I don't get as impatient as before. I just ask myself, 'What's the worst that can happen? I may be a few minutes late for work,' and I try and stay calm."

"That's great," I said to her. "It's much better than the high level of stress you used to experience in the past. The next step for you is to stay naturally calm in similar situations without the need to say anything." She liked the idea.

Avoiding an emotional reaction evolves in four stages.

1. Becoming aware that you reacted in a certain situation after the interaction is over.
2. Becoming aware of your reaction while it is happening and being able to minimize the reaction.
3. Understanding what is happening when the trigger fires off and avoiding any reacting or suppressing. At this level you have accomplished emotional mastery.

4. Your awareness and understanding deepens. You accept what is happening and if another person is involved as a provoker, you develop a sense of understanding, even compassion, for that person. Ultimately you stay calm no matter what. You meet any challenge with great equanimity. At this point you have reached spiritual mastery.

Use these levels to make yourself aware of your own development in mastering your emotional reactions.

Who becomes defensive? The ego, of course. One of the ways to gauge your progress in minimizing ego-based reactions is to compare your reaction during challenging situations to the four stages just mentioned. The ultimate goal is to experience peace even when you are provoked.

A Radical Change in Education

Earlier we considered parents and their expectations of children in the context of comparison. Children these days are driven to success more than ever before. They are also overexposed to materialism, and as a result are removed to a certain extent from spirituality.

I see some of these parents and children in my practice. In many cases, they feel a void that they can't articulate, let alone resolve. A recent patient complained about how she gave her teenage son everything. She claimed she bought him the best brands in clothing and made sure that he was equipped with every technological marvel only to find out that he was doing drugs. He eventually dropped out of school and refused to communicate with her about it.

Many children feel that they are missing something, that just having everything is not enough, but they can't always understand what it is that they are looking for. As a result they engage in risky and unhealthy behavior. The way we bring up our children needs to change. Not only that, but our education system also needs to transform. If it were up to me, I would change about 30 percent of the present curriculum in favor of teaching students practical life skills such as communication skills, stress reduction techniques, and emotional management.

A couple of years ago, I wrote a small book for children called *Max the Guard Dog*, (soon to be published along with an instructional manual for parents) which I have used with parents to use as a tool to teach their children how to identify and deal with feelings. I feel that this is the single most important skill children can learn. Having this ability would, no doubt, make an important impact on future generations.

Recently I heard about a student somewhere in the U.S. who memorized 5000 decimal places of the mathematical symbol π (3.14159..., etc.) for a national competition. Although I admire the talent, I still have to ask myself where the usefulness of this achievement lies. Most schools may be good at loading students with information, but they fail at equipping them with necessary life skills.

In my opinion, this is a huge miss. Some teachers have recognized the importance of teaching children soft skills, but they are few and far between. The changes have to come from within the education system itself and that will probably happen only under growing pressure from parents.

These changes are long overdue, but I am afraid they will take many more years to occur. In the meantime, it is the parents' responsibility to teach young children life skills as much as possible and, of course, children learn best by example.

Stop the Madness!

Now that you have established more awareness about some of the patterns that can pose serious roadblocks, let me show you a simple and effective way to reprogram yourself. I call it the Stop and Choose Technique.

Earlier you read that mental processing is what creates emotions. Cyclical thinking can even create a chain of feelings as well as cycles within cycles. For example, we may get upset with ourselves about feeling sad and then feel guilty about feeling upset. We get caught up in a limiting pattern, which I call *emotional looping*, that can drive us nuts.

Whenever you find yourself processing any limiting pattern, say, "STOP!" Stop is a very powerful word that the mind understands. When you say it, do it with determination. Make it clear that you really mean it. The more severe the pattern the louder the STOP needs to be. Like a mother shouting at a child before he touches a hot stove, "*Stooooooppp!*"

Recall a thought that whirlpools in your mind, yet is unpleasant. Take a deep breath in and say: "I am letting go of this pattern." Then affirm: "I choose peace instead." Lastly, do more breathing to deeply integrate the change and feel the peace.

Wielding this simple tool can be very useful to rid yourself of all kinds of patterns you want to discontinue, such as blaming, comparing, criticizing, and judging—remember those? This procedure is excellent to use when your ego goes into its super-analyzing mode. "What if, how come, why did he, why can't she, when will I?" Try it and see for yourself.

Do you remember the Lysol commercial with the theme, "Germs no, clean yes"? What this exercise really says loud and clear is: "Ego no, soul yes!"

The Independent "I"

It appears that we have what I call an independent "I" as part of our being. This "I" can identify with many different aspects of you. Your independent "I" can identify with the ego or one of its components: a role, a feeling, or a state of mind.

Be certain to understand that the body identifies with the aspect of yourself that you identify with. When you identify with the ego, then the body suffers the consequences, in the form of tension and pain. When you identify with your CoreSelf, the body becomes holy and it too experiences wholeness and harmony. Ego-based identifications are artificial because the ego-based "I" cannot exist on its own. It requires something—a role, a state, some sort of an object—to exist.

> If I am not I,
> who will be?
>
> Henry David
> Thoreau

Instead, you can choose to identify with your real essence, the only "I" that is real. Using the independent "I" to choose what you identify with is the ultimate choice that a person can make. This fundamental identification will determine your behavior and attitudes. When you identify with the ego or one of its masks, you act out a specific part. When you identify with your soul, you choose to live life to its fullest without the complicated dramas created and directed by your ego.

Identification is such an important subject that I want to reinforce it once again. From a spiritual perspective, all suffering comes from false identification.

This is much like a person being misidentified and put in prison by mistake; when the truth comes out he is exonerated. Similarly, our true essence can also be misidentified. The CoreSelf is kept in prison while you play the role defined by your ego.

Choosing ego instead of identifying with our souls leads us to feel miserable, consumed with disappointment and frustration, thinking that we're missing something "out there." Yet all we have to do is understand that we are locked in the prison of our own mind and that we can set ourselves free by connecting with the truth.

One of our greatest fears, the fear of death, is associated with identifying with the ego. The ego is afraid of dying because it is the part of us that really dies. When you identify with your spirit, you connect with eternity and have no reason to fear a physical death.

Recently I facilitated a process of finding her purpose with one of my patients, an artist by profession. When she finally connected with her purpose she felt very happy at first, but then doubts started creeping up. She was filled with doubts about whether she had the talents and capabilities to follow through. I encouraged her, affirming that I believed that she had what it took to achieve her purpose in life.

She asked, "How come everybody tells me I have such great potential and I can't see it?"

"That's because your independent "I" is identifying with your limitations, instead of your beautiful creative side," I said. She realized that identifying with ego imprisoned her and committed to freeing her CoreSelf.

What do you think is one of your limitations that others do not? Could you be choosing ego's prison instead of your soul's creativity in this area?

When you find yourself identifying with your ego through action or a thought process, announce the mistake to yourself and then imagine yourself correcting it in a similar future event. Repeat this exercise each time you duplicate this limiting pattern.

This type of "mental reprogramming" exercise is very effective in breaking the identification with the ego.

Enlightenment

Eastern philosophies emphasize the importance of ultimately attaining a state of enlightenment. This state happens naturally when you connect the plug of the independent "I" with the socket of the spirit. Suddenly, the light turns on and you can see, really see.

The ego can never be enlightened. To be enlightened you have to BE who you are. The ego is what happens when you unplug yourself. To continue using this metaphor, you can say that the ego uses matches instead of plugging into the energy supply. What you get is mostly darkness. Matches provide limited and temporary light and most of the time burn your fingertips. Sometimes matches even cause big fires and great damage.

Lao Tzu said, "He who knows others is wise but he who knows himself is enlightened." Enlightenment represents the light of awareness, also called "the light of consciousness." This special light illustrates awakening from the illusion of perceived reality into Real Reality, the reality of who you are.

I recently noticed a title for a workshop called "Awakening the Spirit" and I smiled, because the spirit is already awake. We just tend to be asleep to its presence.

We experience five levels of consciousness.

1. *Sleep:* In this state, awareness is minimal. The system is occupied with repair and recharging the batteries physically and mentally. This is mostly a state of deep rest without any external awareness. However, a protective mode will react to danger such as fire or a loud noise that may represent potential for danger. In such cases the unconscious mind will respond, acting from its survival mode, immediately awakening to full consciousness to handle the situation.

2. *Awake:* The conscious mind is involved in this state, but it is somewhat numb. The mind is still in low gear but you are aware that you are awake. For most people, morning time, just upon awakening, represents this state. When we go through the motions on automatic mode without deeply connecting with life and creating very little, we actually live in this state. Unfortunately, we then come to believe that this is how life is lived and are unaware that we exist in a superficial, compromised imitation of life.

3. *Wide awake:* Here we are consciously involved in the activities of daily life. We are more aware of what is going on around us. Our psychology is very active in this state. Thoughts common to this state include, "How do we tackle this problem? What do I do next? What would happen if? How do I improve that? Let me come up with a plan." This is a common daily state for most people.

4. *Heightened:* This state is a result of narrow focus. When you perform a task with such absorption that you forget about everything else, time usually ceases. Your creativity is much more involved in this state. This type of concentration is also produced when you're engaged in an activity of high importance. Let's say you had to guard a celebrity. To do a good job you would have to create this heightened awareness of safety, to ensure that nothing goes unnoticed. You can detect this state in kids who play a video game. They are so much into the game that they're disconnected from everything else. You can call them to come

for supper and they will not even hear you. When we're engaged in pleasurable activities, we typically experience such a heightened state.

5. *Enlightened:* This state represents the highest level of awareness. Now your spirit is at the forefront. You have universal awareness as well as focused awareness at the same time. You enjoy looking at a flower and yet have the awareness of all of nature simultaneously. Such combined awareness is the domain of a spiritual experience. You observe and are involved at the same time. This is a state where the experience, the object of the experience, and the process of experiencing become one. Where is the ego now?

As the story goes, after Buddha experienced a state of enlightenment, people who had noticed his transformation asked him if he was God. He replied with a resounding "No." They kept pressing, asking if he considered himself a person if not God, and he persisted with another "No." "So what are you?" asked the confused people. Buddha said, "I am awake."

Since Enlightenment emanates from the spirit, which is a direct extension of the Ultimate Intelligence, it is also a state of very deep knowing. No questions remain. Just one answer exists, which involves you and your relationship to everyone and everything—a deep sense of oneness that cannot be explained using the rational mind or any scientific principles.

In fact, as soon as you try to explain Enlightenment, all of its essence is lost. How do waves sound? For someone who has never heard the sound, the experience will remain unclear. Ordinary occurrences can be explained using language. But deeper experience is beyond explanations, names, and labels, even beyond our five senses. Enlightenment allows you a quantum leap to a high level in which problems and confusion dissolve and even the mundane becomes miraculous.

> Those who are awake, live in constant amazement.
> *Buddha*

Enlightenment varies in degree, as if a dimmer switch controlled it. You can allow faint light or turn it up fully to flood the room with

> The best way to
> make your dream
> come true is to
> wake up.
>
> *Paul Valery*

illumination. The highest level of enlightenment is brilliance. This is a spiritual state that reflects the deepest awareness of who we are, where we come from, and our connection with each other.

No wonder the source of the Jewish mysticism Kabbalah is the book named the Zohar. The word Zohar means brilliance, but it is more commonly translated into "The Book of Splendor." I believe that this was the level of spiritual awareness its author, Rabbi Shimon Bar Yohai, experienced. It enabled him to have deep insights about life and the connection to God and the cosmos.

A few years ago I took a series of photos of trees in the fall. The prints came out vivid and sharp with magnificent combinations of colors. For a few of them, the only word that came to mind was brilliance.

I then realized that deep inside we already have the state of brilliance and splendor and all we have to do is keep going deeper until we connect with it. What is your spiritual dimmer setting, subdued or splendid?

Boredom

We have looked at some of the blocks on the way to spirituality, namely comparison, judgment, criticism, blaming, impatience, attachments, and identification. I suggested that your ultimate choice is to identify with your spirit. Instead of saying "I am a _____," just state "I am." PERIOD. Anything we put after "I am" will just serve as a distraction. "I am" is the part of you that never changes, that knows no suffering, that is completely free, serene, whole, and eternal.

Make a conscious choice to identify with your spirit. Your independent "I" is your choice to make as a human being. What you choose to identify with will determine the quality of your life.

Let's now consider another important factor in the quality of life. Boredom is a strong motivator in Western society. Think about what people will do to avoid it. Modern society offers us ongoing stimulation to overcome boredom. We're bombarded with offers for products and activities to accomplish this one important goal, to make life exciting and interesting.

Why do we run away from boredom? For one thing, in today's pursuit of success, we always need to be doing something. We're driven to accomplish, produce, and constantly move forward.

If you have children you're familiar with the nagging statement, "I have nothing to do, I'm bored." Consider telling a child, "It's okay to do nothing. Just sit down, notice, observe, and breathe deeply."

Why do we really avoid boredom? If you guessed this has to do with the ego, you guessed right.

Boredom time is downtime. It is a time when you are not physically or mentally active. The system needs such downtime to reflect, rest, recuperate, and recharge.

But this is a dangerous time for the ego. Why? Because during downtime, you can go deeper inside. And God forbid, you may connect with your CoreSelf. The ego knows you may find, albeit by mistake, that something is more powerful, more beautiful, more peaceful, and much more real than IT is. Therefore, downtime is not much encouraged by the ego, which turns boredom into an annoying feeling that must be prevented at any cost.

Avoid looking at boredom as an irritating feeling. Instead, see it as time to breathe deeply, reconnect, observe, and be in the deep moment. The very same feeling that you may have tried to run away from will help to transform you.

I Don't Care

How often do you hear people saying, "I don't care"? How often do you say that? Patients sometimes tell me about specific problems they may be experiencing and then quickly add, "I just don't care about it anymore."

I say to them, "Oh no, that's not a good choice. You have to care."

We need people who care. Without care, how can we love and how can we help others? You need to care, but if you don't like something, deal with it or let it go.

"I don't care" is a well-known defense mechanism that serves to push away challenging emotions. Your dad hurt you and so you don't care. Other kids ridiculed you when you were little. It's easy to say that you don't care and push down pain.

Not caring may also represent avoidance of social responsibilities. Recently I found myself in a conversation with a person about world hunger. I remarked that I felt quite guilty seeing so much wasted food during the function we were attending, when so many children die of starvation every day in many parts of the world. The person's comment was quite surprising to me. He told me he did not care. "It is up to the government to do something about it," he added. I explained to him that without people caring, the government was not going to do much.

> So many gods, so many creeds,
> So many paths that wind and wind,
> When just the art of being kind
> Is all this sad world needs.
> *Ella Wheeler Wilcox*

To make the world a better place, we all need to care. I urge you to care a lot. This does not mean that you should take the suffering of mankind upon yourself. Instead, acknowledge it and ask, "What can I do to help?" We have to act reasonably. Otherwise, it's easy to go overboard. When you feel that you are burnt out, you have gone overboard. When you respond in a balanced way, you feel good about your cause and are continuously recharged by it.

Please understand that when you stop caring, you turn off the tap not only for negative but also for positive feelings. When you give yourself permission to open the tap completely, "stuff" will start pouring out, and you may have to face your own repressed feelings. If you want to connect with spirituality on a deeper level, this is essential.

The goal is to develop a state of imperturbability. This is a high state where things don't disturb you, not because you don't care, but because you are beyond that position. You are resolved. No more emotional buttons. This state comes from a state of TruePeace. When you care, you allow love to flow freely.

The Talmud, a collection of commentaries and discussions about the Jewish Mishnah that includes all Jewish oral laws, says,

"The highest wisdom is loving kindness." Buddha said, "The spirit of Buddha is of the greatest loving kindness and compassion."

Our day-to-day interaction with people must be accompanied by kindness. If you want to see people transform, be kind to them regardless of how they treat you. The results will not always show instantly, but through time they will. The concept of loving-kindness can be practiced only through a combination of total avoidance of judgment combined with genuine caring. This engages the soul while completely disengaging the ego.

So please care, would you?

Stillness

The concept of stillness is very well developed in Eastern philosophies. Lao Tzu, regarded as one of the founders of Taoism in the 6th century, is quoted as saying, "To the mind that is still the whole universe surrenders."

Philosophers throughout time have known the importance of stillness. For instance, Jonathan Wolfgang Von Goethe said, "My greatest wealth is the deep stillness in which I strive and grow and win what the world cannot take from me with fire or sword." In the Bible (Psalm 46:10), we find the instruction, "Be still and know that I am God."

This assertion truly summarizes the power of stillness. Stillness allows you to recognize your own spirituality and through that, your connection with God. This is not a command to stop everything and follow God. What the verse really says is that when you become still, you will then know God. This is and has always been your choice.

Stillness means bringing the wheels of the mind to a complete stop. No processing. But note this: your mind can be still even while you are active. I discovered this during my walks, which have always been very inspiring to me. I walk and yet I can bring my mind to just do walking, nothing else. This is true with any activity. Movement happens and yet deep inside everything is still.

In fact, the entire universe behaves similarly. For instance, as you read this book the earth turns around itself while also moving around the sun; the entire solar system revolves around our galaxy at a speed of 137 miles per second; and yet we don't feel anything.

A similar experience occurs in an airplane. Although you're moving very fast, you don't even feel it. That's the nature of stillness in motion.

Everything that has ever been created in the universe, either by nature or by humans, is in constant movement. All matter consists of infinitesimal particles that jump all over the place in constant motion. The only entity that does not have any movement is God. We need to learn to be still, too.

Henry David Thoreau said, "He will get to the goal first who stands stillest." This is a practice that can help us achieve our goals almost effortlessly.

I have found out through my clinical work that the majority of people cannot just sit still. They have to do something. No wonder so many people are so removed from the Real Reality. Just stay still, remove all processing, feel what's deep inside, connect with calm, connect with YOU.

Movement arises from stillness. However, such movement will always be temporary, in contrast to the stillness that is permanent. Ego can paint movement with colors of impatience, hurriedness, and anxiety, but even while this commotion is taking place, you can identify and connect with the essence of stillness, which is peace. Of all choices, always BE peace.

How Do You Be?

> **"If you want to be happy, be!"**
>
> *Leo Tolstoy*

The notion of "doing" is overly reinforced in our society. Our polite greeting is, "How do you do?" How do I do what? A more common and less formal question of greeting is "How are you?" How are we at what? Wouldn't it be more appropriate to ask: "How do you be?"

How are we called as a species? HUMAN BEINGS. Not human doings and not human havings. Yet we spend so little time in "being." Isn't that a bit distorted? Shouldn't we BE more? So how do you be? You already know the answer: Let go of the doing for just a while, eliminate processing, and avoid attachments and false identification. Take a few deep breaths in and exhale slowly, and just BE. It is quite simple to do and so liberating, yet the concept would seem so foreign to many people that they would dismiss it without giving it a fair chance.

The words "be quiet" may trigger a negative association for many people because of childhood memories. And yet this is one of the most important things you can learn to do: BE QUIET!

When the mind is quiet, you can just enjoy a deep state of being. You don't have to do anything. When you are quiet, you are at peace. Of course this does not preclude activities; we already discussed that. Connecting deeper using this method will usually result in making the right choices and, consequently, doing the right actions.

This, no doubt, is one of the biggest advantages of meditation. But please remember that you don't have to go for lengthy meditations. Brief but frequent exercises of connecting inwardly, such as the one I am going to show you in a moment, will be as beneficial.

I worked with a woman who felt she had to put on a strong front to deal with life challenges all her life. Finally she realized that this was only a way to cover up deep insecurity. As we worked through that, she finally said, "I am tired of being strong all the time."

I answered, "You don't have to be strong and you don't have to be weak. Just BE." With more work and deeper awareness she gradually realized that she could let go of one of her major coping strategies without the fear of being considered "weak." This was not just very liberating for her, but it also resulted in improvement of her energy level and disappearance of many aches and pains she had experienced for years.

"How to Be" Exercise

I would like you to try the following exercise.

1. First take a few deep breaths in. Become aware of your breathing.
2. Let go of mind and body.
3. Completely focus on your breathing, while you breathe effortlessly.
4. Begin to "merge" with your breathing.
5. Imagine that all you are is your breath.
6. Stay with it for a while, then come back.

How did it feel?

Repeat the exercise and this time do it while you keep your eyes open. Imagine that you are pure awareness, which means that you are aware of your surroundings and yet free of any thought processes.

How did it feel this time? Can you keep this state while you go on about your day? You will be so much more alert and focused, yet peaceful. Nothing will get to you and you will be even more creative in resolving any challenges that come your way.

The Ultimate Answer to Ego-Based Tricks

Do you want to learn the most important strategy that can offset your ego-based patterns? Get ready to learn the ultimate spiritual attitude.

I am referring to acceptance. Real acceptance is the solution to avoid all the blocks and difficulties the ego piles up on your way to freedom. If the "what" we want to accomplish is peace, then the "how" to do it is acceptance. Acceptance is more than just an attitude or a technique. It is a way of life.

Acceptance presupposes that we can't really control much. We think we can, but we can't. Acceptance is what allows you to be fully in the deep moment. When you accept circumstances as they are, where you are, and how others are, all processing stops. Think about it for a moment. The opposite of acceptance is resistance, which is usually driven by fear. Acceptance enables you to move forward! Resistance gets you stuck.

From teaching it to my patients, as well as from my personal experience, I know that acceptance is not an easy concept to master. After all, if it were, everybody would be totally peaceful by now. The reason it can be a difficult practice has to do with our desires, motivation, principles, and goals in life. We, in fact, are taught not to accept. We're taught to fight and push and always try to get more.

Understand that acceptance does not equal defeat or giving up. Acceptance doesn't mean that things will remain the same in the future. Acceptance means that right now, that's how things are. Acceptance deals with the present, not the future.

Acceptance always results in peace. Non-acceptance equals denial, conflict, and, consequently stress and discomfort. Acceptance takes the anxiety out of the process and allows greater choices. To be in the deep moment means that you embrace a state of affairs as it is, without any judgment. You may want to make changes in the next moment, but first you have to accept the present as it is.

If somebody treats you badly, as an example, you can accept that. Please notice that you don't accept such behavior, but you accept what just took place, i.e., the facts. In the next moment, you may choose to voice your opinion or walk away. But first acceptance has to take place.

The highest level of spiritual connection occurs when you accept the moment no matter what it offers you! Accepting it without thinking, "Why did she?" "Why didn't he?" or "I wish it hadn't happened," is a very important practice. You have to be careful, though, because the ego can pretend that it is not bothered while inside you suppress all kinds of feelings. You have to pay attention.

Please also note that I don't imply that such feelings are bad. If they are experienced, guess what? You have to accept them, too!

I briefly mentioned the Kabbalah earlier. Interestingly, the word Kabbalah means not only "to receive" but also "to accept."

A movie that emphasizes this concept, although mainly for the purpose of humor, is *Holy Man*, starring Eddie Murphy as Mr. G. Aside from contrasting ego-based individuals with a spiritual or holy person who is not associated with any particular religion or practice, you can see who is really happy and content and who is just trying hard to be. The movie demonstrates very clearly who is living in the now and who is living in the future.

A moment that can easily go unnoticed completely represents this ultimate level of acceptance. In one scene, a woman, who was paid by an individual trying to destroy Mr. G.'s reputation, appears in front of the reporters' cameras claiming that Mr. G. was her husband and that he left her and their children. Mr. G. says nothing, although he knows that this is a lie. He is not trying to deny or give his version. All you can see, while watching him, is how he empathizes with the woman. He truly understands where she is coming from.

The movie is worth watching to observe someone who is an example of acceptance and living in the moment. He is a person who does not react and has no need to prove anything. He doesn't get attached to anything or anyone, yet still has much fun. He lovingly addresses what requires his attention and help and always sees the good in people.

Such a high level of acceptance does not kick in just by reading about the concept and agreeing with it. Such deep acceptance develops in stages. As you begin to reduce your processing, acceptance will gradually set in. If you want to speed up the process, just refuse to judge or criticize yourself and others. Acceptance will follow immediately.

Acceptance is the opposite of comparison, complaining, and blaming. Acceptance allows complete forgiveness, because forgiveness is letting go of everything that is past oriented. Acceptance promotes humility, gratitude, and appreciation, and therefore it helps you live life to its fullest in every way. It also leads automatically to spiritual love and to peace. Spirituality is indeed full and complete acceptance, and that is just another powerful shortcut to spirituality.

Can you accept that?

But what about a woman who is involved in an abusive relationship; should she accept abuse? Absolutely not! Acceptance has more to do with feelings associated with the past and with situations that are beyond our control. When a person has choice about a harmful situation, she should then practise acceptance about everything she felt till that point.

Forgiveness

One of the most powerful concepts, well emphasized in all religions, is forgiveness. Simply put, to practice forgiveness, you need to shut your mind and open your heart. Forgiveness is a practice that can change your life.

I would like to share with you a personal example about the power of forgiveness. Overall, I had a good relationship with my father. We shared many experiences together and he taught me many things. My dad was a holocaust survivor, and as a result, he became overprotective and at times quick to anger. On the other hand he was sensitive, good natured, generous, and an excellent storyteller with a great sense of humor. In my late teenage years I found myself harboring resentment and became impatient towards him.

> To err is human;
> to forgive, divine.
> *Alexander Pope*

This all changed when I turned twenty. One day I was able to see my father in a moment of weakness. This was the first time I had seen him crying. He was not trying to keep face or pretend that everything was okay. Suddenly I could see his human side, free of his high-level coping skills and compensation mechanisms. I felt so sorry for him and in a split second all was forgiven. I never mentioned anything to him about my experience. But he noticed, perhaps unconsciously, how my attitude shifted, and after this we developed a very good relationship.

The interesting fact about my forgiveness is that I felt tremendous relief and much joy after I let go of resentment. I could easily find many reasons why I shouldn't forgive, but I am glad I did. It was very freeing for me and I think, for him as well.

Forgiveness benefits everybody; however I admit it is not always an easy thing to do. In the beginning of my career, I recall treating the first few female patients who experienced sexual abuse when they were young. After discussing the abuse for a while, I naively suggested that to set themselves free they should forgive the abuser. I was almost eaten alive. Most of them would not consider forgiveness under any circumstances. I figured that they were not ready, so I got off this high horse and I worked with them on resolving the feelings they had repressed for years. This was a concept they felt more comfortable with. Then, an interesting thing happened. After letting go of the most difficult feelings, forgiveness came out naturally.

Gandhi said, "Forgiveness is an attribute of the strong." This also works the other way around. We become much stronger when we forgive. Forgiveness cuts your losses short. It enables you to let go and move on.

Take time to give this topic more attention. Ask yourself, "Whom do I need to forgive?" What needs to happen for you to do it? ALLOW yourself to forgive whoever you hold a grudge against and let me know how good it felt.

If not now, when? If not you, who?

Self-Forgiveness

In every grudge you hold onto, you hold a part of it against yourself. This is one of the reasons forgiveness is so important. Sometimes you may even be the exclusive object of blame about something you did before, such as mistakes and wrong choices.

Religion teaches us to ask God for forgiveness. The problem is that this externalizes the process. We wait for something to happen, or for a religious figure to tell us we're forgiven. Even then, we may still hang onto feelings of guilt, shame, anger, and resentment, sometimes even hate.

Forgiveness has to be an internal affair. You ultimately have to forgive yourself.

Many years ago, one of my patients brought her best friend to a session. The woman friend, it appeared, had been guilt-ridden for almost ten years. This woman, who came from a very religious Catholic background, had taken something from a department store without paying for it. The cashier skipped the item and the woman saw the mistake but said nothing. The porcelain plate, if I am not mistaken, was worth around 10 dollars.

"Did you bring it back later on?" I asked.

"No," she said, "I was too embarrassed, but I sent them a twenty dollar bill a few weeks later."

"Have you taken anything else from any store since then?" I asked.

"No way," she quickly replied.

"So you are telling me that you paid twice the value of the item, you learned your lesson—never stole again—and you are still feeling guilty?"

The woman smiled and said, "You are so right."

Ten years of guilt and praying for forgiveness and she let it go in a second. When you learn the lesson from a situation you feel guilty about, it's all right to forgive yourself.

Forgiveness is a process of deeper learning that results in letting go. The ultimate learning is to connect with peace. Realize that you don't need prayer, or your priest or anyone else's approval to do it, unless you prefer it that way. What you really need to do is reflect on the experience, learn from it, and then let go. Remember that you already have the built-in mechanism to forgive and let go.

I was asked by one of my patients lately whether I would also recommend that a murderer forgive himself. Of course I would. If a genuine process of learning takes place and sincere regret comes from a deep understanding of what was done, then I say, "Yes, the murderer can forgive himself." We also need to forgive him. I don't claim that we have to suspend punishment when it's due. However, to prevent repeated crime, criminals should be taught these principles, if they are willing to listen.

Notice that the ego can also allow you to forgive yourself. Sort of a quick Hail Mary. However, this kind of forgiveness is not always genuine. It could very well be suppressing the truth where no learning has taken place. Repenting without inner change and understanding is not going to withstand similar future challenges.

Forgiveness is a spiritual act, not a superficial one. If you hold on to stuff that is already obsolete and contributes nothing to your well-being, if you've already regretted, dealt with, prayed...then practice forgiveness.

Forgiveness helps in resolving resentment that we may still harbor towards others and ourselves. Such resentment prevents us from connecting with our inner source of love and peace.

The fact that forgiveness is a process that has to come from within is also implied in the New Testament. Mark 11:26 states, "But if ye do not forgive, neither will your Father which is in heaven forgive your trespasses." You always have to make the first move. As someone once said, "God will do things with you but not for you."

Faith

For "believers," faith represents their connection with God. Faith is a source of hope. Yet for many others it is a charged word with unfavorable connotations.

The following story may help to describe the difficulty with faith. A man is riding his bike on top of a mountain when suddenly the bike slides and the man falls over a cliff. Luckily he is able to grab a branch of a tree just below the edge. As he looks down he sees a long drop below him. First he hopes that the branch won't break, because it would mean instant death. Then he realizes that, unless someone comes to his rescue, he will never be able to climb up and get out of there. So, he starts shouting for help. "Is anyone up there?" he repeats a few times.

> Faith is taking the first step even when you don't see the whole staircase.
>
> *Martin Luther King, Jr.*

Suddenly, he hears a very deep voice responding: "Yes, I am here."

The man is a bit surprised. "Who is it?" he asks. "This is God speaking to you, my son," the voice replies. "Thank God there is a God" the man sighs with relief. "What should I do, God?" "Just let go of the branch, and I will lead you safely to the ground." "Are you sure?" the man asks. "Don't worry, my son, have faith," the voice responds. The man looks down, then up again and finally shouts: "Is anybody else up there?"

One of my patients told me that when she was much younger, she had long conversations with her rabbi from her parents' congregation about the existence of God. The rabbi finally gave up and said: "Either you have faith and believe in God, or you don't." She chose not to.

Unfortunately this rabbi made a fundamental mistake. He wanted her to have blind faith. This is an unfair leap to ask of anyone, let alone someone who is not ready for it. Faith is about much smaller jumps.

It's said that what is science today, was faith in the past. I see faith as a door. You can speculate as much as you want about what is happening on the other side of the door, but you have to open it and step in to find truth for yourself.

Spiritual principles cannot be proven scientifically, although if we look carefully, we can learn a lot about them indirectly even from science. I will talk more about this later on.

St. Augustine said, "Faith preceded understanding." The leap of faith is just a bridge from what you don't know today to what you may better understand tomorrow.

Spirituality does require a certain leap of faith. It is not blind faith though. It has more to do with trust, especially trust in your ability to become who you are. Also, faith in yourself allows you to follow your intuition, to accept difficult moments in the process, and to know that you can eventually realize the ultimate truth. The ego will fight you on that, but you don't have to identify with it.

This faith is about trusting that you can do it, and that guidance will be there for you. Assistance will come from God, nature, the universe, your intuition, or whatever you choose to believe in. And it will be available.

What I have seen in working with my patients is nothing short of miracles. What we view as miracles on an intellectual level are common events on a spiritual level. These so-called "miracles" will be discussed later on when I will talk about "signs" and synchronicities— strange coincidences that can be easily dismissed. But if you pay attention, such signs can guide you safely when you feel that the branch you're holding onto is about to break and dump you into the abyss.

Faith is what connects our psychological mind, which possesses only limited knowledge, to spiritual reality, which consists of immense wisdom that cannot be fathomed by the rational mind. Faith creates a bridge between mind and spirit. Once you cross it, faith becomes a natural resource.

Faith comes from peace. It is not a blind belief. It may seem so at first, but in fact it is a trivial state when you are in touch with peace. A leap of faith is a move from what we know in terms of information and knowledge, to what is known in terms of universal wisdom. The only way you can develop faith, if you don't have it already, is to trust your experience.

A simple example to demonstrate this point could be an argument with a salesperson about whether a shirt is comfortable or not. The sales person may insist that the shirt she is recommending is the most comfortable shirt in existence and you may disagree. But the only way to get out of the debate is to try the shirt on and experience it for yourself. If you are willing to experience a feeling or an option that has been suggested from your gut or through universal signs, without any preconceived notions, then you can leap into the next level of understanding.

As one's spiritual experiences deepen, acceptance of the spiritual world becomes natural. This is the acceptance that everything happens for a reason and that everything will happen just the way it is supposed to happen, step-by-step, moment-by-moment. That for me is the ultimate faith. How much you accept what is happening in your life is the highest criteria of the level of faith you have!

Humor

One of the most powerful aspects of the soul is playfulness and humor. Studies have shown conclusively that when people watch comedies, their immune system becomes stronger.

> There ain't much fun in medicine, but there is a heck of a lot of medicine in fun.
> *Josh Billings*

Anything that originates from the soul is completely positive. In fact, our mind-body system is built to be positive, joyful, and content. If we only let it, the system will know how to produce positive outcomes. Studies have proven that people who suffered from a heart attack were more likely to die if, in addition, they experienced depression.

Dr. Norman Cousins, a physician and the author of the best seller *Anatomy of an Illness*, was diagnosed some forty years ago with a rare, life-threatening disease. He fought the death sentence suggested by his doctors and used humor as one of his main strategies to heal. Many years later he suffered a serious heart attack, which he also overcame using the same technique.

Humor is very powerful because it connects you directly with your soul. A study done by Lee Berk and David Felten from UCI College of Medicine proved that humor is good for your heart. These researchers studied a group of heart patients who watched 30 minutes of humor a day on TV and compared them to a group of similar patients who did not watch similar videos. Those who viewed the comedy not only had fewer abnormal heart rates and lower blood pressure but also required less heart medication. The researcher checked the conditions of the patients one year later and found that just eight percent of those who watched the funny videos suffered another heart attack compared to 42 percent of those in standard therapy.

The ego also has a sense of humor, but it is usually more the cynical type. It is at times sarcastic, the making-fun-of-others kind of humor. A pure soul's laugh comes from deep inside. When was the last time you had a good belly laugh?

Do you know what one of the most important aspects of humor is? To be able to laugh at yourself. When you laugh at yourself, whom are you really laughing at? Your ego, which is indeed worthy of a laugh. With all of its complications, conflicts, and agendas how can you not laugh at it? Why do people laugh so much watching sitcoms on TV? Because these shows emphasize our ego-based, laugh-worthy thoughts and actions.

> **A day without laughter is a day wasted.**
>
> *Charlie Chaplin*

Next time you make a mistake or screw up big time, just laugh at yourself and see how freeing it is.

However, I have to qualify this. At times, people may use laughter as denial, just as positive thinking can be misused the same way. They may laugh at a situation while they bury different feelings inside. An example is burying shame over a mistake while laughing at yourself to look like a good sport. Laughing has to be genuine and accompanied with awareness of what is felt inside.

An offspring of laughing is smiling. A smile is a soul-based quality that allows people to connect on a soul level, thereby bypassing the ego and its constant calculations. Do you smile enough?

You wouldn't expect me to finish a section about humor without some humor, right? Here is a funny piece I received a few days ago by e-mail.

INNER PEACE (author unknown)

I believe that I've found Inner Peace...

My therapist told me that the path to achieving Inner Peace was to finish the things I had started.

Today, I finished two bags of potato chips, a lemon cream pie, the balance of a fifth of Canadian Club, and a small box of Godiva chocolates.

I feel better already....

Selflessness vs. Soulfulness

Since the ego is selfish, are we supposed to be selfless in the process of becoming more spiritual? That depends on how you look at it.

The ego is all about self. Almost everything we do, even when we do things for others, comes from our ego-based tendencies. Somehow we will benefit, now, later, or in the next life. For example, the benefit to self may be feeling satisfaction from doing a good deed or from gaining recognition of efforts.

Selflessness, therefore, can also be a form of selfishness. Many women I have worked with, who used to put themselves last in an effort to do everything for everybody, become selfless to one degree or another. When they finally realized that they would have to take better care of themselves, they expressed feelings of guilt about becoming selfish. First, I would explain to them how important taking good care of themselves is to their physical, mental, and emotional health. Unless you take care of yourself, you eventually expend all the resources you require to help others.

Next I would explain how soulfulness differs from selflessness. Soulfulness is about giving from your soul, without wanting anything in return. You feel so abundant inside that you just want to share it with everyone. Does this sound foreign? I hope not.

In all honesty, I would rather people give out of some selfishness than not give at all, but to give more and feel great without any payback, we must transcend personal needs and wants.

Notice I didn't say suspend them—but transcend them. To do that you have to continue to let go of the ego and one of its major areas of focus—self-esteem.

Transcending Self-Esteem

I mentioned earlier how I used to put a big emphasis on helping people develop and enhance their self-esteem. In recent years I have found myself doing the opposite. I have been teaching people how to get rid of it. Many of my patients were initially quite surprised with my intentions. After spending a lifetime building an acceptable self-esteem, how could they let it go?

Let me ask you a question: On a scale of 0 to 10, 10 being the highest, what kind of self-esteem do you want to have? People usually come up with a number around 8 or 9. A few dare to say 10.

Now here is my next question: On the same scale of 0 to 10, what is the self-esteem of the spirit? It's not 10, it's not zero. It is just not there. The spirit has no self-esteem. It does not need one!

What is self-esteem? Simply put, self-esteem is a concept that describes how you feel about yourself in terms of your abilities, your looks, your performance in different areas, and whether or not you believe yourself to be likeable. Self-esteem is a perception that you have about yourself as a person, as a parent, as an employee and so forth.

Since it is a perception, it is by definition ego based. You may say, "I'm only five feet tall; I'm too short." or "I'm nearly seven feet tall; I'm too tall." These are perceptions. Physical measurements are facts.

Instead, put a big **SPIRITUAL PERIOD** at the end of the factual statement because what comes after is ego-based comparison. "I am 38 years-old and not even married," one may say, "how can I feel good about myself?" You can. The first part is the fact and the second is the perception. Why build your self-opinion on the flawed foundation of perception?

Learn to stick to the facts. The facts are the truth. Perception is a form of a lie you agreed to follow. This concept may be somewhat difficult to accept but you really need to overcome the handicap of believing perception over truth. Practice putting spiritual periods after the facts. It's unnecessary to feel bad about yourself. PERIOD.

Let's talk about assertiveness, one of the measures of good self-esteem. One day I went to check out a secondhand accordion that was advertised in the local paper. When I was young, I took accordion lessons and I felt like playing again. I took my daughter along with me. A very pleasant woman who had put her son's accordion up for sale welcomed us. He had played it many years ago and had lost interest. As we talked with the woman, my daughter, who was about seven years old at the time, saw a beautiful large orange on the shelf. It was so unique in size and shape that I was sure it was put there for decoration. My daughter looked at it and had no problem asking, "Can I have the orange?"

I felt uncomfortable and immediately proceeded to tell her that I didn't think she could have it. But the woman liked my daughter's directness and especially the big smile on her face as she admired the orange, and she insisted on giving it to her. My daughter decided not to take it, based of my faulty influence, of course.

We make too many conjectures. Might we hurt someone? What will people think? Stop processing. If you want something, ask for it. If you get it, fine. If you don't get it, that's fine, too. No processing, no speculations and no uncomfortable feelings as a result.

The other aspect of assertiveness is saying no when appropriate. Let me tell you something important: NO is also a spiritual word! When you are in your deep moment, and somebody wants to move you to his or her moment and it is inconvenient, just say so. On the other hand, if someone is in great need of your moment and you can attend to the person's need, then by all means be there. But don't act only because you don't feel comfortable saying no or because you want to portray yourself a certain way. If it feels right, say yes and if it doesn't, say no.

A few months ago I counseled a young woman about her anxiety attacks. It was very clear that she had overloaded herself with various activities that resulted in stress. She admitted that she could not refuse anything asked of her. Unfortunately, people around her knew how to take advantage and always asked for her help.

The bottom line was that she was on a verge of a nervous breakdown. She felt dejected and anxious and experienced frequent back pain. "I just don't know how to say no," she complained.

I asked her, "Do you want me to tell you how to do it?"

"I would love that," she quickly replied.

I leaned close to her and shouted quite loudly, "NOOOOO-OOOOOOOOOOOOOOOO!" I concluded, "That's how you say no."

After recovering from the initial surprise she started to laugh hysterically. After that she was able to say no more easily, without feeling much guilt.

Self-acceptance is better then self-esteem. When self-acceptance is planted, peace grows. Foster acceptance, despite your perceived shortcomings.

Self-acceptance is better because it is a spiritual practice, whereas self-esteem is a psychological concept. Self-acceptance means that you love yourself unconditionally. This will eliminate all the ego preoccupation with your shortcomings, and therefore, provide the shortest bridge to the true YOU.

When my youngest daughter was about seven years old, she asked me when I kissed her good night if I loved her "no matter what." I always reassured her, and after a few months, she felt confident enough not to ask the question anymore. I kept affirming my unconditional love for her for sometime just to be on the safe side.

I reflected on this exchange a number of years later and realized not just the importance of unconditional love with others, but also the importance of unconditional self-love. Please try the following exercise.

Observe yourself in the mirror for a couple of minutes and notice what you mainly focus on when you look at yourself. Pay attention to your entire body and then look at your face for a few more moments.

From ego's perspective, you can criticize the many aspects of your personality and your body features that you don't like. Spiritually, this type of preoccupation is a waste of time and energy. Just be who you are and accept what you were given. The rest will take care of itself.

Can you tell yourself and fully believe the following statement? "I completely accept and love myself no matter what." If you are not in full sync with this statement, you still have self-acceptance work to do.

The Observer

When we analyzed the different perspectives of who we are, we agreed that we have a personality, an ego, thoughts, feelings, and beliefs. I also asked you, "Who is the one having all these qualities and characteristics? And whose personality is it?" Now I would like to ask you a slightly different question. Who is noticing the flow of thoughts, the change of feelings, the strengths and weaknesses of the personality? Take a moment to reflect on that.

The ego-based self can notice all of the above. But there is a part that's one level higher and it is constantly observing the ego while it notices all that.

This deep aspect of our being, our spirit, is not involved in any of the limiting behaviors of the ego we have discussed before: judging, criticizing, comparing, blaming, complaining, and generally over-analyzing. Instead, it is engaged in observing, but not in the kind of observing the ego does. The ego may observe but it immediately processes the information, draws conclusions, makes comments, and devises strategies. The spirit observes, period.

This observation is a very deep level of awareness beyond all mental processing. The spirit observes from a place of total peace. Such observations are done with great attention and are followed with caring, sharing, helping, love, compassion, and forgiveness, all soul-based activities.

It is important to learn how to observe closely, as opposed to observing from a distance, which is a detached position. Some people, for instance, don't feel comfortable engaging in conversation and therefore observe others in a detached mode. That's ego. I'm talking here about observing what is happening in the moment, while being in the moment. You can learn so much and deepen your understanding when you observe in this way.

I strongly suggest that you practice observing. Remember that this is a sincere way to pay full attention to what is happening, without any processing. Deep connections are made this way, with things that perhaps were not noticed before. With deeper realization, clarity about the interaction sets in.

Does anyone observe the observer? Sure, God does, and observation is done without any judgment or criticism! God does not do any processing either. God's observation comes from the deepest place of peace and love. When you observe in this aware way, you feel one with God.

This is truly a very powerful state of being. All your relationships will deepen by practicing observation with deep attention and no processing. Please try it for yourself and send me a note about your big revelations. I mean it!

Take Half a Step Back to Move Forward

We're always in a hurry to accomplish and progress and move forward. The problem is that sometimes, the more forward we move, the further away we get from the spiritual terrain. When that's the case, all you have to do is take half a step back.

"Why half a step?" you may ask.

A full step may cause disconnection and detachment, and we want to be able to connect and feel. The goal is not to separate yourself from life but to experience it fully. Rushing causes you to be ahead of life. A full step back will cause you to be behind life. Half a step is the right attitude. You observe while experiencing life at the same time. As a result, you will experience joy without restrictions and peace without conditions.

You can take half a step back whenever you feel too absorbed in processing, when you feel the heaviness of thoughts and feelings. Just observe what you experience, without trying to push it away or trying to run away from it. Look at it and allow it to be. You are not the experience, and it is not you. And if you don't believe me, just take half a step back right now and find out for yourself.

The Observer Exercise

> You can peacefully observe what happens around you and how people interact among themselves and with you. As you continue to observe without judgment, your awareness will go deeper and deeper and you will understand more about people and life than ever before.

Equally, if not more important, is to observe yourself. I said earlier that the spirit observes the flow of thoughts and feelings in the mind. We also talked about identification and the "independent I." Now let's do an exercise that will help to integrate all these concepts together.

Observing Thoughts

This very useful exercise will help you to make a distinction between you and your thoughts when you get too involved in them.

1. Close your eyes, take a few deep breaths in, and exhale slowly.
2. What is your mind thinking about? Pay attention to these thoughts for a few moments.
3. Now in your mind imagine yourself stepping back a half step so you can create a small distance between you and your thoughts. In this position you are observing your thoughts instead of being caught in the middle of them.
4. Continue to observe your thoughts from this separate perspective while breathing slowly. Notice what happens.

Does your mind get quieter? Do you feel more peaceful? Do new thoughts come in? Did the old thoughts pull you back in? If you experienced the latter, try the exercise again.

This time, edge further back mentally but not too much, until you feel somewhat separated from your thoughts. Observe them again.

Initially, most people become more aware of how much thinking they do, and then gradually they become more peaceful.

When you feel comfortable with this exercise, you may try a more advanced exercise.

Repeat the last exercise, but this time notice that small pauses occur between each thought. These pauses are totally peaceful, as they don't have the busy vibrations thoughts do. See if you can become aware of them and notice how it feels to observe these pauses for a while.

Observing Feelings

Now I want you to try this exercise with attention on your feelings.

> Repeat the same process as before, but this time be aware of a situation that causes you an emotional reaction—but not too intense to begin with. Assume your observer position and watch the feelings from your half-step away. Avoid analyzing or trying to figure out your feelings, because analysis sucks you back into them. Just observe and notice what happens.

> When you work with this exercise patiently, you will realize that you can be much more at peace despite the emotions, no matter what they are.

To understand this concept better, try an exercise with a physical object as a tangible example.

> Take a basketball or any big ball and bring it very close to your eyes. Can you see that it's a ball? Do you see the object clearly when it's close to your eyes?

Of course not. Your perspective is limited because you're too close to the object. The same limited perception happens when we become too absorbed in thinking and feelings. We tend to lose perspective and subsequently—inner peace.

Use this exercise regularly and you will notice that chaotic emotions will bother you less and less. You will also gain a deeper understanding on how to deal with the situation that triggered the emotions. You may then choose a certain positive action or just decide to let it go.

If you decide that an emotion is not beneficial anymore and it recurs out of habit, you may want to use the Stop and Choose technique to enhance the Observer Exercise.

Love

Manifested through the soul, love is the second major quality of the spirit. I believe that at least one of the reasons God created the world was to exercise love. Peace was always there, even before, when the universe was one vast ocean of no-thing-ness.

> For I have said:
> the world is built
> by love.
> *Psalms 89:3*

Love represents the joy of creation that evolves from peace. It arises naturally as a result of connecting with others on a deeper level. This kind of love is completely unconditional.

The ego's love is very different. It is a kind of love that can make you feel good or can make you feel miserable because it is conditional. It's the love that is based on neediness, ego-to-ego-based love. Compared with the two-dimensional ego kind of love, spiritual love is a 3D type that is given freely and unconditionally. No neediness or expectations are attached to it.

An acquaintance told me that he could never love people in the same way he loved his dogs. He asked me how I would explain this difference. I said that, unfortunately, when practicing love with certain people, he would offer the more ego-type love.

For example, ego-based love expresses itself this way: "If you do all these things for me, I will love you." "If you treat me a certain way, I will love you, but if you don't, or you stop, I will discontinue my love to you." What kind of love is that? It can't possibly be true love.

Spiritual love is pure. It's probably the kind of love this gentleman experienced with his pets. We can experience the same type of love when we remove our conditions on loving.

I asked this man if he were deeply hurt in the past by people who didn't return love to him. He confirmed that to be true. The ego is very sensitive. Don't return what it expects and needs, and it will punish the world by shutting down the capacity to love and be loved. Who is really paying the price of the punishment here?

Essentially, spiritual love is different from what we feel when we fall in love with a person we feel attracted to. Spiritual love is an expression of who we are and the deep connection we all have. This love expands to include limitless numbers instead of focusing on restricted groups. It is that beautiful warm feeling that allows you be kind to others and to help and contribute without wanting in return. Spiritual love springs out of peace, so when you experience this total inner peace, loves flows naturally. Peace is the overall state, and love is its expression and doing.

> Beloved, let us love one another because love is from God and whoever loves is born of God and knows God.
>
> *John 4:7*

When you offer love through sharing, listening, and connecting, then you feel joy. Joy is a sensation the ego can never offer. Never! When we lose our joy in life it means that our ego has totally taken over. It's time we get in the driver's seat and change direction—from searching outside to looking deeper inside. Then, the inside path will lead to beautiful roads we never thought we could ever encounter.

Knowing that I was loved was never a problem for me. My parents always cared for my siblings and me. My mother spared no effort to do things for everybody. She never complained or expected anything in return. She was a true giver.

However, my parents were never strong on the physical aspect of love. Only after I grew up did they start to catch up with hugging and kissing and this was very nice. It took me many years to realize how much I missed expressions of affection as a child. Fortunately, this never caused a problem in my ability to show lots of love to my children, and I am very grateful for that. I also realized that my mother never said to me that she loved me. I guess she believed more in showing it through actions than through verbalizing it.

One day when we were talking on the phone, I said, "I love you, Mom." This was not so easy to do and seemed quite strange at first. My mother was very surprised. I made a point to repeat that when we talked again. Eventually, she too learned to tell me how much she loved me.

The lesson is simple yet very powerful: If you want to experience more love, give it freely!

What Does It Mean to Love Yourself?

I always wondered why it is so important to love oneself in order to be able to love others. Isn't such love narcissistic in nature? When I figured it out, I realized how powerful this truth is.

First of all, self-love equals self-acceptance. This acceptance contradicts the ego's philosophy about "not enoughness," feeling insecure or unfulfilled with what you have and always desiring more. Secondly, and probably most importantly, to truly love yourself you first have to tap into your inner well of love. Not an ego or superficial type love, but the real and pure one.

Once you are in touch with this limitless source of love the rest is easy. You simply want to share it with others and especially with those who have not yet tapped into their own source. Suppose for a moment you now own all the money in the world. What would you do with it? I can bet that you would share it with others. After all, why would you need so much money in your hands? When you tap into this 3D love you immediately understand how shallow and artificial 2D love is and you want everyone to feel it too.

So what do you have to do to connect with this big reservoir of love? Remove the conditions. Let go of your expectations of yourself and of others. Accept yourself now, not when you change, not when you make it in life the way you thought you should, not in the future. Now!

Then offer love to everyone around you, and expect absolutely nothing in return. Expecting is processing. Stop processing entirely, and feel all the peace and love that exists in the world, now! Don't worry about feeling vulnerable. It's the ego that feels that way. Let it. The spirit is as solid as a rock and yet as tender and soft as velvet, so fully identify with it and vulnerability will instantly dissolve.

This idea of self-love, I believe, is indirectly spoken of in the Bible. In Leviticus 19:18 we find the famous instruction, "Thou shalt love thy neighbor as thyself." This message is a very noble—socially advanced—spiritual message.

Unfortunately, many people behave in their daily life as if this instruction said, "Love thy neighbor instead of yourself." They do everything for everyone, but forget to take care of themselves. When you really look at the sentence, you can clearly see that this message presupposes that you are first able to love yourself; otherwise how would you be able to love thy neighbor? You can't give what you don't have.

I hope this makes sense to you, because many people seem to have a problem with loving themselves, and yet it is such an important spiritual principle. I believe that God's love can be experienced only through experiencing self-love; hence the importance of connecting deeply. Over and over, reinforce the concept of going deep inside, deeper than ego territory to find solutions for every challenge, to find answers to every question, and finally to turn from a lifetime seeker to an immediate finder.

We can also find the concept of our innate boundless love in Shakespeare's *Romeo and Juliet*. Juliet says, "My bounty is as boundless as the sea, My Love as deep, the more I give to thee, The more I have, for both are infinite."

When you get in touch with this wellspring of boundless love, you may feel puzzled at first. The reason is that the ego needs to connect it to someone external. We are so accustomed to having an object for our love. Spiritual love is not exactly like that. Spiritual love is about loving all of creation equally.

Sometimes my patients will tell me how accepted and peaceful they feel in our sessions. This is an attempt to attach these feelings to someone or to a situation. I tell them that I am nothing but a mirror, and the object in the mirror is their own CORE, which is always peaceful and loving. I encourage them to continue awareness of that feeling and to work with it; because once they get it, they will become free of any dependency on the external world and yet still stay fully connected to it.

I want to share with you a poem I received from one of my patients after she deeply connected with self-love.

True Love
My heart is filled with joy
Light and free—the essence of being.
Like a sunrise gently breathing life into the morning
Love arises from within.
The love is deep within my soul,
It is a gift given only to myself.
It is not romantic love bound by the smothering ties of
    attachment,
Nor imprisoning like the chains of expectation.
It is liberating, fulfilling and real.
This love must be treasured.
It is the love of self.
Given to me by me,
Not to be thrown away
Or challenged.
It will remain with me,
Comforting and strong.
It is warm like a summer breeze,
And gentle as a soft rain.
My love abounds.
It is mine forever,
Like the sunrise and the sunset.
As the day begins and ends
It will always be with me.

The Spiritual Ego

Sound like an oxymoron? For sure. But trust the ego to pull perhaps
the biggest trick of all.

In all honesty, I respect the ego's capabilities. Such creativity
(by the way, where is it taking its creative power from?) and such
tenacity. Unbelievable. To distract you from getting in touch with
your true essence, something that can bring death to the ego, it can
and will offer you superficial alternatives.

You want love; let's look for it, let's work hard to deserve it. We have to find people who will love us. You want peace? Let's work even harder; we can accomplish it.

Promises pour out and cheap substitutes are occasionally felt. If the ego can get you a little happiness, then you may drop the spiritual pursuit and the ego can start breathing with relief, so to speak. In many cases this mere taste of happiness from the ego is nothing but comfort in disguise.

But what if you are really determined to reconnect with your spirituality? What happens then? The ego will first try to convince you that this is a hoax, that it does not exist, that it can't be found.

> The search for happiness is one of the chief sources of unhappiness.
>
> Eric Hoffer

Suppose you are not convinced. You want spirituality. Be aware that the ego can provide you with the spiritual alternative, a phantom spirituality.

For a long while, I was puzzled by people who were involved in all kinds of spiritual practices, yet at the same time experienced depression, anxiety, fears, guilt, and frustration, even jealousy and hatred. I could not understand how the two could go together. One day it clicked. I exposed the ego's biggest scheme. The ego can give you the illusion that you are becoming more spiritual, by lighting incense, meditating, decorating your room with crystals and such. Now don't get me wrong; I am not saying these practices don't count. They definitely do.

The problem is that once you feel more relaxed with these practices, you enter a comfort zone. As you get comfortable, so does the ego. After all, comfort is one of the hallmarks of the ego. The ego is no longer afraid that you will get rid of it.

You have to expose this scheme too. Demand peace now. Can the ego offer it fully or only its illusion through comfort? You can have peace. It is yours. It is actually YOU!

Try the following paradoxical exercise:

Close your eyes and ask yourself how much you want to become fully spiritual. Get in touch with the feelings of

enthusiasm, yearning, and desire. Then simply let them all go. Take a few breaths in and exhale slowly. Connect with the deep moment. Who do you find after these desires are gone? The ego has left the scene and YOU remain. Affirm: I am already THAT!

The Shadow

Carl Jung said that only when you confront your shadow would you be able to see your own light. What did he mean by that? All ego-based behaviors and feelings that we try to hide, disown, ignore, reject, or deny are part of that shadow. But as logic suggests, if a shadow is visible, a person exists who makes it. Your shadow may include many aspects that others can see in you but you are not willing to acknowledge. Once you're willing to own and face your shadow, all the aspects of your personality that you have tried so hard to keep hidden come to light.

When you acknowledge your shadow, you significantly diminish the ego's power and control. You can see the light that the shadow has obscured, the radiance of your spirituality. Once you have genuinely recognized and accepted your shadow, you will connect with your spirit's brilliance.

This is how I have begun to manage and gradually transform my own ego. Until I started doing work on my SELVES, the ego knew how to take over. It created a stir of emotions when it wanted, directing me into fear, guilt, and sadness. After I decided to confront all the material my ego kept buried deep inside me, and after I learned to accept my shadow, I began to be much more in control of how I felt.

My ego is still there, I have to admit. However, it is smaller. It sits in the back seat and I am at the wheel most of the time. I still satisfy it from time to time to make it feel good and relaxed so that it stays in the background and does not aggressively attempt to take over. I let it have some comfort, but I call the shots. What has been the result of this personal work? I have become significantly more accepting of people and life's challenges and as a result have been experiencing more peace, much more peace.

Controlling the ego is the ultimate control that one can have. To accomplish this goal of reclaiming your personal power you have to start by becoming aware of the role that the ego plays in your life. Next, learn to negotiate with it instead of fighting it. "This is what I want." Be as firm as you would be with a child, because this is what the ego really is—a little child pretending to be an adult. Use the Stop and Choose technique to assert your inner control, the only control ever possible.

What Do You Really Want?

After the question "Who are you?" the second question that causes hesitation is "What do you really want?" Replies are usually "I'm not sure" and "That's a good question." As people recover from the initial consternation, they usually begin to come up with well-known desires. Fulfillment—yes, happiness—naturally, success—sure, healing—yes, good fortune—absolutely.

> We live in a world where people don't know what they want and they are willing to go through hell to get it.
>
> *Don Marquis*

Maurice Sendak said, "There must be more to life than having everything." A great deal of what we want hides in our desires. Desires are sometimes an effort to fill the void inside. But, as you may have experienced yourself, the more you desire, the more the void expands, even if you're able to get everything you believe you want. This is because such desires are very often insatiable.

One of my patients, who spent many years in Hollywood making films, asked me why I thought he, as well as many of his friends and colleagues in the industry, who accomplished fame and a respected economical status, at times felt worse than before they became rich and famous. I explained that one reason could be that these people may have thought that by accomplishing wealth and fame they would overcome the void they had carried from before. Of course, nothing external can resolve that inner void, so after accomplishing all their goals and still not truly feeling fulfilled, such a void could expand even more and drive them into destructive behavior.

Truly, nothing is wrong with desires. We must pay attention to how we feel when we don't get what we want and also to how much time and effort we put into trying to fulfill our wishes.

When we keep pursuing our desires beyond reason, we usually fail to acknowledge and be thankful for what we have. The focus tends to be on what we don't have.

It is not just everyday fulfillment that we're after. Think about this question again, deeply. What do you really want? You might have thought it through and come up with love. That's a fairly good answer, but go deeper into your most absolute necessities.

One of the deepest desires of people is to feel full freedom. Freedom from stress, worries, obligations, and even desires. That would be a pretty good answer, yet another need lies even deeper than that. You have probably figured it out by now. I have mentioned it all along: Peace.

If you had full, complete, and unconditional peace, wouldn't that be the ultimate? Wouldn't that take care of everything else? I have never met a person who disagreed with that.

Now here is the challenge: Can you remember that ultimate desire in your daily interactions? Can you forgo the need to be right, the need to win every time, the need to be in control, the need to analyze and figure everything out, the need to be perfect, and a host of other human desires? Can you let all of that go and just feel peace? Can you imagine peace as the ultimate state of being, as the ultimate attitude, and as your dominant behavior?

Always look for peace because it can be found even in the midst of the biggest storm. Ask yourself constantly, "Will my choice support peace?" If not, just let it go. We all want peace on earth, but even world peace starts as an inside job.

Feel peace, promote peace, be peace. Then the void of the ego is replaced by the fullness of the spirit.

Whenever I teach this material, people ask me a very appropriate question: "What about the principle of right and wrong and fairness, should we let them go?" No, we shouldn't let them go. On the other hand, if everyone had experienced deep peace, these principles would have been followed naturally. You always have to evaluate the choice through the filters of peace.

Gandhi was a man of very strong principles, but he never allowed them to overshadow his relentless pursuit of peace. Therefore, he condemned any action that promoted violence. His actions, directed by his personal state of inner peace, always attracted attention among his own people and the world population. His nonviolent approach eventually brought India its independence.

Gandhi said, "The dignity of man requires the strength of the spirit." Only through the guidance of our spirits can we accomplish great things. Therefore, we have to act from the spirit's territory, which is PEACE.

TruePeace vs. Peace of Mind

At this point, it's of great importance to differentiate between peace of mind that is mainly a psychological state and deep Inner Peace. Psychologically-based peace of mind comes when we perceive we have control over our lives. Deep Inner Peace, or TruePeace, is unconditional and cannot be moved by any circumstances outside of the self. Peace of mind is much more superficial and is a conditional, ego-oriented state with which we should not be satisfied. TruePeace is an internal status that represents a pure, complete, whole, harmonious state of being.

> Until you make peace with who you are, you will never be content with what you have.
>
> *Doris Mortman*

No pleasure in the world will last, no goal in the world will satisfy you forever when attained, unless you find this deep peace first. With this ultimate intention of enduring peace in mind, you will be truly surprised how many times you choose options that do not result in peace. Many times you'll side with the games of the ego instead of the peace that is closer to you than your own nose.

Why is that? Because you may be still following

rules, beliefs, and expectations that you have accumulated through-out the years. Such guides may promote conflict and stress, which typically creates chaos and disarray. To choose peace, you have to learn to let go of your investment in these concepts.

Peace is what you feel when all these concepts are pushed away. Keep asking yourself, "What would be the peaceful choice in this situation?" If you do that, you will always be the winner.

Choosing peace does not mean swallowing your feelings and forgoing your needs when they arise. I'm not talking about an ego-type peace that is nothing but suppression of your feelings to create an artificial, more external peace. True-Peace has to be accompanied with letting go. Remember that the goal is to feel peace inside without anything happening in particular on the outside.

> I long to accomplish a great and noble task, but it is my chief duty to accomplish small tasks as if they were great and noble.
>
> *Helen Keller*

Finding Your Purpose

The issue of finding one's purpose in life occupies many people, since ultimately everyone wants to find it. Some people are connected with their purposes and those who aren't may wander through life feeling dissatisfied and disappointed. As a result of their dissatisfaction, they may change cars, houses, careers, and even partners, not realizing that what they're really looking for is a deep spiritual connection that can turn their life around.

Not everybody's purpose is to save the world. A purpose can be much simpler. Raising kids, working with the elderly, even greeting people when they come to the office can be an important purpose. We don't see the big picture and, therefore, we cannot judge the importance of our purpose, small as it may seem.

A true purpose will always help to complete the universal jigsaw puzzle of peace. Ultimately, our purpose is to do good for others and ourselves, and this can be more completely achieved by deepening our spiritual connection. Remember, you can only give what you already have. Connecting with your purpose and connecting with spirituality are identical.

If you want to connect with your purpose, you have to ask yourself a few important questions. What are you good at? What are your talents? Perhaps you have good communication skills or organizational abilities? Are you artistic? Mechanical? Is your talent in cooking or handcrafts? Maybe you're a good listener.

You have natural talents that are unique, and when used or developed, they could benefit others, directly or indirectly. A purpose is an aim that comes straight from your soul.

After reflecting on the above thoughts, ask yourself the following questions:

1. If you had all the choice in the world, what would you like to focus on, given your background, education, and natural talents?
2. If you had no limitations such as age or financial obligations, what would you be doing?
3. If you knew you couldn't fail, what would you do?
4. What inspires you?
5. What, if you did it, would make you feel better about yourself?
6. What is your true passion?
7. What would be such an interesting occupation that it wouldn't even feel like work?
8. How would you ideally like to be remembered after you die?
9. If you could do anything you want right now, what would you do? If you answered "a trip around the world" or similar, what would you do after that?
10. What do you think is your calling as a human being?

Take sufficient time to answer these questions from your deepest level of awareness. Your answers will lead you to your purpose. Here is an important criteria that will help you determine if you are on the right track: Your purpose is about enhancing, in some way, peace and love in others. The rest, how or where you do it, is less important.

Your unique purpose was specially designed for you, using your own unique aspirations and talents. Do you know what it is? Are you doing it? Understand that you don't necessarily have to change anything in your environment to fulfill your purpose. It's always good to start from where you are right now. You might even be doing a lot of it already without being aware of it.

When you live your purpose, you wake up in the morning and can hardly wait to do your work; and when you go to bed, you can feel warm satisfaction in your heart. Even if this happens only part of the time, it is quite a powerful way to live life, isn't it?

When I guide a patient through this process, various insecurities usually surface. These insecurities take the form of objections. "I'm not good enough, I'm not sure, I don't know, what will people say?" Such objections are normal. By all means, bring all the "yes, buts" out. Then imagine overcoming them. If they did not exist, what would you do then?

An answer always exists. A purpose doesn't have to be as radical as "I want to solve world hunger," although it would be nice if you could. Your purpose has to do with something you're already doing in some way. And by the way, objections that have to do with money and time are not acceptable!

When my patients finally allow their purposes to come out, something in them changes. The radiance cannot be missed. A huge click. Please go back, if you are not sure yet, and repeat this process as many times as you need. Keep asking the questions and be honest with yourself. Don't worry about the execution of the purpose. Connect with it first and later on you will be able to plan how to carry it out.

The pursuit of finding one's purpose is a mental process. The execution is spiritual.

What's the Meaning of Life?

This is a powerful question that has occupied philosophers for hundreds of years. Joseph Campbell asserted that people don't really seek meaning. What they look for is an experience of being totally alive.

I look at this question in a much simplified manner. For me the only meaning of life is the moment. Whatever the moment offers you is what is meaningful, especially when you connect deeper with it. Such connections lead to union with other people, with nature, and with God. That's all the meaning there is.

When people say that they can't find any meaning in life, they're really saying that they live too much in the ego. They may then experience regret, frustration, disappointment, and hopelessness. As a result, they may claim that they have lost any meaning in life. These states are products of the analyzing mind based on expectations that were not met.

Let the mind's processing go. Take a deep breath in, connect with the moment, put a smile on your face, feel the peace. What would you like to do next?

What's In It for Me?

I had an interesting experience a few years ago. I heard a voice. Not a regular internal voice that we all often hear. This was something different. One morning while filling up my car at a gas station, an idea to facilitate a spiritual retreat occurred to me. I liked the idea on one hand, but dismissed it on the other. "Too much work," I thought to myself. The famous question, "What's in it for me?" also came into my mind.

Suddenly, out of nowhere I heard a very gentle and unfamiliar voice say, "This is not about you."

"What?" I asked, surprised.

The voice, which seemed to come from a very deep place inside, repeated in a fainter tone, "This is not about you."

After I recovered from the surprise, I realized what the voice was saying. This had nothing to do with me but purely with what I could do for others. Not that I didn't do that before, but this voice directed me to do more. I could feel it deep in my heart. Now it was all clear.

Yes, I knew that in my work I was able to help many people, but I also gained through that effort. I gained appreciation, recognition, warm feelings of connecting and helping others, even financial rewards.

Now, I realized, all this existed just to get the ego out of the way, to give it comfort so that the soul could do what it knows best: help, share, and do something good for others. This is really what our purpose is all about. It has nothing to do with us (the ego wants to point out that it is not accepting this notion). It has to do with those around us whom we can help in different ways.

> If one man gains spirituality, the whole world gains with him, and if one man fails, the whole world fails to that extent.
>
> *Mahatma Gandhi*

I did facilitate the retreat and all of the participants enjoyed it, but in retrospect we all knew that the retreat was especially geared towards one lady who needed it the most. This lady was praying for help and the retreat was the answer.

I had recently a conversation with one of my patients about spirituality. Being aware of the fact that I was in the process of writing this book, she commented that in her opinion the book would "certainly be a great success." I smiled, and told her that we could never be certain what the purpose of it would be. I added that although the book might eventually help many, it could be very possible that it was especially written for the benefit of one woman in Cheyenne, Wyoming (or Vancouver, or San Diego for that matter), who needed it more than anyone else. By the way, if you feel you are that woman, please write to me, I would love to hear your story.

How many times do we find ourselves asking, "What's in it for me?" The ego always asks: "How is this going to affect me, my life, and my status?" Then it comes up with a plan. Let ego plan whatever it wants. Identify with your soul and follow what's deep in your heart. Nothing is more rewarding or fulfilling.

You can identify your spirit's guidance by asking, "What's in it FROM me?" As for the ego, don't worry about it. It will get used to the changes and probably come up with new plans.

The worse that can happen if you move from ego to spirituality may be temporary discomfort and perhaps uncertainty. What else can go wrong? Now look at the advantages of doing it and evaluate the risk/return ratio for yourself.

The Third Component of Breathing

Earlier I said that breathing has three components. We covered the "mechanical-physical" as well as the "attention-mental" aspect of it. The third component comes from the spiritual realm. I refer to "Intention."

When you add intent to the process of deep breathing, interesting things happen. What kind of intentions can you express? You can convey anything that is stated in a positive way, such as attracting abundance in every aspect of your life, connecting with your ultimate purpose in life, and connecting deeper with spirituality. How about realizing the truth of who you are? Of course all these intentions are similar and lead to the same result.

When setting forth intentions, make sure they come from a place of love and peace and not from lack and fear. Law of focus number two states that if you ask for what you want, then you get what you want; but if you ask for what you don't want, then you get what you don't want. When you ask for something based on fear then you are focusing on what you don't want.

An example for that could be asking not to be lonely. The basis of your request, fear of loneliness, will most likely keep you feeling lonely. However, when you set forth intentions that are based on love, for instance to expand your capacity to love yourself and others, you send very positive vibes that are bound to bring an appropriate response.

After adding this component to my teachings, I realized that intentions are very similar to praying. This took me back to my old days in synagogue when I was so bored praying for hours, without even understanding what everything meant. Hearing the rabbi emphasize the importance of praying with intention only frustrated me more. I just wanted to get it over and done with.

But he was right. When you add deep intentions to the equation, it makes all the difference in the world.

As I thought about intentions and prayer, I remembered a story I heard in school when I was in grade two or three. It was about a Jewish boy, living in a small village in Russia. He was the only boy in the village who couldn't read or write. It was the Day of Atonement, the most sacred day in Jewish tradition, when all of the people in the village gathered at the local synagogue to pray for atonement. They were all dressed in white, all busy praying, and all asking God for forgiveness.

Suddenly, the doors of the synagogue opened. The boy came in, dressed in dirty clothes. The boy looked at everybody praying and became very frustrated. He too wanted to pray to God, but he didn't know how. He stuck his fingers in his mouth and whistled loudly.

All the people looked at him with contempt. How dare he whistle in a synagogue on this sacred day? They wanted to kick him out of the synagogue but the rabbi stopped them. He explained that the boy's intention came from such a deep place in his heart that it surely opened God's heart for mercy and forgiveness.

As the story jumped into my mind so vividly, I realized that I didn't have to recite hours of prayers. My intentions were far more important and prayer is only one method of expressing intentions.

What is the mysterious mechanism by which intentions work? I believe that intentions and prayers are indeed a process of InteliTapping. When they come from a place of love and peace, they enable us to tap into the Infinite Intelligence where universal solutions and resources can be found. Whether you pray or not, adding intentions to your deep breathing practice can significantly enhance the results that you get. The deeper you mean it, by way of intensely feeling your intentions, the stronger the transmission is, if you will. And if you add a sense of gratitude to your intentions, then it makes them even more convincing.

A number of studies have shown the importance of this method of prayer in healing. Dr. Randolph Byrd, a cardiologist at the San

Francisco General Hospital, conducted an interesting study in the early '80s. He divided a group of 400 cardiac patients into two groups. The names of one group were given to people, both Catholics and Protestants, who prayed for them. No one prayed for the people from the second group, which was used as a control.

Dr. Byrd wanted to prevent the placebo effect, which means in this case that only the idea of someone praying for you can promote healing, a powerful phenomenon in and of itself. Therefore Dr. Byrd did not inform either the patients or their treating physicians who belonged in which group. This method of research is called a double-blind study.

The results were quite amazing. The people who were prayed for had fewer complications; they recovered faster and needed less medication than the control group.

Here is a complete framework for setting intention.

1. Begin by doing deep breathing.
2. State what you want, based on love and peace.
3. Visualize yourself attaining what you want.
4. Express gratitude for receiving it.
5. Take positive action to build momentum. Ask yourself, "How can I help in the process? What can I do to make this happen?"

This process can help you to resonate strongly with your intentions on all levels: physically, mentally, emotionally, and spiritually. Eventually, it will help you to manifest your highest goals in life.

Spiritual Intentions

God, open my eyes so that I can realize the truth of who I really am

Expand my mind so that I can connect with my TruePeace

Touch my heart so that I can experience all your love that is in me

And then share it with everyone.

Intention—Attention—Manifestation

Deep intentions connect the ordinary with the supernatural. This state allows things that are beyond our daily control or understanding to happen. Think of deep intentions as a universal switchboard that connects us with the Supreme Intelligence—InteliTapping at its best.

Once you set your intentions, it is important to pay attention. If intention opens the doors, then attention deepens the process. This, in time, leads to manifestation.

Manifestation is the end product of our intentions placed against the bigger picture created by the Ultimate Intelligence. Sometimes manifestation may yield results that you didn't expect. For instance, a "no result" does not necessarily mean that your intentions were not answered, but that they have been answered differently based on high criteria not known or understood by you. It could be for a purpose of a lesson or for the good of others.

Also, when you ask for something, don't necessarily expect to get it the way you anticipate. More often than not, what you seek comes in a subtle way, through an opportunity or through a lesson. Keep your eyes open and be aware. Otherwise, the opportunity to fulfill your intention can stare you in the face and you won't even notice it.

One patient prayed for money to support her while she recovered from a traumatic accident. She had set intentions as taught but complained that nothing was happening. As we talked, she mentioned that she had previously heard a few good tips on stocks but never pursued them. When she checked on the performance of these stocks, she realized that they could have provided her with money to live on.

Set forth your intentions and pay attention. Intentions that are aligned with your soul's desires tend always to be fulfilled one way or another. The manifestation part requires taking action. What can you do now to make your intentions come true?

The Intention-Attention-Manifestation progression (which, as a patient pointed out to me, forms the interesting acronym "I AM") is part of a bigger cycle, shown here.

Source (GOD) ——➤ Spirit ——➤ Creativity ——➤ Imagination
——➤ Thought ——➤ Desire ——➤ Intention ——➤ Attention
——➤ Manifestation

Every part of the spiritual cycle nourishes everyone who is in sync with it, with bliss, and with the ultimate manifestation of all: TruePeace.

The Three Spiritual Truths

"The truth shall set you free." What a deep and important principle this entire spiritual process depends on. Being able to understand and express the truth is the key to full freedom. But truth has many

> The object of the superior man is truth.
>
> *Confucius*

levels. I'm not just talking about telling the truth as in not lying about regular daily events and facts. Important as that truthfulness is, I refer here to a much deeper truth, whole and universal.

Truth can sometimes be quite elusive, tricky, and definitely subjective. Once we take away the complexities of our minds when analyzing things, the truth is fundamentally very simple. Unfortunately, we often see only part of the picture.

Let me illustrate it with an example. Say you pick up a piece of a puzzle and see a dog pictured on it. You might conclude that the picture in the puzzle is about dogs. Somebody picks up another puzzle piece, noticing an image of a child, and concludes that the puzzle is about children. A third person notices flowers on one of the pieces and asserts that the puzzle is about gardens. After assembling the puzzle, you realize that the picture is about a child chasing his dog in a garden.

Each one of three people saw a part of the truth. Each had a limited idea about the puzzle that was only revealed when the puzzle was assembled and the full picture displayed.

The Hebrew word for truth is written **Emet** in English lettering. In Hebrew characters, it consists of three letters: the first, the middle, and the last letters of the Hebrew alphabet. As in the puzzle example, this symbolizes that the truth is a complete picture, not just fragments of it. I have talked about this in other contexts earlier in the book, so the following discussion will serve as a summary for these important spiritual truths.

Spiritual Truth One:

At the core you are spiritual.

You are already complete and whole. You just have to accept your spirituality and identify more with the real aspect of who you are.

What are some of the ramifications of this truth? Many of my patients wish they had recognized their spiritual dimensions earlier. They say something like, "I have spent a big part of my life for nothing."

> If we walk the true way in our inmost heart, even without praying, God will be with us.
>
> *Takuan*

This is not true, for everyone makes an individual journey to arrive at recognition of his spirit. Your journey takes whatever amount of time it takes, and its length isn't a cause for guilt or regret. You have to go through all kinds of experiences and develop certain wisdom until you arrive at this specific realization.

Perhaps the most significant ramification of this truth is that you need to focus continuously on what is really important, to stop putting yourself down, to start taking yourself and life more lightly, to enjoy your true self and to allow it to enlighten your life. You can also let go of the limiting patterns associated with who you thought you were, such as fear, sadness, hurt, disappointment, and self-criticism.

These are the basic truths about YOU:

1. You are good.
2. You are enough.
3. You are whole and complete.
4. You are creative.

5. You are an unlimited source of love.

6. You are intuitive.

7. You are capable.

8. You are eternal.

9. You are beautiful.

10. You are peace.

If you don't feel like these truths apply to you, the problem is only one of misidentification. You can find these qualities in yourself by dramatically reducing your mental processing and allowing all this inner beauty to shine through.

Spiritual Truth Two:

At the core we are all connected; in fact, we are all one.

The famous physicist David Bohm concluded: "Deep down, the consciousness of mankind is one. This is a virtual certainty because even in the vacuum matter is one; and if we don't see this it's because we are blinding ourselves to it."

On the surface, we may not be the same; but fundamentally, we are connected in ways that transcend anything that is physical in nature. We can take this further: We are all made of the same material.

Since what we are made of is essentially spiritual material, and this material is universal, woven from the fabric we call our Higher Power, we are in fact, all the same. Not in the psychological sense, nor on a physical level. On these levels, we are all obviously different. But these levels only represent the packaging, not the deeper content. When we accept Spiritual Truth One, stating that who we are is in essence spiritual, then we are the same.

When trying to explain this truth to my youngest daughter, I created a short story to clarify the idea for her. Now I'm going to share that fable with you.

A widowed jeweler, who lived two hundred years ago in the city of Casablanca, had three daughters. These daughters were quite spoiled and used to spend all day long arguing who was prettier, who was smarter, and who was more popular. The father was quite sad at these futile and sometimes cruel arguments. He tried to teach them to avoid fighting, but nothing seemed to work. One day, the jeweler had an idea. He created three beautiful pieces of jewelery made of gold: a ring, a necklace, and a bracelet. He gave the ring to his younger daughter, the bracelet to the middle one, and the necklace to his oldest daughter.

The young women were amazed at the beauty of the jewelry, but shortly they started to argue again. Each one claimed that her jewelery was more beautiful. They each concluded that their father loved her the most.

This time, their father was pleased to watch them argue. He asked all of them to follow him to his workshop. "Give me your jewelery," he said gently. All three handed him their pieces. To their great surprise, the father took the three masterpieces and threw them into a hot metal pot. The girls were shocked to see the jewelery melting into one blob of gold in front of their eyes.

Then the father poured the molten gold into three cups. He handed one cup to each daughter and said, "Here is your piece of jewelry. Now tell me," he continued, "what is the difference between the three?"

The girls said nothing. They were too embarrassed. After that, they never argued again.

People are very much like snowflakes. Although each snowflake looks different, in essence they are all the same. When you look at snowflakes under the microscope they each look unique, but when they melt, they all become water.

Mental processing causes separation and division. R.H. Blynth said, "Nothing divides one so much as thought." When you stop processing, union and connectedness are natural. Separation is ego. Division has only one purpose: control. Without ego we feel connected with everyone and with every part of creation.

You cannot understand this concept until you're able to feel it. To feel it, you have to let go of beliefs and practices that reinforce the opposite. Self and other are like two sides of the same coin. They are intrinsically connected, forming the one coin.

So what are the ramifications of this truth? Is it that when we hurt someone we actually hurt ourselves? Is it that when we do good deeds we also benefit? Is it that we all share a similar responsibility to promote peace in this world and to protect the environment? Is it that life is really about people, about deeper connections, about bringing a smile to a person, helping to wipe a tear on a crying face? Isn't all the rest just petty?

Recently the mapping of the human genome came to completion. Scientists who were part of the process also mapped other creatures such as mice as well as different viruses. They were astonished to discover that the difference between our gene structure and other living things' genetic structure is not that big. We really all come from the same source.

As long as people feel separated from each other they will continue to hurt others. As long as they feel separated from nature they will not cease harming the environment. We are not just one as a human race but one with nature and all of creation. We all came from the same Intelligence that created the universe. We have to stop believing that we are superior to nature by trying to control and outsmart it all the time. Instead, we must respect its magic and learn to live in harmony with it. Our lives will then dramatically improve in every way.

A good demonstration for both Spiritual Truths One and Two can be found in times of crisis. After devastation caused by floods, tornados, or earthquakes, for instance, helping each other suddenly becomes natural. When we face such challenges, the ego gets pushed away so it is then easy for the soul to surface and motivate us to do what's important.

Not so long ago the entire world was devastated by bin Laden's attack on the World Trade Center in New York. A fanatic extremist killed thousands of people along with his brainwashed terrorists. What was the result? Among other responses, America came through as a united nation, not only to support those in need, but also to fight terror once and for all. Acts of solidarity were expressed all over the world. Without doubt, such challenging times help us connect with the truth of who we really are. I wish we could all connect with our spirits so deeply that we live this unity all the time and not just during crises.

One of my favorite pieces in this context is Chief Seattle's speech to the president of the United States, written in 1854. Its powerful simplicity shows understanding of our unity with all people and nature.

The President in Washington sends word that he wishes to buy our land. But how can you buy or sell the sky? The land? The idea is strange to us. If we do not own the freshness of the air and the sparkle of the water, how can you buy them?

Every part of the earth is sacred to my people. Every shining pine needle, every sandy shore, every mist in the dark woods, every meadow, every humming insect. All are holy in the memory and experience of my people. We know the sap which courses through the trees as we know the blood that courses through our veins. We are part of the earth and it is part of us. The perfumed flowers are our sisters. The bear, the deer, the great eagle, these are our brothers. The rocky crests, the dew in the meadow, the body heat of the pony, and man all belong to the same family. The shining water that moves in the streams and rivers is not just water, but the blood of our ancestors.

If we sell you our land, you must remember that it is sacred. Each glossy reflection in the clear waters of the lakes tells of events and memories in the life of my people. The water's murmur is the voice of my father's father. The rivers are our brothers. They quench our thirst. They carry our canoes and feed our children. So you must give the rivers the kindness that you would give any brother.

If we sell you our land, remember that the air is precious to us, that the air shares its spirit with all the life that it supports. The wind that gave our grandfather his first breath also received his last sigh. The wind also gives our children the spirit of life. So if we sell our land, you must keep it apart and sacred, as a place where man can go to taste the wind that is sweetened by the meadow flowers.

Will you teach your children what we have taught our children?

That the earth is our mother? What befalls the earth befalls all the sons of the earth. This we know: The earth does not belong to man; man belongs to the earth. All things are connected like the blood that unites us all. Man did not weave the web of life, he is merely a strand in it. Whatever he does to the web, he does to himself.

One thing we know: Our God is also your God. The earth is precious to Him and to harm the earth is to heap contempt on its creator.

Your destiny is a mystery to us. What will happen when the buffalo are all slaughtered? The wild horses tamed? What will happen when the secret corners of the forest are heavy with the scent of many men and the view of the ripe hills is blotted with talking wires? Where will the thicket be? Gone! Where will the eagle be? Gone! And what is it to say goodbye to the swift pony and the hunt? The end of living and the beginning of survival.

When the last red man has vanished with this wilderness, and his memory is only the shadow of a cloud moving across the prairie, will these shores and forests still be here? Will there be any of the spirit of my people left? We love this earth as a newborn loves its mother's heartbeat.

> If we have no peace, it is because we have forgotten that we belong to each other.
>
> *Mother Teresa*

So, if we sell you our land, love it as we have loved it. Care for it, as we have cared for it. Hold in your mind the memory of the land as it is when you receive it. Preserve the land for all children, and love it, as God loves us. As we are part of the land, you too are part of the land. This earth is precious to us. It is also precious to you.

One thing we know: There is only one God. No man, be he Red man or White man, can be apart. We ARE all brothers after all.

If you feel a shiver going through your spine, if your mind stops in awe, if your heart just wants to go out and embrace the world while you read Chief Seattle's letter, you are heading in the right direction. When you have achieved a deep and constant feeling of one with everyone and everything—and this feeling becomes your guidance in everyday life—you have fully realized your spirituality!

Spiritual Truth Three:

Everything you really need, you already have.

Perhaps you can't have everything that you want, but you already have everything important that you need. If we skip materialistic objects, what do we really need? We already have within us the seeds of safety, calm, balance, harmony, joy, and healing, as well as love and peace.

So what are the ramifications of the third truth? Perhaps the most important one is that we don't have to be so needy. When we transcend our neediness, we can align with our purpose to help others. When we recognize what we have in us, we feel compelled to offer people around us empathy, understanding, compassion, and most of all, unconditional love.

Technology as a Metaphor

It is interesting to look at technology as a metaphor of how nature and we behave and evolve. For example, cars represent our desire for the ability to move faster, like many animals, and airplanes represent flying abilities derived from the animal kingdom. Electricity and even computers all represent abilities and phenomena found in nature and in us. Electricity can be found in many types of fish who easily produce it. All the messages that flow through the nervous system consist of electrical micro currents. Computers emulate the brain. We know of animals that use sonar and ultrasound waves, animals who use very sophisticated navigational systems, and the list goes on and on.

My favorite example of our adaptation of natural states is the Internet. In my opinion, the Internet represents two things. Firstly, it represents the process of InteliTapping—our ability to tap into tremendous resources that were not within our reach before. For information, resources, and solutions, many people go to the Internet to do the research and retrieve the necessary data. We do the same with InteliTapping. But even more importantly, look at the future of the Internet where all of us, not just the technological front-runners, will be connected through e-mail, telephone, cell phones, videophones, news, databases, and TV.

This is a technical example of how we are really all connected. The good news is that technology is catching up to some of our own intrinsic features, only in an external way. We need to remember what the Internet really represents and learn to respect and make better use of our connection with one another.

In the last few years, the trend has been toward globalization. Enterprises from different countries amalgamate. International agreements and mergers include carmakers, pharmaceutics, communication and computer companies as well as financial institutions. Lately, stock exchanges from North America, South America, Europe, and the Far East have considered a move to create a global stock exchange. Airline companies combine forces to prevent bankruptcies. The Europeans are gradually integrating their economies. Many of them have already started using one currency—the Euro.

As similar trends occur on political and social levels, we will eventually become one undivided planet, which at another level we already are. Star Trek's Gene Rodenberry recognized this essential alliance in his classic science fiction series by referring to our planet as "Federation Earth." This one-world process is nothing but a reflection of our inner connection, which has always existed. We must share and better utilize our available resources on a global level. This can happen only through a serious global spiritual awakening that will enable unification of all people and the promotion of true peace on our planet.

Looking for the Truth

In the New Testament, Matthew 7:7, we find the words, "Ask and it shall be given you; seek and ye shall find; knock, and it shall be opened unto you."

Seek what? I believe this passage relates to The Truth. But which truth? Ultimately, it is the truth of who we really are. No one is so naive as to think that the Bible is talking here about materialistic, ego-based requests (not that anything is wrong with them), right? What door are we supposed to knock on? The door that leads to the heart, to our soul. Confirmation of that may be found in James 4:3: "You ask and do not receive, because you ask wrongly, in order to spend what you get on your pleasures."

When you ask for The Truth and find it deep inside of you, all the rest will be taken care of. Interestingly, the eighth verse in Matthew, chapter 7, repeats the concept, reinforcing that it is open to all: "For everyone that asketh receiveth; and he that seeketh findeth; and to he that knocketh it shall be opened."

The world is abundant if you operate from your heart. Spirituality is there for everyone.

Also notice that in the original statement, "Ask and you shall receive," no doubt whatsoever is even implied. It doesn't say, "You may receive." Neither are conditions imposed. Do you want to know why? It is because what you ask for, you already have! Therefore, the asking and the receiving are one. Think about it for a moment.

When you do your breathing exercise with intention, ask for The Truth, and it shall be given unto you. Or maybe you have already asked and you are being given the way to realize the truth as we share these thoughts. You have the answer right now. So after you ask, just take a few deep, slow breaths in. Let go of your mind's busy-work. Can you FEEL the answer?

A few weeks ago I had a discussion with one of my patients who was in a process of letting go of the anger and fear she had carried for years. When I talked to her about asking for what she wants, she said that she was ashamed to ask God for anything because God had given her such great potential, which she was not fully using. She thought she had disappointed God. I suggested she ask God to show her more ways to utilize her potential. She liked the idea and began to include intentions while conducting her awareness exercises. A few weeks later, she told me about a so-called "coincidence" that enabled her to "see things" in a much different light. The process of letting go became much easier for her afterwards.

Another patient, who was involved along with her family in a devastating car accident, told me that she prayed only for her kids' fast recovery and not for herself, because she did not want to "ask for too much." We discussed the principle of asking and I recommended that she include herself in her prayers. This was a big relief for her and she started to feel better right away.

Our sages knew exactly what the Ultimate Truth was but they had difficulty conveying it clearly to their people. The Bible's stories reflect that attempt. The sages knew that to advance understanding and implementation, they had to include some external, acceptable symbols and rituals. The problem was that, as a result, religion became too external.

Mystics, who also understood the truth, could not lie about it. As a result many were muted and even sometimes persecuted. They were definitely not understood by their church, let alone by the lay individual.

Moses, Buddha, Jesus, Mohammed, and Krishna all knew very well what spirituality really was. They lived it. With the limitations of language and culture, they had a problem explaining to the entire world that what they knew could benefit every human being. Their task was as difficult as trying to teach a baby how much ten plus ten is. All they could do was to sow the seeds and wait. Unfortunately, this wisdom was misused, by people who did not fully understand it and used it for ego-based personal gains. For many of us, thousands of years later, these seeds are still dormant.

It's All One Truth

For the sake of clarification I separated The Truth into three different parts. But in fact all three truths are one. When you deeply understand one, you understand all three. The bottom line of the spiritual journey is to arrive at the realization that *ONE IS ALL AND ALL IS ONE*. When you can feel that deeply—you have arrived at The Truth.

Extraordinary Ramifications of the Spiritual Truths

Earlier I mentioned Dr. Randolph Byrd's study on the powerful use of prayer and intention in healing. Fred Sicher, Elisabeth Targ, Dan Moore, and Helene S. Smith, at the California Pacific Medical Center's Complementary Medicine Research Institute, conducted another study. Forty AIDS patients received distant healing therapy by healers of different religions who were asked to focus on the patients. The healers had only a first name and photo of these people. Miraculously, this group of patients experienced few hospitalizations and fewer complications compared with another group of AIDS patients who did not receive distant healing. In essence, this spiritual healing was nothing but setting healing intentions by the healers.

This study was conducted using rigorous scientific testing equivalent to the standards required for testing a new drug. Neither the patients (who included both males and females from different ethnic groups) nor the scientists who conducted the study knew who was in which group until after the study was completed. Such scientific studies not only prove that spiritual intentions work but they also open the doors of understanding to a very deep dimension that is sadly still disputed by many.

In my opinion, these studies ultimately prove the power of the Spiritual Truths. Otherwise it would be more difficult to understand how such remote healing can take place. I also like the fact that the researchers used healers of different faiths. The healing worked well for all healers, representing different religions. It does not really matter what religion you follow, but how pure your intentions are.

I asked a healer who was introduced to me in a conference how he could heal people who lived miles away, most of whom he did not even know.

He smiled. "They are all within me anyway. I just learned how to channel healing energy to them."

That's InteliTapping at its best. You'll read more about this topic when I present the holographic model.

The spirit is everything, in everyone, everywhere. It is in and beyond time. This concept is really mind-boggling. We can't fully comprehend it but it serves to explain phenomena such as intuition, premonition, and synchronicities in addition to remote healing.

Recently I read in the newspaper about a woman who warned her husband to postpone his flight because she had strong feelings that the specific flight for which he held a ticket would crash. She shared her feelings with many family members. The husband, who decided he "did not believe in superstition," went anyway and the airplane did crash. Fortunately, he was one of the few survivors. This is just one of many documented similar stories.

How can this be explained? Was her prescience just a coincidence? The woman insisted that she had never felt such strong feelings before, although her husband was a frequent flyer. One way to explain it is by assuming that everything that will happen has already happened, perhaps not here but in what is called alternate reality or a parallel universe.

Reserved in the beginning to science fiction writers, but now under consideration by a few daring scientists, this model speculates that everything that happened and everything that will ever happen is taking place right now in a universe that may be more than four dimensional—the three spatial dimensions plus the time dimension. Futurists envision infinite universes occurring in infinite dimensions, which can begin to explain phenomena such as premonitions, or even how prophecies such as the famous foresights of Nostradamus could have been predicted.

Only the spirit has the ability to go back and forth in time without any restrictions. What is my point in all of this? To state that we still have so much to learn, and that what connects us with such unfathomable realities is our spirit, which is part of the infinite source of wisdom.

Infinite Wisdom pervades all that exists. It has the power to create miracles and on a personal level to make your life heaven—now! What do you have to do to connect with it? Let go, forgive, accept, and connect with the deep moment.

You know all this by now, at least rationally. Learn to feel it at your deepest level.

InteliTapping Enhancement

Obviously, we all have powerful abilities within us. They are just not always developed enough. If you like, you can use the following exercise to further develop your InteliTapping abilities.

Choose a question or an area in your life where you want answers, or choose intentions you would like to reinforce, or even choose an area in which you want to increase your awareness. Close your eyes and become aware of your breathing. Then become aware of your thoughts, feelings, and physical sensations. As soon as you are ready, deepen your breathing and allow it to guide you deeper within.

Now imagine seeing a room called "InteliTapping." Enter the room and examine it. Notice what the room looks like and how you personally feel being there. If you happen to be a person who does not visualize well, just allow yourself to have a sense of what it is like. You might see a wise person, an angel, even a super computer. There is no right or wrong; the way you do it is just fine. Make yourself comfortable in that room and then pose your questions, or reiterate your intentions. Then keep breathing deeply for as long as you feel it is required.

When you feel ready, open your eyes. Start paying attention. You may get an idea, a sign, or a dream that will direct you further. Or you may attract the necessary circumstances to make your intention happen or to discover your answer.

If you have chosen a very challenging topic, repeat this exercise a few times. A good time to do it is when you go to bed. You may then get your answer in the form of a dream.

When you keep reinforcing this exercise, you send a message to yourself and the universe that you are interested in enhancing spiritual awareness and everything that it has to offer. You will be rewarded accordingly. Ask and you shall be given!

I am beginning to believe that what the Bible referred to in "Ask and it shall be given you; seek and you shall find; knock, and it shall be opened unto you," is in fact InteliTapping at its best. What do you think?

How Do You Experience Truth?

To experience the truth, you must first recognize it, then pursue it constantly, and lastly speak it. In daily use, telling the truth means not lying, but as I indicated earlier, even that can be very subjective.

> Men stumble over the truth from time to time, but most pick themselves up and hurry off as if nothing happened.
>
> Sir Winston Churchill

In spiritual terms, the truth is absolute. Like the law of gravitation, you can pretend that it does not exist; but when put to the test, the law always proves to be true. The opposite of Spiritual Truth is mental processing. Mental processing is not necessarily lying; it is more distorting. Telling the truth begins by telling sensory-based facts instead of our process-oriented experience.

This is very important to understand. When you say, "She made me so angry," you are not lying in the ordinary sense. The words are not the truth, but your perception of an experience.

What would be the truth-based statement? Remember that the truth is based on sensory experience before processing. Truthful words would be, "She said she wouldn't go to the movies with me. When I heard that, I felt anger."

Two completely different statements, aren't they? The second contains no identification with the problem, no blaming—just the truth. Judgment, criticism, and comparison are always subjective, a result of a mental process, and therefore non-truths.

When you drink a soda or juice you notice mainly the taste. But any drink is mostly water. The rest is flavor. The truth is exactly like water. Truth is 99.99999 percent spirituality and the rest is the artificial flavor we add to it. Unfortunately, we identify with the flavor more often than not.

Albert Einstein, chosen the person of the century by *Time* magazine, was a brilliant scientist. He also understood that beyond the laws of science are more powerful laws that cannot be proven scientifically but nonetheless pervade every aspect of our lives. Here is what he said:

"A human being is part of the whole, called by us "Universe," a part limited in time and space. He experiences himself, his thoughts and feelings as something separated from the rest... a kind of optical delusion of his consciousness. This delusion is a kind of prison for us, restricting us to our personal desires and to affection for a few persons nearest to us. Our task must be to free ourselves from this prison by widening the circle of compassion to embrace all living creatures and the whole of nature in its beauty."

Beautiful, isn't it?

Truth is experienced in the moment, not in the mind. It is only in the deep moment that you can get in touch with who you are, with nature, and ultimately with God. Most people are in constant pursuit of happiness. However, when you seek the truth instead of seeking happiness—you will achieve true happiness. But finding the truth is not always easy, and our biggest block is usually fear.

A while ago, during one of my neighborhood walks, I asked myself the following question: "What if I could manifest 100 percent of my spirituality, now? Without doubts, no ego, just pure spirituality?" As soon as I posed the question, a strong feeling of fear flooded my entire body, followed by many concerns. Maybe I will have to give up my house, my car, and my belongings, maybe even leave the family to do "more important work."

As these thoughts and feelings ran through my mind, I was gradually able to distance myself enough to remember that being spiritual does not mean that you have to give up everything. Things can remain as they are, but your view about their level of importance changes, and what you pay attention to also changes. It is very possible that other changes will take place later on.

You can exercise your spirituality where you are and by doing so, you can affect those who interact with you. That's for starters. Once you have done that, you can consider other options. Bring the

> Peace I leave with you, my peace I give unto you: not as the world giveth, give I unto you. Let not your heart be troubled, neither let it be afraid.
>
> *John 14:27*

spiritual practices to your work environment, to places where they are not well-known. That's where they are most needed.

But remember, don't talk about them unless asked to. Instead, lead by example. When you pursue and practice peace, everyone notices it!

The Unified Truth

Scientists are still attempting to find a unified principle that will include all existing forces in the universe. Einstein dedicated many years to that question but was unsuccessful in resolving this challenge. On a spiritual level, understanding is somewhat easier.

I already mentioned that all three Spiritual Truths are the same. I also asserted that spirituality is peace. Therefore, truth is peace. We are all peace. All of creation is peace.

But just reading about it and understanding it intellectually is not enough. How much is one plus one? Do you have any doubts about the answer? None at all. You need to know the Spiritual Truth as deeply, in the same way.

This level of awareness is accomplished by letting go of old patterns, habits, beliefs, and expectations. When you get in touch with the deeper truth, you will have no doubts about it whatsoever. To accomplish that, you must let go of fear and worry. As you continue to do that, peace sets in. There is nothing more to it.

> Review areas of conflict in your life. What do you need to let go of right now to accomplish TruePeace?

Our Relationship to Nature

Why do we feel comfortable and calm when we relate to nature? Last year I visited with a friend while she took care of her garden. At the time, she was experiencing high-level stress in her work, but as I watched her gardening, she was very relaxed. We chatted a bit and she mentioned that she felt total calm when in the garden. I asked her where she thought the calmness came from. She did not hesitate for even a second before saying, "From gardening."

What do you think? When you feel peaceful in nature, whose peace are you feeling? If you said nature's peace, think again. If you said your own, you are right. I explained that to my friend and she was quite surprised. The idea that she carried all that peace inside and yet was able to connect with it only in certain situations or environments was not easy for her to digest.

Experiencing nature's beauty certainly encourages feelings of serenity and peace. You have the same lovely place of serene peace within you. This is the point of connection between people and all of creation. We simply share the identical "nature." Connecting with this mutual peace is like meeting a beloved after being separated for a long time. The feeling of reuniting, warm familiarity, and oneness never really left; linking just re-ignited it.

When we enjoy the beauty of nature and its profound serenity, we are fully in the moment. When we allow ourselves to be in the deep moment, life slows down as we lose all sense of time. Remember Emerson's words, "Adopt the pace of nature: her secret is patience."

Where do you think patience comes from? Deep inside everyone has unlimited patience. Unbelievable, isn't it? Impatience comes from comparison, judgment, and expectations—all mental processing.

I brought up sex earlier as an example of living in the moment. Also notice that a moment comes when the two people engaged in making love become one. In this connection, the enjoyment is complete. When you and the subject of the bonding—whether a person, a flower, a pet, or a tissue paper of an earlier exercise—intimately connect, you become one.

Find a few minutes every day to connect with nature. This is a wonderful exercise that you can do in your garden, in a

> park, or outside looking at the sky. **Start with slow breathing and then connect with nature using all of your senses.**
> **Accept everything without processing.**

You will be amazed how recharging this experience can be. It will keep reminding you that you and nature are one. You are made of the same essence. We call it: PEACE.

Every morning on the way to work, I make it a habit to look at the sky. This is a tremendous recharging and rejuvenating experience for me. While driving home from work earlier, I felt complete awe while looking at the sky. Just above the horizon lay stripes of brown, then red, then orange, yellow, and light blue turning gradually into darker blue. The sight was breathtaking—a pure spiritual experience.

A couple of years ago I wrote a series of poems I called *Conversations with Nature*. One of these poems will be the basis of the following exercise.

I am like you

I look at the stream flowing through the creek
and I say: I am like you
I see the sun's rays shining through the clouds
and I say: I am like you
I see a flower breaking through the ground
and I say: I am like you
I look at the branches of the tree moving with the wind
and I say: I am like you
I look at a star shining through the dark night
and I say: I am like you.
The stream and the sun and the flower and the branches
    and the star
They all look at me and calmly say together:
We are like you.

Now to the exercise:

I want you to take a few minutes and pretend that you are
the stream. Notice how it feels. Then, imagine yourself being
a sun's ray. After that, a flower. Next, a tree. Lastly, a star.
Take some time to complete this exercise.

What was your experience like? Did you try to be the object in a
physical way? If yes, then I want you also to try being the object in
essence, not in body. What is the difference between the two?

The last thing I would like you to do is to be all of the things
in the last exercise together: a ray of sunlight, a flower, a
tree, a star. You cannot do this in a physical way. Just feel
yourself being all.

Who are you? How do you feel? As you get fully in touch with the
feelings within, say, "I AM." Allow *I AM* to include not only yourself
but also all of nature. Do you sense a feeling of expansion when you
say that?

Please use List 2 at the end of the book now to update your
understanding of who you think you are.

Part 3

Integration

The Principal called the Student to his office. "Who are you?" he asked as soon as the Student entered the room.

Without hesitation the Student replied, "I am you."

The Principal examined the Student carefully. "So who am I?"

"You are me," the Student replied confidently.

The Principal nodded. "Very well, now go back to class."

Whose Beauty Is It?

This poem, which I wrote a few years ago, will lead into our next discussion.

Conversation with a Flower:

> I am in my garden
> Looking at a beautiful flower.
> It's long and has purple silky petals
> I ask: where do you come from?
> I come from no-where
> And what do you like?
> The air, the sun, the wind and the rain
> For how long will you be here?
> Forever
> Then the flower suddenly says: stop asking questions
> Just look and enjoy
> I have one more question to ask:
> Where does your beauty come from?
> The flower whispers: from you

People have always pursued beauty. They look for it in architecture, art, nature, jewelery, fashion, and other humans. Why are we so drawn to beauty? When you see a beautiful painting, whose beauty are you connecting with? Would it surprise you to learn that when you see something beautiful, you are in fact, getting in touch with your own beauty? Did you think it was the painting? The painting only serves to open the door to your own inner beauty. If that's correct, can you fathom how much beauty you carry inside?

The poor ego has difficulty finding beauty that is more than skin deep. Would you buy a box of chocolates, keep the wrapper, and throw the chocolates in the garbage?

The ramifications of this concept are truly great. What this means is that whatever we see outside of ourselves is nothing but a reflection of our inside to its various depths. When you resent something about someone, you in fact resent that part in yourself. The same rule applies when you criticize, compare, and judge. When you see peace, harmony, and joy, they mirror your own peace, harmony, and joy, which project from your spiritual zone where you connect.

Everything that we experience in life is a reflection of the balance that we create between ego and soul. Remember the law of focus #1? Whatever you focus on expands in your life. When you focus more on people's nice sides, what will you connect more with? Your better side, of course. This also works the other way around. Connect with your inner beauty and it will be easier to find it in others.

Raising Spiritually Aware Children

I talked earlier about self-esteem and, no doubt, every parent wants to enhance his or her children's self-esteem. However, from a spiritual perspective a problem exists, a dilemma that one may face when rearing children to have a healthy self-esteem.

Notice that I did not use the term high self-esteem. The reason is that arrogant children and even bullies appear to have high self-esteem. But it is out of balance. A healthy self-esteem has built-in characteristics, which include self-regard and respect for others.

Here is the dilemma: From a psychological standpoint we want to nurture the uniqueness of our children. "You are special, you are unique, and no one is exactly like you in the whole world." But on a spiritual level you want to teach your child that we are all the same. Remember Spiritual Truth Two: At the core we are all connected; in fact, we are all one.

So what do you do?

When I first realized the power and danger of comparison as a torturous ego-based pattern, I also realized that I often compared myself to how smart or how successful others were. This created either a confident or an insecure feeling, depending on who the person was. As soon as I identified my mistake I changed this self-programming. For a while, whenever I interacted with someone, no matter who the person was, I reinforced, "I am like him/her and he/she is like me." After doing this for a while, the comparison habit stopped.

This difference between who we are physically and psychologi-cally as opposed to who we are spiritually has to be explained to children. This will make it easier for them to adopt Spiritual Truth Two and still feel comfortable in developing their unique aspects. You can use the snowflakes metaphor to emphasize this idea.

Regardless of which religion or path you and consequently your children follow, the best way to teach kids spirituality is to first and foremost avoid the ego's blocks to spirituality we discussed before: comparison, judgment, criticism, blaming, and complaining.

This does not mean that you cannot discuss their behavior when you feel it is important to do so. Evaluate the behavior and not the child. When you allow children to grow free of criticism, put-downs, and comparison they will more easily find their path and purpose in life.

Teach kids the Spiritual Truths and the importance of peace. Encourage them to practice basic awareness exercises, which is always much easier when they are still young.

When you demonstrate these practices while interacting with other people, then children learn through observation to accept themselves and others. And what is spirituality if not full and complete acceptance? By all means teach them all the values you ascribe to, but make a special effort to demonstrate that peace has to override everything. Make clear that you have peace of mind not by repressing feelings or avoiding free expression, but by connecting with TruePeace. Show children the advantages when peace moti-vates their daily actions. When you give kids such a solid foundation, you can rest assured that they will be able to tackle life's challenges more calmly and resourcefully.

Where Is Home?

One day a woman I was counseling complained about her high level of anxiety. She was supposed to move to a different city because of her husband's new job. She had sold her house before finding a new one, and the uncertainty caused her a lot of stress.

"I don't know what to do; I don't have a home. I feel as if I don't belong anywhere," she said.

I asked her to stand before a mirror in my office and I proceeded to ask her a question: "Where is home?"

She smiled. We had spent some time discussing and exploring spirituality, so I was not surprised when she said: "In my heart." Her anxiety subsided immediately.

Home usually feels comfortable, familiar, and warm—unless so much conflict is experienced there that we try to run away from it. But home is the physical example of the real home that comes from deep inside, from the warmth and the comfort of the soul, which we are familiar with but may have forgotten. Remove the barricades and you are home. Be there and no matter where you are physically, you will always feel at home.

When we don't feel connected with our real home, it is because the door is blocked with ego stuff, the stuff no one wants to get in touch with. A little bit of cleanup, throwing out old garbage, and you have made yourself the best home in the world.

It's time to connect from within. When you do, you reach a level at which it doesn't really matter where you are, or whether you are by yourself or with people. You simply feel very comfortable with yourself.

> If a man happens to find himself, he has a mansion which he can inhabit with dignity all the days of his life.
> *James A. Michener*

As an example, many people I work with express feelings of loneliness and sadness because they live alone. They look for mates to share their lives. Many have been in relationships that didn't work out, thereby intensifying these feelings. Being motivated by the fear of loneliness and neediness is almost a guarantee to attract the wrong person. I explain that before they can find someone suitable, they have to feel comfortable inside.

After they feel inner comfort, two things might happen. They may find someone based on their new level of development and what they want in a life partner. Alternatively, if they're meant to stay by themselves, at least they won't feel bad about it anymore. They come to terms with it—accept and feel peace.

Are We God?

Even the ego would admit that we are not God, although I must admit, it sometimes acts as if it is. We do have a strong godly part.

> "He who knows his own self knows God."
>
> *Muhammad*

Let's see what the Bible says about that: "So God created man in his own image, in the image of God created he him; male and female created he them." Notice that the Bible mentions the fact we were made in God's image twice, just to make sure that we get it! He created both male and female in his image because God is a perfect mix of both.

The reason, in my opinion, that some people have difficulties finding God is because they look outside of themselves. I have already emphasized the point that the only way to find God is by finding yourself. When you become who you really are, you will be the closest you can ever get to God. Since you are created in God's image, when you become who you really are, you will engage in godly behavior: helping, sharing, and caring that come from a deep state of peace and love. Unfortunately, most religions have failed to fully teach us this truth.

It is interesting that the Bible did not attempt to describe more precisely who or what God is. We can only understand the nature of the Higher Power from the descriptions of God's behavior and inter- action with some of the Bible's characters. Since God is not quantifi- able, any attempt to describe Her would be grossly distorted. God is often described as omnipresent and omnipotent, but what exactly does this mean?

The answer to the question, "Who is God?" can come only from a deeper experience. If you want to experience God, you need to behave like Her. Do you know what God's main state is? Staying in silence! You need to silence your mind to get in touch with God.

Furthermore, when God does talk to us, it is in a subtle way. To listen to this subtle language, stay quiet. We pray to God and ask for all kinds of things, but so often we forget to keep silent so we can hear the messages or answers.

One of my biggest realizations about God is that He is not religious. God is the source of all spirituality but does not support any specific religious practices and rituals. If God wants anything, it is an intimate connection with you. Such a connection comes from your sacred place of peace and love.

The intimate love of God is a major theme in Sufism, the mystical aspect of Islam, which promotes a direct and close experience with God as a way of achieving higher consciousness. As the famous poet Rumi put it, "In the thirst you drink water from a cup, you see God in it. Those who are not in love with God will see only their own faces in it."

The Ice Cream Effect

In my attempts to better understand the way the ego thinks and operates, I came to a very interesting realization. Here is the question I asked myself: "Why do we seek freedom, peace, love, harmony, and beauty with such fervor?

The answer came to me one day as I treated myself to an ice cream, hence the term "The Ice Cream Effect." Think about the following question for a moment: Why do you eat ice cream—or chocolate or pizza, for that matter? The answer is very simple: because you like it, right?

But how do you know that you like it? The answer for that is also not complicated: You tried it before. Let me repeat that: You eat ice cream because you like it and you know that because you have had it before. And here lies the answer to the question I asked earlier: We seek all these wonderful states (freedom, peace, love, harmony, beauty and so forth) because we experienced them before and liked them.

You may say, "Yes, I had them before when I was a child and so I am still looking for these "tasty" things that give me a good feeling." Well, not quite. Even people who were deprived of them still look for them. How is that possible?

Here is the explanation I came up with. We all tasted these wonderful states—before we were even born. That was a time when we were pure spirituality with no physical constraints, just pure peace, freedom, and perfection. We had it all.

If you can allow this idea through the gates of your belief system, you may begin to understand how the ego tries to mimic everything you had and still have within your spiritual domain. The ego cannot stop you from searching, so it directs you outwardly. "If you do all these things...if you work really hard...if you achieve perfection...you will find it."

Baloney. You will never find TruePeace outside. Can you see why people may stay frustrated for their entire lives? We have all heard about people who achieved wealth, power, success, and fame but still experienced big emptiness inside and as a result engage in risky, unhealthy behavior such as abusing alcohol and drugs. Where are the promises, Mr. Ego?

Why do we keep searching for an answer to the question of who we are? It is because deep inside we know we have made a mistake in identifying ourselves. Is it Larry; is it Angelo? St. Augustine was obviously very aware of the Ice Cream Effect when he said, referring to God, "If you had not already found me, you would not be seeking me."

I have a personal, actual ice cream story that exemplifies this point. When I was about eight years old, my father took me to a place to eat parfait ice cream. This was the most delicious, superb ice cream I had ever tasted. This place was closed down the next time I went to visit it.

Throughout the years, I tried numerous ice cream places in search for an equally good parfait ice cream. I went to any restaurant that had parfait on the menu with the hope of finally finding that special ice cream I had when I was a child. But I could never get something even close.

A few years ago, after yet another attempt to locate an equivalent taste of my first parfait, it dawned on me that it would be impossible ever to find such an ice cream. My search was futile, not because of quality differences, but because of the unique situation: experiencing parfait for the first time and doing so with my dad. I wasn't really looking for the ice cream anymore; I sought that very special experience.

All yearning, longing, craving, and desire are in fact for that "first-time ice cream experience." It is not about food, or a lost love, or adventure. These are all great things that can bring pleasure and enjoyment. But don't be fooled by the physical aspect of it. The only way to repeat the real original experience is to reconnect with your CoreSelf.

What do you prefer, chocolate or vanilla?

A Few Good Words About the Ego

I have been very harsh with the ego in this book. My purpose was to make sure that you can bring your ego a few notches down, to be able to focus more on your truly powerful side.

I will let you in on a small secret. I was never extremely angry at my ego. As I said earlier, I even have respect for it. I know that it served me well at different points of my life, but I also know that now I can do better with less of its involvement. I really feel sorry for the ego, for working so hard to accomplish so little. I feel sorry, because it just goes in circles aimlessly, consuming tons of energy and producing nothing but havoc.

As I indicated earlier, a little bit of ego could be necessary to be able to communicate with other society members, to go to work and support the family. But notice I said "a little bit!"

To continue with this important trend, let's talk about conflicts within ourselves.

Conflicts

All inner conflicts are ego-based, and outer-based conflicts are no different. For instance, conflicts between two coworkers, neighbors, even countries usually represent a clash between different, typically contradictory, beliefs, values, needs, or preferences. These conflicts represent different parts of the same ego.

Here is a classical example. "Shall I work late to make more money or finish early to enjoy home and family?" This example represents one of the biggest conflicts of modern society: living to work or working to live. Success demands sacrifice and the sacrifice is usually about our personal life.

Studies show that the number of people who die from overwork in Japan is four times higher than 20 years ago. Several Canadian studies show that people are grossly overworked. The cost of health care in North America is higher than ever before. Obviously if this trend continues, the health system will hit crisis. Some claim this has already begun.

Conflict is the flip side of balance. Any system—a person, workplace, society, or a country—that is out of balance becomes sick and sooner or later pays a high price for it. Sometimes the system even dies.

Another big conflict also arises when facing the dilemma between looking after your own interests versus serving others. Some people will first take care of themselves and then, to various degrees, help others. Some will sacrifice their own well-being for the benefit of others. How much of doing for others is too much?

Want the bottom line? Essentially, all conflicts fall under one category: the silent conflict between our ego and our spirit. Selfishness versus soulfulness. Materialism vs. simplicity, commercialism vs. spirituality.

Conflicts create war. Did you ever notice yourself in a state of war? When one part of you wants one thing and another part wants another, many times exactly the opposite? How is one to handle such inner wars, which tend to wear the system down?

First let's find what the opposite of war is, so that we can be clear on what we want. That's easy: The opposite of war is peace! How do you achieve peace? Through the acceptance of the moment. And in the case of a conflict, the acceptance of the conflict.

You see, you can have a conflict and still feel peaceful, if you don't identify with the conflict. When you identify with it, you feel stuck in the middle; but when you observe it and accept it, you feel peaceful. When you feel peaceful, clarity sets in and you can then more easily decide what you want to do about the situation. Sometimes you can take positive action and other times you have to let it go.

Peace, deep moment, acceptance, truth, spirituality. By now you have completely realized how intertwined these terms are.

Conflicts consume a lot of energy and cause much stress on an ongoing basis. Remember this: There are no conflicts in the moment, only in the mind.

Now let's talk about another factor that occasionally causes us conflicts and consequently stress and anxiety.

Time

Time is a human invention of measure. We use time as a reference to the duration of or between events. The Webster's Dictionary defines time as "the physical quantity measured by clocks."

Does that mean that before clocks, time didn't exist? Of course it did, but up until then, the standard reference to time was, "Let's meet when light follows darkness again near the big rock."

The next definition of time reads, "finite (as well as earthly) duration as distinguished from eternity." This makes the concept more understandable. Notice the parallel between "finite" and "earthly."

Since the industrial revolution, how people use time has become more important, and now the clock controls the show. Our concept of time is what can turn us from human beings to human doings. Our "to do" list can never be completed. It is filled with tasks upon tasks, projects, household chores and so forth. Couldn't you do much better with an extra two hours a day? If you said yes (I know I did) then let me ask you this: How long do you think it will take for you to get used to it and then require additional hours to be able to catch up?

How we relate to time can change according to how we process the activities during the passage of time. For instance, we can be engaged in a pleasant activity and three hours will seem like minutes.

Or we can wait for a few minutes in line and it can feel like hours. This phenomenon is called time distortion. Another example of time distortion can be found when we look forward and back in time. If we are reasonably healthy, when we look ahead it seems that we have plenty of time left to live, but when we look back it seems that ten, twenty, thirty years passed in a flash.

We all have periods of involvement where we lose track of time. The reason is that when we are absorbed in the deep moment, regardless of the activity, the clock keeps ticking, but for us it feels as if time does not exist. Also, engaging in soul-based behavior seems to slow down time and we then feel that we have more of it available to us.

Since our sense of happiness is too often measured in modern society by how much we have accomplished, we may easily become slaves to time. When we feel rushed, or that we have no time, or that time has passed us by, we are not living in the now. The moment itself is eternal. Spirituality has no time constraints; it is timeless and boundless.

Our struggle with time is nothing but a subtle process of comparison. For instance, when you are in a hurry, you are comparing where you are or what you have accomplished, versus what you have to do or where you ought to be. The discrepancy will evoke a feeling: anxiousness or relief depending on the result of the mental process.

In my efforts to conquer my own rushed mentality, I have realized that I can be working fast and still be fully present in the moment. This happens in two ways. First, I'm fully engaged in the activity, whatever it is that I am doing; and secondly, I take breaks and do some of the awareness exercises described earlier, especially if it is an activity that demands a lot of mental work or if my mind is racing because a number of things have to be accomplished.

A final step to avoid negative comparison is equally important. At the end of the day, I appreciate everything I accomplished, instead of dwelling on what I didn't complete, and I look forward to continuing the next day.

With this attitude of acceptance, I feel time is on my side and I don't have to fight it, which is altogether futile. When you enter the mind zone, thoughts of "should and shouldn't" begin to go in circles and as a result stress kicks in.

Look at these examples of mental processing and living in the moment in relation to time in order to appreciate the difference.

Processing: Oh my God it's already six o'clock. I am dead.

Moment: It's six o'clock; I need to work faster. PERIOD.

Processing: I am late for the appointment; I am going to be fired.

Moment: I am late for the appointment; whatever happens I will deal with it the best that I can. PERIOD.

Most people living in Western society have a great need to learn how to slow down in order to catch up with life. This task is not easy since the pressures and expectations from society and the work-place increase constantly.

I worked with a patient, a teacher, to slow down her fast-paced life. She would get into severe anxiety if she were late for work or for a meeting. She explained that she had to do a lot of self-talk to cope with her stress. "Deep resolution is better than coping," I explained. After addressing feelings she had buried many years ago, she confirmed being able to slow down her pace, yet accomplish more, by better using all the energy she saved through reducing the need for coping.

"That's great," I said to her, "yet rationalization is still a method of coping. The next goal would be to feel calm naturally, without the need to say anything to yourself."

The amount of coping you have to use to meet different challenges in life is in many cases an indication of unresolved issues, which brings us to the subject of challenging emotions.

Challenging Emotions

Emotions can be very trying. When things don't work our way, especially in important areas of our lives like relationships, career, and our health, we may encounter difficult-to-handle feelings. Most people refer to them as "bad" or "negative."

If you want life, expect pain.
Midrash Tehillim
16:11

However, such emotions are not necessarily negative. They usually tell us that something is wrong; that we were taken advantage of; that we need to change something about our behaviors or environments, or that we need to pay more attention to deeper aspects of ourselves. The problem is not with feeling these emotions. It is how we handle them that can, in many cases, work against us.

These so-called "negative emotions" can include sadness, hurt, guilt, anger, shame, despair, hopelessness, helplessness, resentment, frustration, disappointment, rejection, and fear. Many emotions can be experienced together, at times creating more intense states such as depression, panic, and anxiety. Although it is normal and natural to experience such feelings when hit by adverse circumstances, realize that these emotions are always formed as a result of a thought process. With the exception of severe organically based chemical imbalances, which accounts for only a small percentage of the cases, all the rest are really caused as a result of a mental process: "I was treated a certain way; therefore, I feel angry." "I was fired without any justified reason; therefore, I feel sad." "My girlfriend left me for another guy; therefore, I feel hurt and frustrated."

I have already discussed the fact that if you were living more in the moment than in the mind, you would not experience such emotions so much, or at the very least, not so intensely. Again, I have to emphasize that it is normal to feel them; after all we are humans who were given the capacity to feel. The problem is not one of feeling any emotion; it is hanging on to them for too long, which can also be considered a process of attachment and identification. By breaking these attachments to painful emotions, you make it easier to let go.

When you identify with a feeling, you become it for any length of time. When you are it, you fuel and strengthen the emotion to a degree that you may lose control and perspective of a situation. For instance, a person can be so grief-stricken by the break-up of a relationship that he may ignore future opportunities for new and potentially even better ones.

Often people prefer to suppress such negative feelings instead of resolving them. This may cause long-term damage. Push the feelings away as much as you want, but they are still there, taking a toll on the system. Ignore them and watch how they come back indirectly, in ways you never suspected: tension, pain, dis-ease, psychological disorders, isolation, alienation, or just general unhappiness.

People do get too attached to emotions. Even though one should avoid any attachment as much as possible, I can see how people would want to attach to pleasant ones. But can you imagine individuals wanting to attach to so-called "negative emotions"?

Every so often I work carefully with patients to elicit long-buried emotions. When I suggest they let go, they sometimes respond, "I don't want to," without being able to explain why. Many times people believe that hanging on to such emotions will somehow improve or benefit them. Absolutely not! Such emotions drain the system and make a person susceptible to all kinds of health hazards.

For instance, many times when I suggest letting go of anger, I get the response, "Anger makes me strong." I explain that holding onto anger does not make a person strong; it actually weakens the system that retains it. It may give the illusion of strength though it actually acts like mental acid, burning away one's energy and personal power.

To deal properly with difficult emotions, a totally different attitude is required. Instead of fighting them, trying to push them away, or running away from them, which never works for long, treat such emotions with empathy. They are locked up in your system like innocent prisoners in a cell through no fault of their own. These feelings exist, without harm in the mere fact of existence. Comfort them, be gentle with them. Stop the war and unlock them to set them free. You can do it.

Who is becoming free now?

Enhancing the Reprogramming Technique

The earlier Observer Exercise is a good way to deal with any type of feelings. When you combine it with the Stop and Choose technique, it becomes an effective approach to dealing with nagging emotions that you have dragged until it's time to remove them from your system: guilt, fear, shame, anger and so on. The two exercises are also a useful approach when you get frustrated or disappointed about things you cannot change. Lastly, they are also helpful in dealing with recurring thoughts or behaviors you want to let go of.

Here are the steps:

1. Become aware of an unwanted emotion or thought pattern and observe it for a while.
2. Say with great determination, "STOP." (The stronger the pattern, the stronger you are to pronounce it.)
3. Take a deep breath in and confirm, "I am letting go of (state the feeling or thought pattern.)
4. Proclaim, "I choose peace instead."
5. Do a few moments of deep breathing for reinforcement.
6. Assume the observer position again and notice what you feel.
7. Keep breathing deeply until the thought or feeling subsides.
8. Repeat the process whenever the unwanted feeling or thinking pattern reoccurs.

This technique is also very useful in dealing with addictions. Repeat it a number of times until the reprogramming process is achieved. Be patient. Addictions may take longer to change.

It is so important to understand the following: Peace is real. Emotions are not! They may feel real but you give birth to and continue to nurture them by your thoughts. Emotions are simply your reactions. They can exist only when attached to a story, an experience, and a thought process. When you say, "You make me so angry," the reality is that you allow yourself to react with anger in this story and experience it through your thoughts. Let go of the mental process and the emotion will be gone, too.

Very Challenging Emotions

At times we have to face very challenging emotions. Such emotions may include deep pain, despair, grief, rage, and hatred that surface as a result of present difficulties or after recalling past traumatic experiences. Such emotions are usually felt around issues of abuse, loss, separation, nonfulfillment of goals and dreams, or as a result of personal tragedies.

I can still remember how I felt when my father passed away. After the initial shock and deep sadness faded, I began to think I was coping well with it. But I got accurate feedback six months later when I went to see the show *Forever Tango* by Luis Bravo. I was enjoying the show when suddenly I felt my eyes well up. I started to cry uncontrollably. The show reminded me of my dad, who liked tangos, especially when I played them on the accordion when I was much younger. I treated my tears as feedback, realizing that I still had more grieving to do.

According to Jewish tradition, the period of grieving is one year. I find this very reasonable. Many people grieve for years. Others just bury the feelings and pretend that everything is fine. Both extremes will cause indirect problems or ongoing unhappiness.

We can turn our losses into very powerful spiritual learning, but this requires courage. I worked with a woman who, as a result of an accident, was in constant pain and very depressed about her deteriorated health. I was able to help her deal much better with her pain and stress and accept her condition.

But as the therapy progressed, it was apparent to both of us that one of her favorite ways to deal with her feelings was to push them away, basically suppressing them so that she would not have to deal with them. When I poked a bit, she admitted that to feel and to cry was always a sign of weakness for her. She was determined to "be strong" and move on.

I explained to her that the suppression of feelings, not the act of feeling, weakens people. She agreed to explore that idea further and we composed a list of everything she had lost as a result of the accident. The list was quite long. I told her that she could turn all the losses into a tremendous gain and that she could find something more valuable than all of her losses, but that she would have to resolve her deep pain first.

She was resistant. She didn't want to "go there." She was afraid to get in touch with her vulnerability. With more coaching, a sad story of horrible abuse came out. The accident was just the last straw. She had never been allowed to cry even when her father died. She had to be strong to be able to "move on." I asked her if she would rather go back to how she felt before or face her deep hurt, consequently accomplishing total freedom.

This was a moment of truth. The choice was between settling for a superficial perception of strength or resting in the real strength of her spirit. She took the step toward peace. The guards came down; she acknowledged a lifetime of abuse, loss, and repression. She cried for a few weeks as if her system was trying to catch up with all the crying she skipped. And then it was all over. The hurt was gone, the guilt was gone, the protection mechanisms were gone as they were not needed anymore. Even the physical pain subsided, and she felt a deep sense of peace she had never felt before. Later on she acknowledged that she found her true self in the process, a self that was free of pain and suffering of any kind.

I have worked with many individuals who had no idea how much hurt and anger they carried deep inside. We can be angry about many things that happened to us in the past, but probably the biggest, and mostly unnoticed, is anger about losing our true self.

One patient was a woman who, during the process, realized that since childhood she had to suppress who she was to be able to please her father, in order to get his approval. The sad thing was that not only did she try hard to become someone she really wasn't, but no matter how hard she tried to please him, he never showed approval and affection in return. As she got in touch with that situation, she was able to let go of the anger and hurt and to reconnect with who she really was before she decided to push her feelings away. Such a process is always accompanied by a big release of false perceptions and limiting beliefs followed by a deeper realization of who we are and what's really important in our lives.

What to Do with Such Difficult Emotions?

Deeper awareness is the key to releasing difficult emotions. But sometimes we can get very overwhelmed when in touch with such feelings. The built-in mechanism to deal with loss is called grieving.

The process of grieving consists of two stages, the loss stage and the recovery stage. During the loss stage, a variety of challenging emotions are often experienced. Many of the patients I have counseled were stuck in the loss stage for a long period of time. Some people can get stuck in this stage, at least to some degree, for the rest of their lives. One of my patients, whose brother was killed by a drunk driver, told me that her parents, for over 10 years, would not talk about him. They even locked his room and no one could get inside. We call this denial, and denial is indeed one of the ways people remain stuck in the loss stage.

To be able to move to the recovery stage, a bridge has to be built. We call the bridge acceptance. Acceptance leads to letting go and consequently to peace. That's ultimately where we want to land. After all, what choice do we have? We cannot change the past and the choice of long-term suffering is a poor one.

What you can do is to change how the past is affecting your present. Your goal is always to arrive at peace. We sometimes try hard to hang on to things, people, positions, and certain conditions, but life is nothing more than a series of ongoing changes. Every moment is different. Change is the only constant in life.

The one thing that never changes is our spirit. Many times we hurt as a result of losses, but as we accept and let go, peace sets in and we can then move on.

Recently I worked with a woman who became ill a few years ago and had to quit her job. She admitted that with all the stress it had created, her work was the only source of satisfaction in her life. We talked about how she used work as the main reference for her self-esteem, and she understood why she became depressed when she was told by her doctors that she would not be able to go back to work, at least not for a while.

As I began to suggest a let-go process, resistance to change surfaced. When we explored this further, she admitted she didn't want to let go of her past, because if she did, nothing would be left. I explained to her that hanging on to an illusion never got anyone better. I acknowledged her difficulties; after all, in times of crisis, acceptance and letting go could be the most difficult thing to do. I reminded her that if she chose to hold on to memories and keep comparing her situation with the past, she would always stay in the loss stage and never be able to move on.

For her, the choice was either being able to go back to her old job or stay the same. This block to her recovery required much effort and courage, but only when she was able to fully accept the fact that life would never be the same as before, at least not for a while, she started improving.

> And you would accept the seasons of your heart, as you have always accepted the seasons that pass over your fields. And you would watch with serenity through the winters of your grief.
>
> *Kahlil Gibran*

People sometimes try to push away, or use rationalization, to put the past behind them. This works only when it's accompanied by acceptance and letting go. The alternatives include suppression and denial.

Many times we are taught to do that by our parents. Here is a recent example. In conversation, a woman told me that her child was too emotional when a rabbit that he had become attached to disappeared. She tried to reason with the child, offering to buy him a new rabbit. I suggested that instead of pushing her child to "put the incident in the past" too quickly, she allow him to grieve before other solutions were offered. Otherwise, these feelings would be pushed down and remain unresolved.

Strong feelings have to be dealt with first and the only healthy way is to face them, acknowledge them, sit with them for a while, express them, and then let them go. With kids, expression is almost always necessary before they can completely let go of their losses. In a few moments, I will describe a powerful exercise that will help you in dealing with challenging emotions.

Yes, But...

I know I should let go, but...
I know I should take the time to practice, but...
I would really like to____(fill in the blank), but...

These are just a small fraction of the "yes, buts" I get from patients when discussing change. It appears that people are attached to their habits, lifestyles, and routines for better or for worse. I discussed resistance to change earlier. Whenever a deep part in you knows that you have to let go of something to progress spiritually, and a "yes, but" pops up, at least know that it is your ego who is resisting change. "Why bother," ego says. "You are so busy," "It won't work anyway," "You can't afford it," "You don't have time," "It's taking too long," the ego says.

Does any of that sound familiar? The "yes, but" is usually very loud and very adamant. The soul's voice is more of a whisper, a suggestion or a gentle nudge, but it is trustworthy. It knows what you need to do to get to the next level. You have to help it. When you get a "yes, but" from your ego, reply with a "yes, but" of your soul.

The ego says, "Yes, but I am so busy, I have no time." Your answer would be, "YES, BUT, this is important and I am going to find the time to do it." The ego's voice may sound loud and determined but it is all a show. When you hear the voice of your soul that points out what you need to be doing, never ignore it, as it holds the key for a deeper understanding. Try "YES, BUT-ing" your ego's nebulous "yes, buts" and watch yourself grow rapidly.

Circle of Peace

I would like to teach you a very powerful exercise. To do that, I want you to take a few moments and connect deeper.

Take a few deep breaths in and exhale slowly. Get in touch with your breathing. I want you, as you continue to breathe deeply, to notice where the source of peace is in your body. Do more deep breathing if you need to and find the source of peace. Perhaps it is deep in your chest, or your heart, maybe your stomach. Allow the waves of peace emanating from this source to spread to every part of your body. Let every cell of your body,

> We dance in a ring and suppose, but the Secret sits in the middle and knows.
>
> *Robert Frost*

every fiber of your being, bask in peace. As the waves
continue to engulf all of you, allow them to flow through
your body outwardly and create a circle around you. See if
you can picture the circle. Get a sense of it. Imagine its color.
I call it The Circle of Peace. You are now in the middle of
that circle.

This is a very important exercise, so please take the time to practice it until you experience the Circle of Peace. Now you're ready to
deal with difficult emotions through a continuation of this exercise.

Begin with deep breathing and go into your circle of peace.
Now I want you to call up any challenging emotions you
would like to deal with. As you experience the emotion, call
up your circle of peace. Allow the specific feeling to rest in
peace without judging, criticizing, or attacking it. Keep reinforcing the process by continuing your deep breathing. Take
the role of a facilitator. Avoid getting sucked into the feeling.
As you repeat the process of connecting a challenging
feeling with peace, it will diminish in intensity and finally
completely dissolve into peace.

Peace is the only healer. What would happen if you connected
with your circle of peace regularly?

I recommend that you deal with one challenge at a time. Also,
start with less intense feelings in the beginning and gradually build
your experience to deal with more challenging ones.

What this exercise does is allow you to feel and express emotions
peacefully. This is a radical change in how people relate to their feelings. Although it sounds paradoxical, for instance, to "feel anger
peacefully," spirituality allows the ego to feel. By accepting the
emotion and allowing the ego to connect with peace, the process of
reacting negatively, or denying the feeling, or letting the feeling
control us, is eliminated.

Widening the Circle

Wouldn't it be satisfying to dissolve all existing difficult emotions in peace? You read earlier about studies showing that our intentions could effect healing in others; could the same spiritual intentions impact others' peace? Surely that prospect makes it worthwhile to widen your Circle of Peace.

> Get in touch with your circle of peace. Then gradually widen it to include your family in it, your immediate as well as your extended family. Now extend it to take in your entire neighborhood. Slowly expand it to include all the people in your city or town. Even further, encircle all the people in your province or state. Keep going to bring in all the people from your country. Then your continent. Do it slowly. Expand the circle to include all human beings. Don't stop here. Now embrace all of nature in our planet. Then let the circle gradually encompass all the planets around us and the rest of the universe. Can you feel one with all?

I noticed that over a billion people usually watch the Oscars. Wow! If five minutes in the middle of the show could be used to remind people how important it is to connect with peace, and with each other, what a momentum that could build. Such global reminders can shorten our evolutionary process dramatically.

The only way humanity can truly progress is one person at a time. We all want to accomplish peace on earth, but such a desired goal cannot be accomplished externally before we all accomplish it internally first.

And the Oscar goes to...world peace!

The Good News About Difficult Emotions

For a long time even after I finished grieving my father's death, I would occasionally experience feelings of sadness. When I thought I had resolved this issue, I would realize that something still remained. It appeared that a deeper feeling of longing still existed. When I looked carefully into it, it became clear to me that this longing was for my childhood. My longing was for being taken care of, for a life that was free of obligations, commitments, and responsibilities where Mom and Dad took care of everything. I was quite surprised to have such feelings and so I worked on resolving them.

Then I noticed that certain songs triggered yet a new set of even deeper feelings that were somewhat similar in nature to longing. As I kept exploring, I discovered something that had no time, person, or event related to it. It was an amazing feeling pouring out. I finally figured out what it was. This was pure energy coming straight from the soul. I knew that this energy always wanted to come out. I also realized that I could mold this energy any way I wanted, but only in a positive way. Such a feeling compels us to create and do good.

Finally, I realized what I always knew at a deeper level: Deep inside us is tremendous creative energy that is locked up under all the hurt of the past. We call this energy love, but it is even more than that. The "more" cannot be explained, only experienced. That "more" is what makes spiritual love so different from ego-based love.

Don't be afraid to feel and to look deep inside. You can find what has always been yours. Do you have a musical composition, a picture, or a poem that penetrates so deep inside that you feel it takes over? Such a feeling, pure and completely unattached, represents the energy I am talking about. Our ultimate goal is to be able to feel it without the need for any external triggers or stimulation, and to be able to feel it naturally and more regularly. We can then feel unconditional peace, love, and joy.

I am reminded of the story of a father whose son was exceptionally positive. The father decided one day to test the limit of his son's special attitude. He took a pile of horse manure and dumped it in his son's room. He then followed the boy to see the result of the test. When the child returned home, he went straight into his room, and of course it didn't take long to notice the addition. The father watched as his son jumped up and down with a huge smile.

"What are you smiling about?" he asked his son. "Didn't you see the horse manure?"

The boy nodded. "Of course I did."

"Then why are you so happy?" the father asked.

"This means that there is a pony around," the son happily replied.

When you feel the insecurities, doubt, or any of the challenging emotions we have discussed earlier, don't despair. Just remember that below all that, you can find a treasure chest full of goodies. Just sit down, take a deep breath in, and dissolve whatever is bothering you into peace. Do it again and again and watch what comes out. Give yourself permission to be surprised and you will.

I worked with a woman who was experiencing depression. She kept repeating that she saw no point to continue living in a world filled with problems, which she figured could not be resolved. Her depression worsened after the September 11 bombing of the Twin Towers in New York. She described a deep sense of helplessness because she could do nothing about what was happening in the world in terms of people dying every day due to wars and famine.

> There is nothing the body suffers that the soul may not profit by.
> *George Meredith*

I told her that although it was normal to feel helpless after such devastating events, she could do one thing to help the world, in a small yet meaningful way. I explained to her that her prime responsibility was to connect with her inner peace. This would not only help her in solving her personal difficulties, but as she and many others did the same, eventually enough spiritual momentum would be created to form the necessary changes that would bring an end to many of the difficult challenges we still face worldwide.

With our world as it is, can we afford not to make this effort?

Dis-ease and Healing

Perhaps one of the most difficult challenges to deal with is a chronic condition, or even worse, a terminal disease. I have seen many courageous individuals struggle with such challenges. I have seen the anger, frustration, hopelessness, tears, the constant search for cure, and the courage to face it all. So many emotions can be experienced in the process, and trying to tell people to accept what they are going through is quite difficult.

I would like to tell you something about the body. In essence, the body is a pure physical manifestation of our spiritual energy. But when we allow the ego to control it, tension, pain, and ultimately dis-ease set in. The body becomes the victim of our emotional struggle. Stress and bad habits such as poor nutrition, lack of exercise, or addictions only accelerate the process. The body also has its own genetic code that, for better or worse, also affects this process.

But please do not underestimate the effect of the emotional make-up on the system. Feelings are, indeed, felt in the body.

The body can become sick because it is the storage house for all the problems of the ego. It is very much affected by repressed emotions. Contrary to common belief, such repressed material is not stored in the mind, but in the physical framework. The mind is like an index of all the experiences and emotions, but the actual storage is in the body.

To heal the body, we need to become spiritual. When we treat the body with full respect, when we look at it as the physical extension of the spirit, we can expect it to work properly and to perform at its best. Healing does not come from medicine, herbs, meditation, or visualization, although all of them can, no doubt, help in the process. Healing comes from wholeness and wholeness is a spiritual state of being. The last definition of spirituality was PEACE. Therefore, healing always comes from peace.

One of my patients, a young man who was battling chronic pain and fatigue, and I had a conversation about praying to God for healing. I asked him what he expected from God, and he answered, "A miracle."

As we worked on some of his difficult emotions and he let them go, he relaxed. I asked him how he was feeling.

He replied, "At ease."

"What is the opposite of dis-ease?" I asked. He realized what I was getting at and quickly replied, "Ease."

"And how would you create ease?"

"By having peace," he confirmed. He understood that what he needed most was to connect with peace—the antidote to dis-ease—because healing can come only from the inside. Miracles happen when we can accomplish this deep inner state of being.

I mentioned earlier that the Hebrew word for peace is *Shalom*. Shalom is actually derived from the word *Shalem*, which means *complete and whole*.

The process of healing can be summarized by using this H.E.A.L. acronym.

H—stands for harmony. Harmony on mind and body levels. This is ultimately the state you want to accomplish, both physically and emotionally. Harmony is achieved by peace and it leads to wholeness, which then leads to healing.

E—stands for expression. Expression helps in releasing everything that is bottled up inside. Such expression can use different forms such as writing, talking, art, movement, music and so on. Many people perceive being spiritual with shutting up. Although we want to stay still and practice observation, expression is part of our creativity that has to be cultivated and nurtured. When all of the inner pain is resolved, the need for expression will subside, and we will then continue to create for the benefit of others and our personal pleasure.

> Peace, peace for him who is far off and for him who is near, says the Lord; and I will heal him.
>
> *Isaiah 57:19*

A—stands for acceptance. This is not a passive acceptance of doom. Rather, it is an active process during which you do what you can about your condition and yet you accept where you are and what you are going through. Acceptance also implies a letting-go process of which expression is an important part. Deep acceptance always leads to deep peace by letting go of the stress and anxiety associated with a difficult condition.

L—stands for love. All soul-based expression is an expression of love. Love dissolves bitterness, anger, guilt, resentment, shame, and fear. Love allows for forgiveness. Loving yourself and your body regardless of the challenges you face leads directly to acceptance, harmony, peace, and healing.

And here is a summary of the healing process:

Awareness ⟶ Letting go ⟶ Acceptance ⟶ Peace ⟶ Wholeness ⟶ Harmony ⟶ Healing

This process is effective in healing any part of your life including physical and emotional health, relationships, and overcoming loss and trauma. It also applies to healing the world from conflict and wars.

This process is almost a chain reaction that can be triggered by its first two components: awareness and letting go. Once you do that, acceptance kicks in automatically, leading to peace and all the way to healing.

Dr. Andrew Weil, in his book *Spontaneous Healing*, concludes that people who healed spontaneously experienced a sense of acceptance prior to the healing. The acceptance is not that the condition is going to stay as it is, although it might. Acceptance is in the moment. You accept what you are experiencing now; the next moment can be different.

> Behold, I will bring health and cure to it, and I will cure them, and will reveal to them abundance of peace and truth.
>
> *Jeremiah 33:6*

Acceptance defuses the conflicts, the struggle and anxiety, and promotes the opposite, which is peace. Healing of any system, be it a corporation, a country, or a person's life can only take place with peace. The body is no exception. Acceptance of the condition enables a person to accept himself and his life completely, despite the limitations and challenges. Since healing comes from our spiritual terrain and what leads us there is acceptance, it is very important to experience full acceptance to promote healing.

"When you are sick, surrender does not mean giving up the hope of renewed health. Rather it means accepting all circumstances of

your life, including present sickness, in order to move beyond them"
Andrew Weil, *Spontaneous Healing* (paperback), Ballantine Books,
New York.

So how to do it? If you are experiencing a physical challenge, the
most important truth for you to understand is that under all the
pain and the symptoms, you can always find peace. This peace is
your source of healing. You need to transcend the emotions associated with your condition, truly let go. Otherwise, you are in conflict.
Conflict is war, and war is not conducive to healing.

Many people who go through severe adversities are fortunate to
realize that such conditions could be a spiritual wake-up call.
Through looking deep inside and evaluating your life, your question
(whether you are sick or not) should be, "How much peace am I
experiencing in my life?" And also, "How much unconditional love
am I offering?" The answer to these two questions can be a gauge to
how you have advanced in reducing ego and expanding your spiritual connection.

What kind of changes, both internal and external, do you have to
make to expand your own connection? If you don't want to make
changes, use the ultimate shortcut: stop processing! Let go of
grudges, anger, resentment, bitterness, guilt, and shame by committing to living in the deep moment and getting in touch with the
peace inside.

The ego blocks the path to healing, through heavy loads of repression and thick layers of protection mechanisms. Letting go of the
ego's defenses is not always easy to do, I know. But it is possible. The
feelings you experience daily are a good indicator of where you are
blocked by ego, and if you are not feeling anything, that's not a good
sign either.

You have to understand that the body cannot speak English—or
any other language for that matter. The body speaks indirectly in
two ways: through feelings and through symptoms. If you can
understand this unique language then you can work on improving
your health. Physical tension happens as a result of lack of attention

to your inner world. Physical pain can be a manifestation and an indirect expression of inner pain and hurt. Dis-ease can occur when you carry too much uneasiness and burden, and premature aging happens when you move faster than life.

Over and over we see that when one lives life too much in the mind, the body pays the price. High-level stress finally catches up and causes much unhappiness and a gradual deterioration of the body. When continuously ignored, the body at some point breaks down and more severe conditions are then experienced. Why not stop this process now?

A word of caution here: Many people who were trying to promote healing using different holistic approaches, and did not succeed, experienced not only feelings of discouragement and disappoint-ment, but also self-blame for not being able to make it happen. After all, the books and holistic therapists told them that with the right diet, and the right supplements and the right visualization they would heal. If they haven't, they assume that they were not doing it correctly, or didn't try hard enough.

That's a dangerous trap that we have to avoid falling into. It is also the reason the accomplishment of deep peace is so important in such circumstances. If, for whatever reason, physical healing has not been accomplished, peace will allow the person to feel good about him or herself no matter what. Peace is always a win-win solution.

What About Traditional Medicine?

Millions of people turn every day to different types of alternative medicine because of dissatisfaction with the traditional health care system. The reason is either because they didn't get well; they couldn't get the answers or the results they were looking for; or perhaps because, to a certain degree, the health care system has lost the "care" element. Alternative disciplines include Homeopathy, Chiropractic manipulations, Naturopathy, Acupuncture, Shiatsu, Reflexology, Aromatherapy, Therapeutic touch, Craniosacral therapy, Ayuverdic medicine, Chelation, and many more. Thousands of herbal and megavitamin combinations are claimed to possess healing powers for all kinds of illnesses.

We have to give conventional medicine a lot of credit. It has helped us a great deal in overcoming many health-related difficulties and improving our longevity. Traditional medicine, however, is still facing many challenges. It may never be able to overcome some of them, at least not before medical doctors begin to treat not only the symptoms but also the person as a whole.

Medicine is still too drug oriented and medical practitioners over-blame chemical imbalances for many conditions, especially psycho-emotional difficulties. As a result, conventional medical practitioners are very quick to prescribe medication.

The emphasis has to shift towards healing rather than just fixing or maintenance. Emphasizing the importance of looking at a problem from a more holistic approach by examining both mind and body, Hippocrates, who is regarded the father of modern medicine, said, "Don't tell me what disease the man has, tell me what man has the disease."

A few years ago I met a physician specializing in allergies, who told me that for a while he could not understand why patients told him about their everyday problems during their regular visits. These problems seemed unrelated to his treatment. One day it dawned on him that the different difficulties his patients experienced were part of the physical health problem and he started to pay more attention to them. He stated that since he started to do this he noticed improvement, not just relief, as a result of his medical intervention.

Health centers with an "integrative approach" that combines traditional as well as alternative medicine are becoming very popular. But we have to be careful. Since alternative modalities can represent a potential for big money, many jump on the bandwagon trying to make a fortune.

It is absolutely unbelievable how many "we can fix all your problems" therapies and products exist. You can go on the Internet and see many questionable health aids for yourself. I believe that consumers should check carefully before engaging in any protocol that is not performed by reputable professionals. Hopefully, more traditional, qualified practitioners will learn to enhance their skills and be able to offer a more holistic approach.

I have been fortunate to work with a wonderful team of professionals headed by my good friend Dr. Gordon Ko, MD, a specialist in rehabilitation and chronic pain, at the Canadian Centre for Integrative Medicine in Markham, Ontario. He is a living example of how powerful the combined knowledge of traditional medicine and alternative approach can actually be.

We have to remember that in essence all healing is self-healing. The body knows how to heal itself, but it is sometimes blocked and therefore unable to complete the healing process. Such "blocks" could be one of the following: old injuries, chemical or metal toxicity, nutritional deficiencies, emotional trauma, and genetic predispositions.

I strongly believe that in the future, doctors will have to include the "peace" ingredient in their prescriptions. We have to remember that the word "doctor" comes from the Latin word "docere," which means to teach. Medicine for many years has been mainly physically oriented. Now the emphasis on the mind-body connection is widely accepted by most professionals. Many healers have the ability to engage the person's natural healing mechanism to promote deeper healing. Future medicine will have to include a very strong spiritual element, only because deep healing is in essence a spiritual process.

Right now, I would like to teach you a powerful self-healing exercise using The Circle of Peace.

Circle of Peace Healing Exercise:

Get in touch with your circle of peace, then imagine your physical symptoms, whether muscle tension, fatigue, pain and so forth, saturated in peace. Let the symptoms completely dissolve into peace until they too become peace.

Do the same with any feelings associated with your
condition such as anger, frustration, guilt, fear, hopelessness
and so on. Do you feel inner peace each time you do it?
Please repeat this exercise frequently.

More Uses for the Circle of Peace

You can bring into the circle anything that bothers you. It will help you with a problem, a weakness, insecurity, regrets, confusion, and even with decisions. When you bring the problem into peace it may help not only in feeling better, generally, but also in connecting you with your intuition and creativity. As a result you may come up with more creative solutions to the challenges you currently face.

Another very powerful way to use this method is to bring into The Circle of Peace people you need to forgive. You can also help friends and family members who are sick, or experiencing any type of difficulty, by bringing them and the challenges they face into the circle. This type of remote healing is a very powerful process to help yourself and others.

In time, you become peace and peace becomes you. You will not have to do any practice to feel peace. Peace will be your only practice. Spirituality needs no exercises or special attention, unless you have not fully manifested it. Your symptoms, your problems, and your difficulties want nothing but peace. When they experience it, they no longer suffer. They can heal themselves. Just show them how to connect with peace and all the rest will occur naturally.

But what if a condition is incurable? This can happen too. Sometimes all the healing power that one has, with all the possible help, care, and support, are not enough to cure. Still, the same approach has to be practiced. Then the person can live peacefully and when the time comes, die in peace. This will also allow everyone related to the person to feel peace too. Cure is not always possible, but healing certainly is!

End of the Day Routine

Why do you regularly wash your hands or take showers or baths? To keep your body clean, of course. Shouldn't your emotional system be treated the same as your physical body? You can use the Circle of Peace to "cleanse" yourself emotionally by putting all of your daily stresses, one by one, into the circle just before going to bed. It's a brief exercise that can prove to be very beneficial. You will feel great and sleep so much better.

Suffering

In certain circumstances we may experience severe suffering and pain. Pain in its physical form is a sensory-based experience. But suffering has a lot to do with how we relate to pain, how we perceive circumstances around it, and how we allow it to affect us.

One of the best examples of how a spiritual individual copes with pain is described in the Bible. I refer to the book of Job. God tested Job, after an ongoing debate between God and Satan, on whether or not he would keep his faith after sustaining severe afflictions. Job lost his fortune, he lost his family, and as the ultimate test, he contracted a terrible skin disease. But throughout the ordeal he refused to curse God.

This idea of God testing us is a difficult concept to understand. I don't take the stories of the Bible at face value. I cannot understand a God who plays games with humans. This is a story, and as I suggested earlier, we need to look at the spiritual principle the story portrays rather than get stuck in the packaging. Perhaps the true moral here is that a place exists in us that is not affected by any external circumstances. When we learn to connect with it we can then face tough challenges without letting them rule our lives and demoralize us.

"Acquaint now yourself with him, and be at peace; thereby good shall come to you." *Job 22:21*

Job clearly equated knowing God with finding inner peace. He also recognized that this type of peace is the foundation of all goodness in life.

What Is the Ultimate Letting Go?

The ultimate letting go is to let go of YOURself. What a concept, isn't it? And you may ask, "So what is left when I get rid of MYself?" "Wouldn't I feel bad, go through identity crisis, feel empty?"

No, no, no. You will be left with your real, authentic "I." I am. You are. PERIOD! We always let go of OURselves when we die. Can you do it when you are still alive? Letting go of YOURself will result in letting go of your inhibitions, fears, anxieties, and hang-ups. You become fully spiritual without any need for a philosophical, religious, or scientific belief system.

> The true value of a human being can be found in the degree to which he has attained liberation from the self.
>
> *Albert Einstein*

Dealing with Difficult People

My patients often ask me how they are supposed to deal with difficult people around them. Such people can be an employer, a sibling, a spouse, or a coworker. These patients also express their frustration at the fact that as they continue to evolve, they want other people to feel like they do; but this doesn't always work. The first advice that I give them is to stop all attempts to change others. Firstly, because the more you try to change people the more they resist. Secondly, trying to change others involves judgment, and we have already discussed this point in detail.

> It is being dead to self that is the recognition of God.
>
> *Hazrat Khan*

A woman I counseled worked in a very stressful environment. She held an executive position with a boss who was putting a lot of unnecessary pressure on her. She didn't want to leave her job as some of her friends had suggested, because she looked at the situation as an opportunity to grow.

First we worked on improving her assertiveness skills which, in turn, improved the situation to a certain degree. But the real change came when she deepened the connection with her inner peace. She simply stopped reacting to her boss's remarks and put-downs. Instead she felt sorry for him, realizing that all of his behavior was not really about her but about his own insecurities. She chose to go into her place of peace whenever she was provoked. No defending or offending.

Her boss kept trying to push her buttons for a while but gradually started treating her with greater respect. This woman reported she felt that she started living life on a "higher plane of peace" as she described it, and began to truly enjoy her work. She also reported that many of her coworkers came to her with their problems, seeking her advice. I suggested that instead of advice she teach them how to connect with their own peace.

On Death and Dying

It is impossible to write a book about spirituality without talking about death and dying. The question of what happens after death has occupied people's attention and speculations since the beginning of mankind. I have already shared with you my ideas about heaven and hell, so you know that's not how I view the afterlife stage. My "Ice Cream Effect" principle implies that we existed before we were born and continue to exist after we die.

> The dust returns to the earth where it came from and the spirit returns to God who gave it.
> *Ecclesiastes 12:7*

So what really happens after death? Obviously, I can't tell you for sure. What we know is that the body as well as the ego die—total death. I do believe that the spirit does not die. It is just there as it was before, spreading to every edge of the universe and beyond. How does one feel "out there"?

We have never received scientifically substantiated, direct messages from "the other side."

However, we can learn more from people who went through a near death experience (NDE). NDE refers to an out-of-body experience by individuals who were pronounced clinically dead as a result of physical trauma such as an accident, surgery, or cardiac arrest. During the experience, these people usually reported going through a tunnel after which they connected with a source of light. Sometimes they encountered spiritual beings and deceased relatives on the other side of the tunnel. Almost always they experienced an extraordinary sense of peace and love. After some time the individual would return to his or her body, waking up with a deep sense peace. People who went through such an experience noted that they could be in more than one place at a time. They also reported that they continued experiencing peace and love in their lives. This powerful feeling is consistent in most near death experiences and I believe this outcome indicates that these people lost a big part of their ego in the process.

NDE puzzled many scientists who could not explain how individuals whose brain had stopped working could have such a powerful experience. This immediately ruled out the explanation that these individuals just "hallucinated" the experience.

From NDE indications, it appears that when the spirit is disconnected from its association with the body it just spreads out to eternity. It is everywhere yet nowhere. We become the energy everything is made of, experiencing a true feeling of pure awareness, a no-body fully aware of everything from the beginning to the end of time.

This model may also serve to better understand the process of life and death. We start as a no-thing. Out of this "no-body," body and ego are created. They gradually develop throughout life and at the end return to becoming a no-thing, only to start the process all over again.

I like it when certain patients who come to therapy complain that they "feel like a nobody." "Good," I say. "In my book, no-body means spirit. That's tremendous progress. Let's now look at how it all works." More often than not, the patient will start laughing and can then progress in understanding the source of his or her difficulty and where to find the real solutions for it.

Life is full of all kinds of deaths. Time, experiences, sometimes relationships die. Every such death includes an end and a new beginning. The ultimate physical death at the end of our own lives is not any different. It also symbolizes the end of a certain form of life and a beginning of a new one.

We can use the water cycle to better understand our life cycles. Since nature acts cyclically and since we are a reflection of nature in specific and of the universe in general, I believe that this example clarifies the stages we go through. Water pours from the mountains through creeks that connect with rivers that ultimately pour into the ocean. In the ocean, all water becomes one, indistinguishable. Some of the water evaporates along the way, becoming vapor as invisible as the spirit. Then the vapor turns to rain that goes back one way or another into the creeks and rivers to rejoin the ocean, completing another cycle.

> All the rivers run into the sea; yet the sea is not full; to the place from where the rivers come, there they return again.
>
> *Ecclesiastes 1:7*

We are born out of the unseen Supreme Spirituality taking on physical form like the rain that feeds the streams. Our life then flows and progresses much like the rivers until we join the ocean. Without awareness of our spirits, we remain alone in a sea of spirits. When we recognize our spirits and respect those of others, we're at one with the great indistinguishable ocean of all creatures. At some point in the physical cycle, death transforms us to pure spirit, and we reconnect with Supreme Spirituality. We then separate again, taking on physical form once more like new rain; we are reborn to start the cycle all over again.

This metaphor only describes the big picture. As for the details and how exactly it all happens, I guess we will know only when we get to experience it directly.

Even if nothing really happens after death, still the only way to live is in the now. When you live your life experiencing peace, you feel no fear of dying. You live in peace and you die in peace.

The doctrine of becoming constantly aware of one's death as an essential component for living is a well-known principle in many religions. Such awareness is supposed to clarify what's important to focus on in life.

Death is the ultimate act of letting go. But you don't have to wait for death to let go. As we learn to let go of our egos, we also lose the fear of death. Coming to terms with death enables us to live life without the nagging fear of death in the background.

During a trip to Mexico, I bought a three-dimensional mask inspired by Mayan tradition. It is comprised of three masks, one on top of the other, that symbolize the three stages of life: birth, living, and dying. But this symbol can be also looked at as the process we go through during each day: being born in the morning, living the day, and dying at night into sleep. An even more powerful way to look at it is what happens moment after moment: a moment is born, you experience it to the fullest, it then dies and a new moment is born.

What a perfect way to live life, though not so easy, I admit. Unfortunately, we tend to accumulate millions of "dead" moments inside ourselves that take space and energy to maintain and have very little or no usefulness to our systems.

When you identify with your ego and your body, you may experience fear of death. The ego is terrified of death, because this is when the ego dies for good. But when you realize that you are neither your body nor your ego, this fear goes away.

The notion of totally losing one's fear of death after near-death experience has been well documented. Interestingly, many of the people who went through the experience also recounted that when "coming back," they felt they could then become whom they really were. This feeling is a result of losing their egos in the process of the NDE. They didn't lose only the fear of death, but also the fear of life itself, and they began to live life more fully.

The Near Death Experience is a remarkable phenomenon that has to be looked at seriously

> I existed from all eternity and, behold, I am here; and I shall exist till the end of time, for my being has no end.
>
> *Kahlil Gibran*

because people from different cultures and age groups, including children, have experienced the essence of the experience. Trying to replicate such experiences using various methods such as drugs, big electromagnetic fields, even hypnosis, failed to achieve even a close result. The importance of these extraordinary experiences is not just that they strongly indicate a continuation of consciousness after life, but also that they contradict neuroscientists' assertion that consciousness is only an offspring of the brain. NDE proves, in my opinion, that our consciousness is part of the Supreme Consciousness that never dies, only changes forms.

From Stress to Spirituality

I mentioned in the introduction of the book that we have become an over-coping society. Coping is appropriate, but over-coping means that we are paying a high price for stress.

With busy schedules, increasing demands, and a bombardment of information, the mind becomes more and more crowded. Symptoms begin to surface until at some point in the process you may be pushed against the wall. Then you have no choice but to deal with stress more seriously; only at this point it is more difficult to do. If at all possible, let's start the process before it's too late.

A recent study done for the Canadian Heart and Stroke Foundation reveals that four in ten Canadians, 30 years of age or older, feel overwhelmed by stress. More than half of the people questioned in the study admitted that they don't spend enough time with their loved ones and don't have enough time for themselves either. The cost of stress to the Canadian economy, in terms of lost work time, not even including health care cost, is about 12 billion dollars. In the USA this number is believed to be 10 times higher.

Once the process of stress is understood, the route for moving from stress, which is always ego-based, to spirituality is clearer and easier to do. In a lecture I once gave, a S.T.R.E.S.S. acronym came to my mind. It is divided into two parts: the problem part, S.T.R., and the resolution part, E.S.S.

The problem part:

S—*senselessness*. Thinking that you can control others or circum-stances is senseless. Senselessness represents our "over-processing" mind that tries to impose control on life and along the way misses the real principles that can make us not only stress free but more importantly—truly fulfilled.

T—*tension*. Tension is a result of irrational and unreasonable expectations, which is part of our senseless thinking. This kind of thinking inevitably causes mental and physical tension and if not resolved properly, expands into pain and dis-ease.

R—*repression*. Repression is always a big factor that colors not only our decisions and behavior, but also our general well-being. Repression represents the unconscious mechanism that keeps unresolved issues and feelings associated with it out of the conscious mind on the one hand, but constantly strives for reso-lution on the other. Repression has to be expressed one way or another, and therefore will come out in the form of physical and psychological symptoms.

The resolution part:

E—*expression*. I have mentioned this in the H.E.A.L. acronym. Expression is the opposite of repression. When you express what is kept inside, you free the locked-up energy. Expression represents our creativity. As more and more of the repressed material is expressed, either verbally or artistically, a shift occurs toward expressing love, kindness, and compassion towards others and self.

S—*surrender*. I referred to this concept earlier. People often use the term "go with the flow." This can be modified to "go with the right flow," and the right flow is that which fully surrenders to the experience of the moment regardless of its content.

Surrendering is about embracing the flow of change. It repre-sents the ultimate acceptance and it automatically connects you with your infinite source of peace. Please remember that surrender is not defeat or giving in. Surrender is the deep realization that we are just one tiny part in an enormous system, and that we cannot always understand how this system works. Surrender is, first and foremost, letting go and accepting that which cannot be changed. It is also the realization that we are part of a magnificent universe operating from Divine Wisdom that by far transcends our little needs and agendas.

S—*spirituality.* Spirituality is the opposite of ego and the true solution for all stress. Spirituality is the sum-total of letting go of S.T.R. and the manifestation of E. S. Spirituality manifests itself in the physical world through the soul, which knows how to put things in a lighter and higher perspective, how to laugh and find goodness in all of creation. At such point, all elements of spirituality are present: peace, love, creativity, and joy. Where is stress now?

So there you have it. From stress to spirituality. To make this formula useful when you're in a stressful situation, ask yourself the following questions:

1. What's in my thinking that is causing me stress and tension, and how can I change it?
2. What do I have to let go of, to be able to move to the resolution part of the S.T.R.E.S.S. formula?
3. What kind of feelings do I still keep bottled up that relate to the issue at hand?
4. What do I have to accept about the situation, to be able to avoid conflict, pain, and tension, and to feel peace instead?
5. Am I in the moment or am I in the mind?

Take a few minutes right now to try this model on something in your life that is causing you stress at the present time. Start with a simple stressor and you can gradually work through the more challenging issues. Remember: At all times do your best, then let go of the rest.

Observe Instead of Absorb

When you begin to follow the S.T.R.E.S.S. concept naturally, you will be able to be in the midst of crisis and chaos and become aware of what is going on instead of absorbing the stress. You will be able to observe and respond in peace. Can you picture yourself doing that?

The most terrible storm has a spot in it called the eye of the storm. If you could get there, you would still be moving at the speed of the storm, but you would not feel it, because the eye of the storm is a peaceful place in the middle of all turbulence that is going on around it. Every challenge, problem, or difficulty has peace in the middle of it. When you connect with it, you stop paying the price of stress and you become much clearer about what would be the best approach to deal with the situation: Take peaceful action to resolve the situation or accept and let go if there is nothing you can do about it.

Recently, I acquired a serenity fountain for my office. It is built with five semi-levels, three levels projecting out from one side and two from the other, which allows the water to flow from level to level all the way to the bottom and then up to the top again through a small water pump. Small rocks on each level and on the bottom allow every owner of such a fountain to arrange them according to his or her taste. Water trickling over stones is really very peaceful to look at. Aside from that, I use it to demonstrate the flow of life as I explained earlier.

But another interesting aspect to the fountain makes a big point. You have to arrange the stones on each level so that the water can move smoothly from level to level. Then, if you move any of the rocks even a little, the water starts to spill all over and everything around gets wet.

In a way, life's energy flows through us perfectly when we are aligned with it. But when we put blocks in its way (and these are always mental blocks), it starts splashing, so to speak. My office fountain needs occasional fine-tuning. From time to time, the flow loses its focus and I have to readjust the stones. Our daily practices, in a similar fashion, need constant examination and realignment to maintain focus. The water pump, which is hidden in the fountain, makes it all work. This pump represents the Supreme Intelligence that makes us all work. We cannot see it but it is always working deep inside for us.

Another interesting thing to notice in this context is that the metaphor of success in our society has to do with moving up. We talk about climbing the ladder of success. Spirituality is the opposite. We are moving down, to deeper levels of awareness within ourselves, much like the water going from the mountains to sea level, following the water cycle I described earlier. Applying the principles of the S.T.R.E.S.S. formula allows our spiritual energy to flow without effort, and then we always feel energized and rejuvenated.

An allegory is attached to this fountain. When I first installed it, nothing happened. The pump seemed to work properly but the water didn't flow. I played with it for a few minutes but since it wasn't working, I decided to let it go until I could ask what to do at the store where I bought it. About ten minutes later, I was into a session when I heard a sound coming from the fountain. Turning around, I saw that the water had started flowing. I was quite surprised, but the story doesn't end here. Later, I noticed that the fountain didn't make enough waterfall sounds and this was somewhat disappointing. I rearranged the stones but nothing changed. Again, I decided to let it go and later on, to ask about it at the store.

The next day as I entered the office, I heard the musical sound of water spattering from one level to another. I realized that this fountain symbolized a significant lesson for me. We're accustomed to pushing a button and getting an instant reaction. We expect things to work immediately for us. More often than not we just have to allow events to take their course and everything then falls into place. We need to learn to work at the pace of life. That requires a good measure of acceptance, which then allows us to accomplish anything we want, at least internally, which is the only place that really counts.

Signs

Many people pray to God to send them a special sign, a lightning bolt striking their heads, as if a specified manifestation will strengthen their belief in God. That's not how God works. If we could all get strong signals that left no room for interpretations, the process would be too easy. The evolution of spirituality is such that we have to figure it out and choose to get there, even though other, more short-term choices may tempt us in the process.

Having said that, we do get signs, in fact daily signs, which are usually subtle in nature. Nonetheless, these signals can point out to us whether we are moving in the right direction or not. They can also tell us what we need to focus on in order to jump to the next level. They could even be warning signs about situations or people to be aware of.

Many of these special signs are hidden in what we commonly call coincidences. Someone once said that coincidences are God's way to stay anonymous. Another term that describes this phenomenon is synchronicity. If we are willing to look at such synchronicities a bit deeper, we can learn a lot about a level of communication that the scientific mind has no explanation for.

I receive such signs on a regular basis. In the beginning, I didn't think anything of it; but as these experiences continued, I had no choice but to pay closer attention to them.

Early in my work I noticed that I could think of a person, say a patient that I had not seen for a few years, and then the person would call me right after. One time could be regarded as a coincidence but when it started to happen regularly I knew it was something greater than just a simple coincidence. The last time this happened, I was looking for a misplaced chart when I came across another chart of a patient I treated five years ago. As I noticed the name, I wondered how the patient was doing. A few hours later, I reviewed messages on the answering machine and found a message from this patient asking me to give her a call.

Many people have similar experiences from time to time. This, in my opinion, is one of the many examples of how we are all deeply connected. We transmit and receive messages with each other and when we are tuned into the universal connection, as you would tune a radio to a particular station, synchronicities happen.

Signs could be even stronger and more meaningful messages for you. Here is one personal example. A friend told me about a certain professional who wanted to sell his practice and thought I might be interested in his office, since at the time I was looking at a possibility of changing offices. I went to see the house, located at Falcon Street in Toronto. The place wasn't exactly what I had expected, but I enjoyed meeting the people who occupied the premises.

While there, I noticed a big, old radio in the office. I commented about how beautiful it was. Fixing vintage radios used to be my hobby when I was a teenager. As I drove home, I passed a small old-radio repair shop. These shops are very rare these days as most shops repair TV's, VCR's, and more sophisticated electronics. I made a mental note to visit the place one day.

Suddenly I realized that within less than an hour I had come across the "old radio" theme twice, and I wondered if any special meaning was implied. I thought that perhaps the message related to reconnecting with my old hobby, but this did not fully click with me.

As I looked at the name of the store I was surprised yet again. It said "Falcon Radio Electronics." This was the second Falcon in less than an hour. Then I recalled that the day before, a lady had left a message at my office, asking me to call her back. Her name was Mrs. Falcon. Three were too many falcons to ignore in such a short period of time, so I wondered what significance they had.

When I researched it, I discovered that the falcon is regarded as a very talented diver. It can dive towards its prey at a speed of 200 miles an hour and it has a wonderful ability to focus and quickly reach its target. It didn't take me too long to realize the implication of the recurring falcon theme. I realized I was too scattered at the time. The message was very simple: I had to FOCUS. As a result, I went through a crystallizing process that resulted in deciding to write this book.

It's debatable whether the Supreme Intelligence sent this message or whether we are able to tune more carefully into things as we grow and develop spiritually. Like anything else from this intangible territory, neither can be proven. But I have certainly realized that the more I progressed spiritually, the more interesting and meaningful these signs became.

I discussed tuning into signs as messages with one of my patients. The following week she told me that after our session, she went grocery shopping and a jar of jam dropped from her hands and splattered over the entire floor. She felt embarrassed at first but she remembered our conversation, so she decided to check the ingredients of the jam. One of the ingredients was something she was very allergic to. It was an ingredient that one would not normally expect to find in a jam.

We all receive all kinds of messages. They arrive from where intuition comes from. Receiving them cannot be rationally explained but as we learn to notice them and trust them, they can enrich our experience and guide us well.

How do you recognize such signs? A sign is an occurrence or an out-of-place object that calls for your attention. It can be one or even a series of ordinary, or not so ordinary, events that will somehow be connected to an issue or a challenge that you are dealing with, or to intentions that you had set previously. Sometimes a sign can be very strong and leave no room for interpretations, and other times it can be more subtle. If you click into a "suspected sign" you will have a feeling that says, "Pay attention to me; please do!"

If you encounter a sign, ask yourself, "What is the meaning of that for me?" If the situation is indeed a sign for you, the answer will always have something to do either directly or indirectly with increasing your spiritual awareness and connection.

If you encounter an animal you usually don't see often, pay attention to it. I remember noticing a ladybug one day sitting in my car's keyhole. A week later, I saw a snake in the woods while I was taking pictures of autumn's display. This baby snake froze just in front of me as if waiting for me to go away.

Ladybugs represent metamorphosis and change. A snake represents death and rebirth. Both appeared while I was in the midst of my own spiritual transformation, so I decided to view them as signs of support and reinforcement. If you want to learn more about

262   Shortcut to Spirituality

animals and their spiritual meaning and symbolism, refer to the book *Animal Speak* by Ted Andrews (Llewellyn Publications, Minnesota, 1993).

A few months later, at a time when I went through a period of doubt, which is very typical while going through spiritual transformation, something exceptional happened. When I came to the office one morning, I found the ledge of the window flooded with ladybugs. How they got there, I don't know. But I was very surprised and thankful for the universal gesture and reinforcement that change was the right path for me.

A woman I worked with told me she had encountered a "weird experience" the previous week just after our session. As she drove in the countryside on her way home, she suddenly saw a hawk diving in the sky that somehow stopped in mid-air and stayed still for a long time. She asked me what it meant.

I wasn't surprised at all with her story and showed her a note I had written during the previous session. The note said, "Next week discuss the concept of stillness." In a way the universe showed her the next spiritual practice she had to learn, which "coincidently" was the subject I planned to discuss with her the next session.

Noticing signs can accelerate the process and simplify it, unless you become too obsessive and begin to analyze every little thing that happens in your life. That's not really the purpose of this kind of awareness.

Another patient I worked with described experiencing remarkable coincidences on a weekly basis. She wanted to know why she experienced so many such signs. I reminded her about the doubt and fear she experienced during her rapid process of growth and personal development. The signs, in my opinion, were there to tell her that she was on the right track, to suspend her fears, and trust the process. She needed the reassurance because people in her family resisted the changes she experienced. My answer motivated her to deepen her understanding even further to a point at which she felt no doubt in her mind that she was doing what was completely right, even if some people did not agree with it.

Many of my patients receive messages in the form of hearts when they are at a fork in the road, trying to decide whether to follow spiritual-based choices or to just stay where they are. These are usually quite strange experiences.

For instance, one of my patients encountered a strong fear of change as she contemplated some drastic changes in her life. She told me that the day before our appointment, she stepped out of the house and found a ring near her front door. She showed me the ring. I was not surprised to see that it was heart-shaped. I told her that this was a spiritual sign that she had to follow her heart. She promised she would.

Another patient bought a crystal and when she looked inside, a beautiful, natural part of the crystal formed a heart. This inclusion shone when you looked at it from a specific angle. I have seen many crystal formations, but this was a unique one.

If you find unusual signs involving hearts, the universe is hinting loud and clear: Put your mind-oriented choices aside and follow your heart. You will not regret it.

Dreams

I don't intend to write much about dreams, although I could easily write a book about them. But in this context of signs, it is important to mention that dreams are an excellent source of signs and messages.

Dreams represent the depth of our unconscious mind. They can show us what we need to deal with to be able to free ourselves from our fears, inhibitions, and other repressed material.

For example, a woman I counseled told me about a series of dreams she had been having. These dreams had to do with strangers visiting her bedroom. She said that the dreams were so real, she would open her eyes in the middle of the dream and still see them.

"Did you ask them what they want?" I asked her.

"They wouldn't tell me. I tried talking to them, but they don't want to listen to me," she replied.

"Who in your life is not listening to you?" I asked.

The woman thought for a moment then said, "My kids, my husband, my parents… I guess everybody," she recounted, sobbing.

The dreams clearly indicated that she needed to trust herself more, especially to feel more comfortable asserting herself and to stop trying to please everyone so much. After we discussed the issue for a while and came up with creative solutions, her dreams about the strangers disappeared.

The unconscious mind can also point to the direction of answers and solutions through dreams. A young boy was brought to me because he constantly had nightmares about monsters and bad people coming into his bedroom. These dreams were mostly inspired by movies he had watched, but although he knew the source of the dreams, he was not able to stop them. I advised that before he went to sleep that night, he ask his dreaming mind to come up with a good and safe solution to the problem. The child dreamed that night that he built the most secure alarm system, which could detect anyone coming even close to the house and immediately call the police. We perfected the security system during the following session. The nightmares stopped immediately. I have since used the security system idea very successfully with many kids who had similar nightmares.

When we sleep, our analytical mind is not active; so an opportunity exists to connect with our intuition and creativity. Many inventions and great ideas came from dreams.

You can direct your dreams if you want to, by setting intentions of what you want your dreams to deal with. The most powerful intention would be asking for what I call "dreams of transformation." You may encounter, at first, some uncomfortable material, which relates to your repressed feelings, since they tend to be blocks that may interfere with the process of deepening your spiritual experiences. But as you become more comfortable with the true meaning of your dreams, powerful and transformative dreams will follow and allow you to begin to see creative solutions to life's challenges.

Dreams may sometimes appear to be very direct and clear, but frequently they use metaphoric language that we need to learn to understand. A while ago, in my dreams, I was offered a flattering appointment that would be entirely different from the counseling I did. I was appointed as a government official to take care of a certain territory and I was very proud of this prestigious job. But I was then told that actually my job would entail doing a lot of gardening, which I found to be strange.

When I woke up in the middle of the night, I pondered the dream and concluded that the message was to shy away from glory and stay focused on the "gardening," which was a metaphor for my professional work.

But this was not a new idea. "Tell me something new," I contended inside, before falling back asleep. The dream continued. In it, I developed innovative methods to do the gardening so that people could cultivate their grounds more easily.

At that point I didn't care about the official appointment any more. The message was simple but powerful: Improve your work and make it easier for people to cultivate their life-gardens. As a result of this dream I developed newer approaches that have helped me become even more effective in my work.

Not too long ago, a patient whom I had worked with for a while began to have many spiritual experiences. One session, even before she had a chance to sit, she exclaimed: "I had a very strange dream; it almost felt real, and you were in it." I was curious and asked her to tell it to me. She dreamed that as I was going down the stairs in my office, the staircase broke and I fell down "into the deep," as she described it. She rushed towards me since she watched it happening and found me in a big puddle of water, throwing up, and so she helped me stand until I felt better.

"Isn't it strange that I was helping you in the dream?" she asked. She continued explaining that she thought perhaps this was a sign she had completed the therapy, and asked for my opinion.

I asked her to tell me exactly what day she had the dream and at what time. She confirmed it was the previous Friday early in the night. I was shocked. That Friday, I went to do night diving in Florida with a few friends. It was a long day for me because my flight got canceled the night before and I had to go back home and wake up early to take the morning flight. That evening I was very tired, but I decided to go for the dive anyway. The first dive was fine, but in the second one I couldn't equalize my ears. I tried a few times and when I realized it wouldn't work, I decided to go back to the boat. I felt nauseous and threw up.

After the dive, we went to a restaurant. I didn't order anything, because I didn't feel very well. I also felt very tired, and almost fell asleep on the table. Suddenly, I felt a strange, gentle energy flowing through me, pulling away the fatigue and nausea. I felt fully awake at once, and very hungry. My friends, who watched me eat with great appetite, commented at my fast recovery.

My patient was quite surprised, to say the least, at my story. We both realized that something very powerful happened, and I thanked her for her "spiritual assistance." We discussed the three spiritual truths, and she had no problems accepting them even more deeply.

The Choice of a Simple Life

When I was diving in Mexico, I bought a new underwater camera. Photography has always been one of my favorite hobbies (do you like my picture on the front cover?), and I thought that combining it with scuba diving would just be natural. As I was diving in Cozumel, I pulled the camera out to take a shot of some beautiful fish, only to find that the camera had filled with water. What a disappointment it was, especially because the film included nice shots I had taken a day earlier while diving in caverns not far away. The next day on my second diving trip my flashlight filled with water. A coincidence, you might say. Maybe.

> Manifest plainness, embrace simplicity, reduce selfishness, have few desires.
>
> *Lao Tzu*

A week later, I spilled a glass of water on my laptop computer. Interestingly, this happened while I was talking to a person I met a week earlier in... Mexico. The next day, my car's remote control, fairly new, stopped working. Somehow it got wet and the contacts were not working properly.

As you may have guessed, I viewed this as a very strong sign. What was the message? Since it all involved mechanical instruments—camera, flashlight, computer, and a remote control device—I realized I was focused too much on technology at the time—a powerful reminder that life does not take place in things but in the heart. Water often represents spiritual flow and technology can be an obstruction to that flow. Nothing is wrong with computers and cameras, cars and remote controls as long as we don't lose sight of what is really important.

A while ago, I had a conversation with my brother. I asked him why he thought our sages were so wise and how come it is so rare to find such wise people these days. My brother said that our sages were really focused. They had no distractions in the form of TV, Internet, newspapers, magazines, investments and so forth. They were, therefore, able to look really deep and understand the true principles by which we operate. These days, many of our gurus come mainly from the area of technology and finances, two areas that, if not put in the right perspective, can distract us from our true paths.

Simplicity reinforces humility, and being humble is a soul-based characteristic. In some Buddhist monasteries, the more a student progressed, the tougher the cleaning jobs he got, to make sure he remembered to stay humble. Many people have traded high-powered careers for a simple life.

To be able to be "in life" you must learn to reduce distraction, to avoid the information overload, to reduce clutter, and to make it okay to accomplish less. Living in the present always simplifies life and living in the mind always complicates it. What can you do to simplify your own life?

> There are two wings that raise a man above earthly things—simplicity and purity. Simplicity reaches out after God: purity discovers and enjoys Him.
>
> *Thomas A. Kempis*

Holograms and the Supreme Intelligence

The field of holography is an excellent, more scientific simile to help us understand the Spiritual Truths. A hologram is a three-dimensional picture that is produced using laser technology. The word hologram is taken from the Greek words holos, which means "whole," and the word gram which, means "message." A whole message. Quite an interesting choice of words for this phenomenon.

A regular photographic negative and a holographic film are quite different. Suppose you have a photo showing two buildings. If you tear either the picture or the negative into half, you have a picture of one building on one hand and the second building on the other hand. However, if you have the same two buildings on a holographic plate and you tear it apart, you still have the complete picture on both parts. If you break it into a hundred parts, still you can see the whole picture in every piece. This holistic message is how our innate intelligence works.

Let's further look at the concept of the whole within each of its parts. If you talk to an acupuncturist, a specialist who uses acupuncture needles to treat various conditions, he will tell you that you can access every organ in the body through corresponding points in the ears. An acupressure therapist will tell you that you can do the same through pressure points in the body, and a reflexologist will indicate the soles of your feet for the same purpose. A chiropractor will explain how specific body areas can be treated through the spine. In essence, the entire intelligence of the body can be found in each of its cells. Another proof for that comes from the field of genetic engineering and the successful experiments of cloning mammals. The sheep Dolly was cloned from an adult sheep using a cell taken from the sheep's udder. Dr. Ian Wilmut in Scotland headed this revolutionary experiment.

Theoretically, any cell of the body can be used to do the cloning, because each cell in the body contains the complete copy of the genome. Therefore, every cell contains the genetic information of the entire body.

As an aside, scientists observed four genetically identical cloned sheep and realized that, with age, the sheep grew to become quite different in their temperaments. They looked alike, but they behaved quite differently, just to show that genetics doesn't determine the entire being. The environment and its specific experiences also shape individual characteristics, with parents and other authority figures as most influential for humans.

We can, with accuracy, refer to a person as one big hologram. Further, we can say that our specific hologram is part of a larger hologram, called human beings; or bigger than that, nature; and largest of all, the universe. According to the holographic model, we all share the entire intelligence that can be found in the universe. This could explain how we are "the same" and how we are "connected," in a more scientific way. An important implication of this model is that when one person changes, all of humanity is affected for better or worse— depending on the changes.

Another important aspect of this technology is the ability to store numerous pages into one hologram. Such pages can be recorded in different angles using special laser technology. These pages can then be accessed separately by illuminating the hologram in different angles. You might have seen a sample of this in holograms that have two, even three different pictures, which you can see by tilting the hologram in certain angles. Theoretically, you can embed an unlimited number of pictures, or pieces of information, using this technology.

In a similar way, the Supreme Intelligence that makes this universe go around is one immense hologram. We, as human beings, are definitely part of this hologram, and with the right knowledge and technique can access this amazing intelligence by looking at it from a specific angle, so to speak. This may be a speculation; but it is possible that within the general holograms also exist all of our past lives arranged in different angles, if you will. We can even go further to explain the hypothesis of parallel universes, which I have mentioned earlier, using the same model. Perhaps each such universe happens in an angle, and most of us only know how to connect with one at a time. I believe that InteliTapping is that unique ability to "change angles," to be able to access information which is not available to us directly. This Creative Intelligence is fully ingrained in us right now.

Let's go back to the Supreme Intelligence. What is it really about? *EVERYTHING*! Einstein said that invention has nothing to do with intellect. It is based on a brilliant, spontaneous idea that, most inventors would agree, comes from "nowhere." *Nowhere* is composed of two words generally accepted as *no where*; but by moving the "w" to the left, you get *now here*. Interesting, isn't it? I believe that everything we will ever need, solutions to every problem in the next billion years and beyond, are available now, here. We just need to learn how to tap into this Universal Source directly to find them.

The entire technological development in communication, computers, and transportation is a direct result of connecting with the Supreme Intelligence and then manifesting it physically. This unfathomable intelligence surrounds us and permeates our lives, offering infinite possibilities for tremendous growth on all possible levels. To connect with it, we have to "polish" our spiritual prisms, so to speak, and we can then see the beautiful colors of this amazing Intelligence.

In his book *The Holographic Universe* (Harper Collins Publishers, New York, p. 54), Michael Talbot quotes Karl Pribram, a brilliant neurophysiologist at Stanford University, and David Bohm, a quantum physicist at the University of London and a protégé of Albert Einstein, who both arrived at the holographic model separately. Considered together, Bohm and Pribram's theories provided a profound new way of looking at the world:

> "...our brains mathematically construct objective reality by interpreting frequencies that are ultimately projections from another dimension, a deeper order of existence that is beyond both space and time. The brain is a hologram enfolded in a holographic universe."

And Then There Was Peace

The "whole message" of perfect health and abundant joy is thus embedded in you "holographically." All you need to learn is how to connect with it.

Many spiritual scholars ascertain that the material we are made of is love. I disagree. If we don't have complete peace, can we offer unconditional love? Love is a second order. Love is the creative part of peace. Creation is a manifestation of love but it can only arise from peace.

I believe that everything is intrinsically made of peace energy. Just look around everywhere in nature and in the universe. What do you see? Peace. Out of peace other energies are created. Everything rises from peace, even love. Love is no doubt a very powerful force; still it takes its energy from peace.

At times, turmoil in nature occurs. Animals fight, tornados sweep through land creating devastation, stars explode, galaxies collide, but soon everything returns to peace. That is, unequivocally, the foundation in all of nature. Humans are a little different, because out of peace energy, humans created ego energy and forgot what the true base was.

Peace is home, the truth, the way of life. Peace is the core of our being. It is what everything is fundamentally made of! This profound peace is not just a state of calm. It is an intelligent nonmaterialistic essence, which in the Bible, Philippians 4:7, is referred to as the "peace that passeth all understanding."

In nature, peace comes naturally. In us, it has to be discovered and cultivated until we too can become one with it.

Before me peaceful
Behind me peaceful
Under me peaceful
Over me peaceful
Around me peaceful

A Navajo Prayer

Quantum Stuff

Quantum physics is another popular field that can serve to explain some spiritual concepts. Quantum theory is complex and I have no intention to get into too many details here. If you're not particularly fond of science, you can skip this section. I include it because I want to bring in everything we know from science in order to better understand spiritual reality.

In general, quantum theory was developed and then enhanced in the beginning of the century by high caliber scientific thinkers such as Albert Einstein, Max Plank, Werner Heisenberg, Niels Bohr, and David Bohm. It was considered a breakthrough that served to explain phenomena that traditional Newtonian physics could not.

In principle, quantum theory explains what happens on a sub-atomic level. On such a level very interesting paradoxes occur. Unlike classical physics that offers formulas and specific concepts to define location, speed, and direction, quantum physics determines that on a subatomic level, particles do not really have a defined location, speed, or direction. It merely focuses on the chances, the likelihood, that such particles will behave in a certain way.

In the subatomic reality, uncertainty and chance rule. Everything that can happen actually happens. According to quantum theory subatomic objects can be in two places at the same time, or even go in two different directions at the same time. I believe that quantum physics brings spirituality and science much closer together. At some point they may even converge.

The term non-locality is used in quantum theories to describe the above-mentioned subatomic phenomenon. It is also used by spiritual teachers to describe the fact that the spirit is nonlocalized, meaning that it spreads beyond time and space.

Particles operating in a way that is contradictory to how we think may demonstrate how we can be spiritual beings and yet at the same time do absurd things such as hurting other people or the environment. I was fascinated studying the quantum world because it served to explain paradoxical realizations I have observed during my work. I will expand more on the paradoxes of the spiritual world in a few paragraphs.

Change vs. Transformation

The reason people find changing so difficult is that they are trying to change aspects of their ego. This is not easy to do. It is like the joke, "How many therapists does it take to change a light bulb? Only one, but the light bulb must want to change." And here, of course, lies the problem. The ego is not fond of change. In fact, it is so afraid of change, it resists it. The ego prefers the comfort of the known, so it usually fights change.

> We cannot solve our problems with the same thinking we used when we created them.
>
> *Albert Einstein*

Transformation is different. Instead of trying to change one thing, be it behavior or a habit, you completely change how you view things. This shift is like the famous Transformer toys, where you have a car and with a few clicks, turn it into a big robot. Transformation occurs when your point of view changes dramatically.

A while ago, I worked with an individual who was agoraphobic, which meant that he was very scared to go out in public, especially in crowded places. He was quite paranoid, believing that everyone was there to get him. After doing some work, and especially revealing and releasing childhood fears, he realized that people were busy dealing with their own issues. They were not really interested in an unknown person walking on the street and most people didn't even notice him, let alone try to hurt him. This new viewpoint was a big transformation for him. His fears didn't completely go away. But he knew very well that they were only an echo from the past, which he could ignore, because they limited his life. As a result, he actually began looking forward to going out and interacting with people.

We cannot completely conquer ego. Instead we want to transcend it and jump directly into spiritual territory to transform our lives. Some of the biggest transformations happen when we understand the nature of the spiritual paradoxes. Let's explore these paradoxes now and discover how understanding them can create fast transformation.

Spiritual Paradoxes

Paradoxes are not necessarily contradictions. They may only contradict a belief or common knowledge. Spiritual paradoxes can be easily looked upon as absurdities, but they also can be better understood in light of the quantum theory I briefly described earlier.

> Out of the tension of duality life always produces a "third" that seems somehow, incommensurable or paradoxical.
>
> *Carl Jung*

The main reason we're confused by these paradoxes is that our scientific-logical world focuses on dualities, so it cannot explain such anomalies. But spirituality is not contained within this realm of linear thinking. Spirituality begins where this thought process ends. The paradoxical patterns we'll consider can cause you to spin around yourself for a while, but when you transcend them, true transformation occurs. Take your time to fully understand them as they offer a solid bridge from psychology to spirituality.

Paradox 1: When you completely let go of a need, you become fulfilled as if the need had been fully met.

How is that possible? Please understand that I am not talking about repressing needs or giving them up unwillingly. I am talking about a complete letting go.

What are some common needs we have as humans? Aside from our day-to-day physical needs, we tend to have needs for approval, recognition, accomplishment, fulfillment, success, security, power, and respect, to mention just a few.

What happens when you resolve these needs? You find its equivalent inside. You feel self-fulfilled and free of any external conditions. This is one of the most difficult paradoxes to understand. I hope it makes sense to you. What we are doing here is replacing conditional, externally based needs with unconditional spiritual fulfillment.

Enhancement of paradox 1: When you completely let go of a specific need, not only do you become self-fulfilled, but also other people will offer it to you freely. For instance, when you let go of the need for respect, people begin to respect you naturally. It is the same with the other needs. When you fully let go of a need, you become free, you stop interacting based on neediness and hidden agendas; and you can do what is right. Say you let go of the need for approval. You will, as a result, stop doing things that are not necessarily important for you, just to satisfy others in order to get their approval; and they will then approve of you more freely.

Letting go of a need is synonymous with healing childhood wounds that originally created the need. We will do an exercise to enhance this process very shortly.

Paradox 2: When you let go of your fears you will be safer than you were with them.

People have some sense of security holding on to fears. But in fact, fears do not save or protect you. Nor do they offer any guarantee that challenging events won't happen. They just make you more vulnerable because you start avoiding situations and so often, they prevent you from trying new opportunities. Fears block your creativity and intuition and ultimately prevent you from living life to its fullest.

Paradox 3: Every internal defense mechanism eventually contradicts what it is trying to accomplish.

For instance, when an individual shuts off his feelings because he wants to avoid any possible contact with deeply buried hurt, the person can never feel good about anything. Shutting off feelings disables the positive ones too. He is hurting himself that much more.

Such protection mechanisms could have been useful at an early age because the child lacked any other protection or support. But as adults, they become very limiting and ultimately prevent people from feeling fulfilled and joyful.

Paradox 4: The more you give up the need to control, the more in control you get.

Even though this one also has to do with needs, it deserves separate attention. In this case what you are giving up is external control. What you are gaining instead is internal control. The ultimate control is accomplished by understanding who you are and doing what is right, based on the Spiritual Truths. When you give up the need for control, you surrender yourself to the deep moment and experience full peace. Who needs anything else?

Paradox 5: When you let go of the need for security, you feel completely secure.

Here is another famous need that requires more attention, since security is such a big issue for so many people. The security we are trying to find is more artificial, where true safety, security, and ultimately freedom, come by drawing from the strength of our infinite spirit.

If you knew beyond a shadow of a doubt that God follows you every step and fully protects you, would you feel secure enough? Since your spirit is an extension of God, when you practice your spirituality you are the closest you can get to God. Can you get any safer than that?

One of my patients just asked me if this means that spiritual people won't get hit by a car. My answer was very short: NO! But God will make the necessary resources available for you if you are.

Paradox 6: To find yourself, you have to give yourself away.

Think about that for a moment: Which part of you are you giving away, and whom are you finding instead? This principle has been thoroughly discussed earlier in the book.

Paradox 7: When you stop fighting yourself...you win.

In war, all sides eventually lose people, resources, etc. When you fight against yourself, both of your "selves" lose. Therefore, stop being so critical of yourself; stop putting yourself down; and start treating yourself with patience, love, and kindness. Now you are a winner!

And here is the bottom line: The ego can get what it really wants by letting go and surrendering to the higher self—the spirit. Unfortunately, the ego has created all types of coping skills to deal with its own neurosis. Can you imagine how much energy is wasted for nothing? When the ego is released from its needs, you stop living a life of coping, covering up, dealing, hiding, pretending, and needing. All is replaced by total inner peace. Ego cannot heal ego. Peace can!

There is no good or bad, lucky or unlucky, winning or losing. Dichotomies belong to our psychological dimension. Learn to relinquish the need to be right or to win all the time. Spirituality begins when such dualities are transcended. Once they are left behind, a new reality is experienced. What is the field Rumi referred to when he said, "Beyond ideas of wrongdoing and right-doing there is a field. I'll meet you there." The answer is PEACE.

St. John of the Cross referred to these paradoxes in *Ascent of Mount Carmel*.

"To reach satisfaction in all, desire its possession in nothing. To come to the knowledge of all, desire the knowledge of nothing. To come to possess all, desire the possession of nothing. To arrive at being all, desire to be nothing."

The great Leonardo da Vinci also reinforced this notion: "Among the great things which are to be found among us, the being of nothingness is the greatest." When you are willing to be nothing, you are everything. What this means is that when the ego, which always wants to be a "somebody," disappears from the picture, you become the spiritual everything.

As soon as you can fully integrate these paradoxes, you transform. I have to be honest with you and tell you that this is not always easy to do. The reason is that you have to change your thinking by 180 degrees. On the other hand, please understand that the reason people are still struggling so much is because they are either not aware or not willing to fully adopt the lessons embedded in these spiritual paradoxes. Our thinking has to evolve towards integrating these teachings, which will in turn enable us to surpass the chaotic world our egos have created, so that we can eventually shift from disharmony to a state of balance.

Letting Go of the Past

Letting go of needs for security, control, and approval is about healing the past. Such healing has to do with letting go of the pain, guilt, anger, sadness, shame, and rejection we still carry with us. Guess what medicine can heal all that? Peace!

Let's use The Circle of Peace to transcend our needs and heal the past.

> To do that, first connect with The Circle of Peace. Then invite into the circle everything you believe you still carry from the past. Unresolved feelings, insecurities, people, neediness, traumas, everything! Avoid processing this material while doing the exercise. Just bring it out and connect it with peace. As you repeat this exercise over and over, more deep material will be cleared. At some point your unconscious mind will be able to take over and clear the rest on its own; then your past will be healed.
>
> When you practice this exercise make sure you avoid mental processing such as judging, blaming, comparing, and complaining. Just become aware, and see if any realizations or positive lessons come up. Note them down as they appear.

I recently worked with a woman on resolving issues from her past. She was releasing some pretty intense emotions associated with her niece who used to constantly put her down when they were younger. As she brought her niece into the circle, she realized that her niece, just like her, was also abused as a child. Recognizing this, she could accept that her niece's actions were a reflection of her personal pain. She was able to let go of her hurt and anger towards her niece right away. She described it as lifting a ton of weight off her shoulders.

Clarity is usually obscured by repressed feelings. Once you let go, deeper realizations will allow you to make amends with your past so that you can begin to live in the present, fully.

I Wished...

Another important and mostly ignored aspect hinders letting go of the past: everything we ever wanted that has never come true for us. People carry all kinds of unfulfilled dreams as well as regrets about things they did or did not accomplish, commitments that got broken, wishes and ideas that never materialized. When you carry such unresolved material you are indirectly violating the important practice of acceptance. No acceptance—no peace, remember?

People expect relationships to be a certain way; they may have expected to accomplish a certain status or financial goals. They may have had wishes to live a certain way or have their children develop according to certain standards and values. When these desires are not met and we don't accept it, we then have to suppress our disappointments.

Use the "I Wished..." list at the end of the book to write down all these wishes that never materialized and that you might still, on some level, feel frustrated or disappointed about.

I worked with a gentleman who was experiencing a variety of health-related issues. He told me that it all started when he decided to renovate his country house. It took a lot of effort on his part to do, and even though he felt burnt out, he wouldn't stop. Eventually his health deteriorated and he had to stop the work, which caused him continuous frustration. When we talked about it, he told me that it was always his dream to have the house done similar to his grandfather's house. As we further delved into it he realized that he was trying to reconstruct the pleasant feelings of love and encouragement he felt when he was a child visiting his grandfather's house. We did a letting go process that he described later on as a big burden lifted off his head.

Use your "I Wished" list to let go of what you cannot accomplish at the present time. You can use The Circle of Peace to facilitate the process.

When you truly let go, you feel the release and subsequently—peace.

Intimate Relationships

A certain woman came to see me because she wanted to break away from her existing boyfriend after a few years of trying to make the relationship work. She was very dependent on him and was too scared to break up. We worked for a short period of time on different issues and she seemed to progress very nicely. One day, she showed up for the appointment and before I even had the opportunity to ask her how she was feeling, she said that she had finally decided to tell her boyfriend she was leaving him. She intended to do it in the coming weekend, but I had different plans for her so I asked her to delay her initiative.

> Take each other for better or worse but not for granted.
>
> *Arlene Dahl*

She was very surprised. "The entire reason for coming to you was to arrive at this moment," she said. "And you suggest that I postpone it? I cannot understand that."

"This gentleman obviously knows how to push all of your buttons," I explained. "If you let go of him right now, a lot of the repressed material will just stay there, who knows for how long. This is a wonderful opportunity to find out everything that needs resolving."

She understood my point and was willing to put off her decision. Interestingly, as we progressed, she changed her mind about leaving. She became calmer and apparently less threatening to her longtime boyfriend and he finally agreed to seek professional help.

Challenging emotions can make someone's life quite miserable; but if understood and worked through, such emotions can provide a powerful bridge into deeper spiritual awareness.

Only when we become involved in an intimate relationship do we realize what we are really carrying deep inside. More often than not, we tend to blame our partner when we feel a certain way. But the truth is that these are all our feelings, and we don't just produce them because our partner did or said something. In fact, he or she just helped fire off such repressed feelings. Our partner can help to bring out the best in us or the worst in us or even both.

But you need to understand that your actions, reactions, and feelings are all your stuff, not anybody else's. Always!

I mentioned earlier that when two people fall in love, it is usually the soul that they fall in love with. When the ego rears its head, the real challenges begin.

From this perspective, relationships may be sorted into three major types.

1. A relationship that is based mainly on soul interaction. This is a positive, warm relationship where both partners will help and encourage each other, which will in turn allow the relationship to grow and develop.
2. A relationship that is mainly based on ego interaction. This is usually a cold, sometimes destructive relationship that goes nowhere. It is filled with blame, conflict, anger, resentment, arguments, and alienation. The partners grow increasingly bitter until one day they separate.
3. A mixed relationship. One partner is more ego-oriented and the other more soul-based. In this instance, the latter will always take the responsibility to make the relationship work, but may feel frustrated and disappointed at the lack of cooperation and understanding from the significant other.

Naturally, we want to strive to develop any relationship based on spiritual principles. This would be an honest, open, direct, attentive, warm, and mutually supportive relationship.

Almost no one is free of ego behavior; nevertheless, in such a relationship, the ego's activity is not a basis for bitter fights. Both partners accept mutual limitations and help each other to overcome them. They learn to use their own unique strengths to balance each other's weaknesses. They encourage each other's personal development, which in turn will promote a healthy growth of the relationship itself.

> **Close your eyes and picture such an environment for you and the other person in your most significant relationship. What is the nature of the actual relationship compared to this mental picture? How do you want to change in order to create that environment?**

Yes, the question is "How do YOU want to change?" Common complaints I hear regularly are "If only she would understand me; If only he would listen to me." I explain that we cannot and should not try to change others, not only because it doesn't work, but also because it makes things worse.

The more you want your partner to change, the more likely that your partner will stay the way he or she is, and sometimes even get worse. This is a fundamental principle based on how the ego operates. But paradoxically—and by now you understand how these paradoxes work—if you stop pressuring for change, if you genuinely accept your partner just the way he or she is, the change will probably occur naturally. I have proven this principle many times to my patients. Note though that the key word here is "genuinely." Genuine acceptance is something you can't fake.

Many relationships are based on control. If you check carefully, you may find that in almost every intimate relationship, one person appears to have higher energy and to be more controlling, and the other appears lower in energy and more submissive.

Usually, two people who are controlling in their behavior cannot stay together for too long. Both control and submissiveness represent neediness that has to be cleared in order to transform the quality of the relationship.

Control is based on fear. It always reflects insecurities that people tend to deny or ignore. As is the case with many other patterns, the need for control represents deep situated issues that we need to resolve to be able to break free from our servitude to fear.

A woman came for an initial consultation with her husband because she thought he had many problems with self-esteem that affected their relationship. I suggested brief counseling with the man to be followed with marital therapy. Since during the consultation the woman was the one doing most of the talking, I indicated that I would have to speak with her husband alone. She did not like that, and later left a message for me that if she couldn't be present when I did therapy with her husband, she would cancel it altogether. Naturally, this woman not interested in her husband's progress. She was afraid she might lose the controlling role that obviously was so important for her.

Generally speaking, you always have to remember that your sole responsibility is to upgrade yourself. You can then become an example to others. People, and especially kids, don't go by what you say, but by how you behave. So you have to do your own inner work and everything else will fall into place one way or another. I have had many instances where one mate's growth helped improve a relationship the soul's way. I have also encountered many instances when one of a couple realized that the relationship was too ego-based and decided to separate. I am usually the last one to recommend a break-up; on the other hand, I have seen many times how my patients were just hitting a brick wall. Finally they chose to exit.

Many times people get married, or are involved in a relationship, to complement what they lack. They expect their partner to complete them. Such expectations will continuously create ego-based behavior. I talked earlier about the paradoxical principle that explains it, and here is its relationship application: Everything you want from your partner (nonmaterialistic), you may get only after you find it within yourself. When you do finally find it inside, you will stop wanting it and, in turn, will be able give it freely to your partner and to others.

When we look for approval to build our self-esteem, we act vulnerable and dependent. Even if we get approval from our partner, it will never be completely satisfying because it is not the real thing. Find it within yourself and you will stop needing it. This could be then a wonderful opportunity to step up the relationship to a soul-to-soul level.

Marriage symbolizes the unity between the male and female energies which every man and woman have. When we succeed in harmonizing these energies before we get involved in an intimate relationship, then the relationship will be spiritual in nature. Very few individuals have this prerequisite. As a result, we are supposed to learn from our external conflicts and become able eventually to integrate these energies internally.

The method to accomplish that is, as in every other purpose, to connect with your inner peace. TruePeace IS the perfect mix of male and female energies.

I'm often asked if we can also expand this notion to include same-sex relationships. The answer is positive because the integration takes place between male and female energies and not necessarily between a man and a woman.

The Relationship Bottom Line

One day one of my patients turned her back in the middle of the session, and asked me: "What's the color of my eyes?"

"Brown," I immediately replied. "Why are you asking?"

She told me that her husband was completing an official form and asked her what the color of her eyes was. She was shocked at the fact that after spending thirty years together, her husband did not know that.

When confronted, her husband replied that he wasn't sure, and he couldn't understand why she was so upset about it.

I'm sometimes asked what is the single most important principle in an intimate relationship, or in any relationship for that matter, that can improve the communication, mutual understanding, and as a result the overall quality of the relationship. I have two parts to the answer.

First and foremost would be listening. You have to learn truly to listen, free of preconceived notions and expectations, with little or no mental processing. We need to find out what is really being said and respond to the underlying need. This can be done only while paying closest, unbiased attention, which I admit is not always easy to do.

For instance, let's take a woman who constantly complains about her husband's working long hours and he in turn complains that his wife is always on his back. If you are that woman, you need to realize that deeper inside, your husband wants some acknowledgement about working hard. Do that and he will be much more cooperative and helpful, as long as there are no other major issues of conflict. If you are the man in this example, understand that your wife may feel neglected and lonely. While you are busy at work, she has to deal with the house and the children, not always the most rewarding job in the world. She wants your attention, a hug, to be able to tell you how her day was, to feel important too, without you saying, "Yes, but I have to work all day to support us." Do that and she will complain less about your work. Even if she is also working, as many women do these days, the picture is not that different. In this case she would want you to appreciate how hard it is to juggle work and home responsibilities.

If I look back at all the couples I have counseled, the most common underlying theme I have seen, that resulted in numerous arguments, fights, and sometimes even break-ups is lack of mutual acknowledgement and appreciation. This is part of our basic need to be accepted without criticism or judgment. When you acknowledge your partner without any conditions, you are working from a soul level. This is the transition from psychology to spirituality in relationships.

I encourage couples I counsel to take time throughout the week just to acknowledge each other, which is definitely much more productive than put-downs, blaming, and name calling.

Here is the second principle to improve the quality of a relationship: Ask yourself, "What is the most important thing I want from my partner?" When you know what it is, start giving it freely to your partner and expect nothing in return. No ego-based agendas. To get what you want, you have to give it. Another paradox? Sure, but we are in spiritual territory here.

Something interesting happens when you give your partner what you want. Firstly, you learn to tap within yourself for what you need. Remember spiritual law Number One? Secondly, when you give it freely, you make it okay for your partner to give it back to you. In addition, you become a walking example of how powerful connecting with your CoreSelf self is. You want love, offer it first; you want understanding, begin by understanding your partner. Are you seeking approval without judgment? Express it towards your partner first. Does this make sense to you?

This powerful approach is based on a well-known spiritual principle: We receive when we give. In Luke 6:38 we find the concept: "Give, and it shall be given unto you." This will not necessarily happen as God's direct reward for your good deeds. It is already a built-in mechanism that will kick in automatically, unless it is clouded by unreasonable self-expectations, in which case letting go will be required first.

Let's recap these two very important principles: Acknowledge your partner and everyone you have a meaningful relationship with, unconditionally. This represents deep acceptance. Secondly, what you want to get, give! If you like these principles and intend to practice them, start right now and build a spiritual momentum that will contribute to your general progress on every level.

The Spiritual Body

I mentioned earlier that the body will usually identify with what the "independent I" identifies with. If this "I" identifies with the ego, the body will seek instant gratification without considering the long-term ramifications of the stress caused by the ego. This may include all kinds of addictive behavior such as smoking, overeating, and excessive alcohol consumption. The body always pays for the stress the ego creates.

In many instances tension, pain, and especially burnout are indications that the ego is out of control. In a way, the body is saying that it can't cope with ego anymore. The body becomes spiritual when you do. You can accelerate the process if you start treating your body with respect. Are you aware of the tensions in your body? Do you know when your body is hungry? When it's thirsty? When it needs rest? Do you go to bed according to the clock or when you body requires it?

Did you know that you can develop a very deep physical awareness that will allow you to recognize which food your body requires at different times? Even which supplements are good for you, if they are indeed necessary? I believe that this is how Shamans once found the kind of herbal remedies they used in order to treat the people in their tribes for various health problems. They had a deep intuitive sense of what worked for each problem. When you pay attention to your body's messages you will feel less tense, more vital and energetic, which will add more quality years to your life.

Clearing Tension

Our bodies carry a lot of tension in them. This tension is a result of all the stress we have accumulated throughout life. Here is a good exercise that can increase your awareness and also help you let go of some of this tension.

> Close your eyes and connect with your breathing for a while.
> Now begin to focus on your body, becoming aware of how it
> feels. Where do you carry tension? Which parts feel achy?
> Heavy? Sore? Which parts of the body feel comfortable?
> Do some deep breathing and direct it towards any tensed
> or problematic areas.

Do that for a few minutes and notice how it feels. Make sure you are not trying to force anything. This is a process of "allowing" and whatever you get—accept. If you listen closely, you might notice your body saying "thank you" for this little attention. A good time to do this exercise is when you go to bed. Do it along with the Circle of Peace. It will allow you to unwind yourself from the tension you have accumulated throughout the day. At first some people feel increased tension or pain as they practice this exercise. The reason is that most people tend to suppress a lot of the tension to avoid discomfort.

When you increase your awareness, some of that tension which you may have repressed, resurfaces. That's good. Now with more attention you can begin to clear it. It is much more difficult to deal with what is covered up, i.e., repression and suppression; hence the importance of facing the truth, accepting it, and then letting it go.

What About Money?

This book is almost at the end and I still haven't seriously discussed money. I only mentioned it briefly in other contexts, so this is a good time to focus on the subject— especially after discussing how to deal with tension. For many people money is one of the biggest sources of stress.

> Money is a good servant, but a poor master.
>
> Dominique Bouhours

Financial gurus want you to believe that money makes the world go around. If it does, it would be the ego's world. I do not want to tell you that you don't need money because you do. We all do. All I would like to say is that you cannot make it the main focus of your attention, because if you do you will become its slave. I discussed in the beginning of the book how materialism and commercialism can detour us from attaining a deeper spiritual connection because the pursuit of riches is usually a superficial process.

People have all kinds of concepts about money so I would like to clarify one important thing about it: Money is neither good nor bad. It is just a way to buy necessities and comfort.

The ego loves comfort, yet it never feels comfortable for long before it pushes us to go for the next level of comfort. Money can indeed give you some peace of mind, but never inner peace.

I used to run a workshop called *The Psychology of Money*. If you want to know the basics of the program in one sentence, I will tell you that right now. With only a few exceptions, the money that you make is in direct relationship to what you deeply believe you deserve. For the most part, money is a self-esteem issue. If you truly believe that you deserve to have more money, you will be more likely to make it. But if you have deep-situated negative beliefs about it, for instance that money is evil and that only bad people have lots of money, then you may sabotage your finances one way or another.

I once worked with a lawyer on some emotional issues. One day she asked me if it was possible that she was sabotaging her income. She explained that she was making about forty thousand dollars a year. When I asked her how much she thought someone else in a similar capacity earned, she said that her colleagues made at least two hundred thousand. As we delved into her negative beliefs about money, a sad picture emerged of a person who was exposed to much financial struggle and many negative messages when she was a child. We worked on all these issues. Three months later she was making an average of over a hundred thousand dollars a year. By feeling more comfortable about money she started undertaking bigger cases and charging accordingly. She indicated to me that she could make even more than that but chose not to.

After facilitating my workshop for some time, I upgraded my program and called it *The Psychology of Money and the Spirituality of Abundance*. The goal of the program was to switch people from focusing exclusively on money, to broaden their perspectives, and to expand their abundance. This represents just another bridge from psychology to spirituality.

When you strive for abundance in every area of your life, money will also be amplified. I have proven to many of my patients that when they really needed it, money always came to them. If you have financial issues, set your intentions accurately, explain why you need the money, and then pay attention for signs and opportunities. Make sure that if you pursue an opportunity presented to you, that it really feels right and it is not motivated by a sense of greed that may compel you to make hasty decisions.

I knew a teacher in high school who used to buy lottery tickets every week and was teased because he would be the last person expected to spend his money on the lottery. He explained that one day when he meets the Creator and asks why he never had more money, he doesn't want to get the excuse that he gave God no way to channel more money to him. The point is that with positive intentions, at the minimum, your needs will always be supplied.

Gandhi said, "Nature will always satisfy your need but not your greed." The opposite of greed is, in my opinion, charity. When the soul's generosity is allowed to pour out, we want to do good for others and financial support is one of the ways. Our charity is how others get their needs met. I like the saying, "When you die you can take with you only what you gave."

> Success is measured not by what you have achieved, but by who you have become.
> *Author unknown*

Many years ago I flew from the Far East to Europe and had to stop for a few hours in Bombay, India. When I got there I was told that due to a strike, all passengers would have to stay overnight in Bombay. On my way from the airport to the hotel, I noticed by the side of the road, many tiny huts. I was surprised to learn that people actually lived in those little huts. I could not help but feel sorry for these people. A local official, with whom I talked about the subject, told me that the people living in the huts, who were obviously poor, were very happy people. I did not know anything about Hinduism or spirituality then, and it was difficult for me to grasp that. The official said that if I visited anyone who lived in one of those huts and all they had was a bowl of rice, they would gladly share it with me. I was quite impressed, realizing that generosity had nothing to do with what one has, but with how much one is in touch with their soul. I'm not rationalizing poverty by sharing this story. As happy as those may be who have accessed their spirituality, we still need to remember to help the poor in every way possible.

Are You There Yet?

In the beginning of the process of shifting from ego to spirituality, you will get many opportunities and consequent experiences that will gradually transform your belief system and deepen your connection with your CoreSelf. As this happens, more things will change: You will let go of grudges you may still be holding onto, and you will not get so upset, irritable, or frustrated if this was a previous issue for you.

As you reach even higher levels of awareness, you will experience more often a deep sense of peace and fewer incidences will disturb it. If your inner peace is not disrupted, unease will not last as long. Your capacity to love people, even those who were not nice to you, or tried to harm you in some way, will increase. You will look for ways to be of service and help without expecting anything in return. You will stop reacting. You will stop giving advice.

Instead, you will share your peace with others by giving them warm attention. You will recognize depth even in the mundane. You will feel more grounded, stable, and balanced.

Make no mistake, you will still feel emotions; you may still cry or become angry or fearful. However, these emotions will not be so intense anymore, and you will be able to deal with them with patience and kindness. You will stop being hard on yourself and you will treat yourself with more gentleness and understanding.

> Close your eyes and breathe deeply. Imagine the next level of awareness you want to experience. What needs to happen in order for you to get there? Include in your answer something you have to let go of. Picture yourself releasing it like a balloon into a wind that catches and carries it off. How do you feel now?

**The more you detach from ego-based attachments and
patterns, the deeper you go into awareness of your spirituality.**

When delving deeper into spiritual water, many meaningful things happen. Some are clearly significant and others more subtle. A patient with whom I'd had a few prior successful sessions told me that for the first time in her life, she stopped making excuses and stopped defending herself when interacting with her family and friends, which she used to do regularly before. She described what she was feeling as a very freeing experience.

Freedom is a very typical feeling when you let go of the bondage of the mind. This sense of freedom is at the bottom of spiritual awakening. You'll feel freedom from burdens, worry, and from chasing your own tail. You will feel at ease with yourself and with others. You may find yourself listening more, with less need to make your point. You will feel good without anything in particular happening to prompt it.

Over a year ago, I had an interesting internal experience that led to some deep realizations. A few hours later I went to visit friends. As we conversed in their living room, one of their cats jumped on me and sat calmly while I stroked it. My friends were very surprised. Apparently, this cat never interacted like that with strangers. I smiled, realizing that the cat sensed the peace I was feeling inside and was connecting with it.

You will understand yourself much better. Comparison, judgment, and criticism will gradually become part of the past. Things that used to bother you will cease to disturb you. Fear will gradually diminish or, at least, be significantly reduced. You will deal with issues one moment at a time. You will feel so much better about yourself, you'll forgive personal mistakes, even in areas you found difficult before. You'll be more forgiving with others as well.

Probably the most important feeling will be acceptance. You will accept other people and their opinions even if you don't agree with them. You will get excited about the smallest things and feel in awe looking at everything in nature. Peace will be the most dominant state of being. You will also have more spiritual experiences. You will feel a deep sense of love that just wants to flow out. You may even get some out of body experiences, being able to observe yourself and others from a higher plane. You will connect very deeply with nature and animals.

One of the best ways to know that you are transforming is through other people's feedback. A teacher I worked with told me that many of her colleagues approached her on different occasions, asking if she had lost weight or if she had changed her makeup. They realized something was different but couldn't put their fingers on it. Other patients told me how people changed their behavior towards them, wanting to be closer, and showing them much more respect and appreciation than before.

When you're peaceful inside, people, especially good friends, notice it. They can't always understand what the change is but they can feel something is different. This change has to be fundamental and consistent, not just a temporary change, to affect people around you in a positive way.

Sometimes negative things also happen in the process. Taking the time to practice your spiritual exercises and changing how you interact with others can definitely antagonize members of your family. A number of patients informed me that as they progressed, they lost some friends. Of course, these friends used to take advantage of them, and when they couldn't do that anymore, they removed themselves. Many had to face a partner who resisted the changes, because he or she could not tolerate the fact that their spouse was actually enjoying more peace and became disinterested in petty arguments. This typically happens in an ego-soul-type relationship and could be very trying for a mate who doesn't understand your alteration.

If you are going through such an experience, don't worry. Because people close to you will constantly challenge you, your opportunities to grow will be much greater than if you were on your own. At a later stage you will have a clear idea of what to do next.

Another thing that will occur frequently will be synchronicities. You will think about something and it will happen. You may even be, at times, a mind reader. You will have strong feelings about different issues without necessarily being able to explain them. You will get many signs that will reassure you in the process. You will take the time to smell the roses more frequently. Your state will be peace and your actions will be love. You will notice things on a deeper level.

Are you there yet?

A more advanced patient was going through very tough challenges. She came to see me and asked whether I thought she was in denial because she couldn't feel stress about her particular situation. We chatted for a while and I realized she was actually feeling calm and confident that things would work themselves out for the better. I assured her that she was not in denial. The memory of how she used to deal with stress was there, but her mind had become spiritual. She had no need to think how to react, she just responded to things with peace. When the processing mind becomes spiritual YOU ARE FULLY THERE. Or shall I say, *HERE*!

> Life is a creation.
> Self and
> circumstances—
> the raw material.
> *Dorothy M.*
> *Richardson*

I always wanted to take up ballroom dancing but I never got around to it. I think fear was one of the reasons I didn't. I just thought I couldn't do it. One day I went to a dancing school and signed up. I had always used dancing as a metaphor for how we are supposed to relate to life, i.e., to dance with it, and while taking lessons I realized how true this analogy was. I found out yet again that there is no such thing as *I can't*, only *I am afraid of*, *I don't want to*, or *I am not willing to put in the effort*.

I also noticed that I tried too hard to dance with my mind. I had to work on learning to allow mind and body to integrate with the music and become one with it. I still have a lot to learn; and according to my instructor, this process never ends. To be really good at it, one needs to practice continuously. Coordinating various aspects of myself to FLOW with the rhythm of the music is quite similar to the way we grow; but the most important rule is to focus on enjoying the process, rather than wait for the accomplishment of an ultimate goal.

Life is indeed a dance. Surrender yourself to it by accepting what you're experiencing, realizing who you really are, and dancing with the moment through mind and body. When you feel joy in the dance with life, you have arrived.

What Do You Need to Learn?

One of my patients, who had been making very good progress in therapy, came one day for her session feeling quite upset. She said that she had applied for a higher position in her workplace and was not accepted, so she experienced feelings of rejection and unworthiness. We discussed her experience briefly and I advised her that from a spiritual perspective, she could consider two possibilities: First, this was not the right position for her at the time and if that was the case, a new one would present itself instead. The second option was that it was very possible that there was more that she needed to learn in her working environment before she could move on. It didn't take more then a few minutes to discover which one it was. She had to learn how to deal with a few challenging colleagues at work without feeling so stressed. Three months later, following a few interesting coincidences, she was promoted to a position she never believed she could ever get.

> There are some things you learn best in calm, and some in storm.
>
> *Willa Cather*

Life has a strange way of throwing situations at us that will help us go deeper within, to help in heightening our inner awareness. Many people tend to blame the circumstances, especially when they cause discomfort, rather than to look at them as opportunities. If an important lesson is not fully processed, don't be surprised if you encounter different experiences that basically teach the same theme. Alternatively, you may just remain stuck for a long time in an unfavorable environment to repeat the class.

Every person in your life, every interaction with another human being, can be a tremendous opportunity for growth. Typical areas that we need to learn include patience, kindness, opening up, giving without expecting anything in return, forgiving, and trusting. Additional areas include letting go of ego-based behaviors, which we discussed earlier. The bottom line is that learning will always, one way or another, be about ACCEPTANCE and about GIVING unconditionally.

A good exercise right now would be to take some time to review major areas of your life such as relationships and career.

Ask yourself the following questions:

1. **What can this (relationship, person, environment, circumstances) teach me on a spiritual level that I still have not mastered?**
2. **What do I have to do to learn fully that lesson?**
3. **What do I have to change in my thinking to transcend the challenge?**
4. **What do I have to let go, to be able to transform?**

Another way to do this is to look back at your life and find common problems that repeated themselves. Ask what you could learn from them. It will usually be one of the above-mentioned items. Watch as your life changes in some significant way when you complete your learning.

You Are a Bad Ego

As the ego's influence on your life diminishes, you need to avoid a dangerous trap. I talked about how many masks, roles, and agendas the sophisticated ego can come up with, including becoming a "spiritual ego." Knowledge about the tricks of the ego, and trying at times to avoid them unsuccessfully, can lead to an upfront attack on the ego or some of its aspects. Such an attack will take the form of self-criticism, put-downs, and feelings of disappointment and discouragement. Who does that?

The ego has appointed a part to criticize itself and the part is voicing its discontentment through you. This would be equivalent to appointing a thief to protect us from crime.

Remember that it's okay to experience emotions, all kinds, from both sides of the spectrum. Make sure that you don't identify with them, don't react too much to them, and are able to connect them eventually with peace to let them go.

Self-criticism does not help you to grow. Self-acceptance does. It is very possible that with all the work, some of your ego-based behavior will persist. You will have to accept that. Instead of criticizing the ego, you will be better off connecting with peace. That will take the anxiety out of the process, and will diffuse and gradually eliminate any chain reactions caused by self-struggle.

The famous psychologist Carl Rogers reinforced this notion, saying, "The curious paradox is that when I accept myself just as I am, then I can change." Avoid falling into that trap of self-criticism. There is never a good reason to criticize yourself. You can look at your behavior and decide to change and you can learn from your mistakes. But when you change using negative motivation, either the changes won't last, or new problems will form.

As radical as this may sound, ultimately, you must fully accept the ego. This will lead to a point at which the ego will finally recognize and be willing to admit two things: Firstly, its role as the *"know it all, I'll protect you, trust me, I know what is good for you,"* is over. Secondly, the ego itself would be better off re-integrating with spirit—like a lost child coming back home. That's a profound transformation. Now the ego has real peace. Welcome back; ego has sprung from the spirit, and it has returned to its source. More on that soon.

> The only limit to our realization of tomorrow will be our doubts of today.
> *Franklin Roosevelt*

Last Minute Doubts

A patient came into my office one day complaining that the "spiritual process" was too slow for her. I reminded her of the deep peace she was able to tap into, perhaps for the first time in her life, just a few weeks earlier. She calmed down and I explained to her that she had just fallen victim to her own ego's plot. She laughed and was then able to move on.

As your spiritual awareness and practice increase, you may encounter some doubts. "Is that it?" "What's next?" "I'm bored." "I thought there would be more." I have heard these comments numerous times from my patients and always assured them that this was a good sign. I myself have heard it from my own ego many times. The ego is really trying its last futile attempt to detour you, to discourage you, to get you to quit. "What's the point? It's taking too long." Or, "What's the big deal?" it would ask. Please don't give up. This is a last minute attempt to trip you. Tell your ego, "Yes, yes; I understand. Don't worry, I am doing just fine."

Many people, as they dip deeper in spiritual water, feel really good and very peaceful. But the ego may not be dead yet. Don't be discouraged if this happens to you. By all means acknowledge the doubts; you don't want to repress them. Then go back to do the work that led you that far. It will be well worth it.

How Deep Is Spirituality?

Spirituality is as deep as space and beyond. It is indeed boundless. Reuniting with who you are is like getting married. You marry someone you really love, and then you begin to explore your partner and learn more about him or her while both of you grow and develop. If you don't fall victim to complacency, this process of connecting with your deepest levels never really ends.

But here is just another paradox. Naturally, you want to constantly deepen the process by asking, "What do I do next? Where do I go from here? How do I get deeper?" After asking such a question, instead of trying consciously to figure it out, just breathe deeply and allow your deeper core to reveal itself to you.

I have come across many people who were trying too hard to become more spiritual. This would fall under the "spiritual ego" category. Just allow deeper awareness to surface and it will.

I received a call from a woman who had made significant progress in therapy. She told me she was working hard on deepening her spiritual awareness. At the time she was taking courses and reading books, and she wondered why she was "plateauing." I told her to stop everything for a little while, even to stop wanting to arrive deeper. Instead, she was just to acknowledge and accept and focus on where she was and on what she had accomplished so far.

Deep spiritual awareness cannot be a result of mental hard work. The opposite is true. When we stop working so hard with our minds and take ourselves more lightly we get there faster.

This woman called me again a few weeks later. After our talk, she had connected with a deep sense of acceptance and as a result enjoyed greater inner peace. She understood the principle that acceptance leads to peace, but for the first time was able to integrate it. "What next?" she then asked me. My advice was to start looking around her and asking how she could share her peace with people she came in contact with.

> If you scramble about in search of inner peace, you will lose your inner peace.
>
> *Lao Tzu*

I like the story about a student of martial arts who wanted to learn swordsmanship. He went to one of the best teachers in the country. "How long will it take me to learn the fine art of swordsmanship?" he asked.

The teacher replied, "About five years."

"That's a very long time," the student said. He then asked, "But what if I worked really hard and put my best efforts forth, how many years would it take me then?"

The teacher thought for a moment and said: "Ten years."

This is a famous Zen saying: "Before enlightenment you chop wood and carry water; and after enlightenment you chop wood and carry water." I have a small enhancement to this saying: After enlightenment everything may still stay the same, but somehow everything becomes more joyful. Life is not lived as a routine anymore. Joy is spirituality in the doing. Nothing is too much, nothing is too little.

Nothing is boring. Everything is met with acceptance and peace. That's the spiritual depth we are all able to connect with.

Where Does the Ego Come From?

I implied earlier that the ego originates from the spirit. Does this sound totally absurd, that the origin of the ego is also our spiritual essence?

Religion looks at Satan as the enemy of God. In Christianity, Satan, who represents all evil, is an angel who rebelled against God. In Judaism, Satan is considered to be on God's payroll and is regarded as one of God's sons. But who is Satan if not a metaphor for the sum total of all "ego energy"? We can, therefore, assert that the ego was part of the Spiritual Intelligence that decided to rebel against its own source, much like a child rebelling against his own parents.

Here's another way I like to look at it: Since the Supreme Intelligence has all possible options built within itself, an ego manifested in the physical world is one of those options. The ego shouts loudly: "I know what's good for you, I can show you the way!" Spirituality is humble. It hides behind a two- inch screen compared with a full thousand-inch ego's screen. No wonder we pay attention to it so often.

But the ego is all hype and has no substance. The ego is more like a house of cards. It may look nice and solid, but it is actually very shaky. One little touch and it collapses. The table the cards are placed on is, on the other hand, a very solid structure you can trust.

Taming the Ego

Taming the ego is much like taming a wild horse. In the beginning when you try to ride, it resists and throws you off its back. The fall can even hurt you. But as you gradually train the horse and it becomes more relaxed, you can start riding it for longer periods of time. After a while the ride becomes smoother; the horse has accepted your leadership. Gradually, the horse learns that it is much better off when you are in command because you know what's good for it. Now both of you can enjoy a ride through a beautiful meadow.

Here is another metaphor. The ego is much like an orchestra without a conductor. Every player is playing a certain part of the masterpiece, but quite often with poor timing and lack of coordination. The ego has many uncoordinated parts doing different, sometimes even opposite, things at the same time. It needs a conductor.

Do you care to pick up the baton and start conducting your ego? You have the ability and power to do so, and I am sure that Beethoven would be proud of you.

Identity Crisis

The spiritual quest for most people is not without challenges. Just a few moments ago I talked about doubts. One of the most challenging crises many people experience in this process is an identity crisis. This should not be a big surprise when you reflect on how most people identify with the wrong self. When such crisis occurs, feelings of confusion are not uncommon.

I received an e-mail from one of my patients. She sounded quite perplexed, not sure about what do next, how to behave and how to relate to people around her. She realized she was going through an identity crisis. This kind of crisis is very important. It clearly points to the direction of transformation. I reminded her that what she called an identity crisis was nothing but the ego's attempt to throw in fear and confusion so that she would give up. This fear was based on some of the ego's own deep fears and especially fear of the unknown, which is part of the fear of change.

While I was personally going through a similar process, I had a dream. In my dream, I lived in an apartment building, which suddenly collapsed in an earthquake. As I experienced the earthquake, I tried to run away to safety, but it kept chasing me. Luckily, I was able to jump over a big crack on the ground and save myself. Then I felt a sense of acceptance of what was happening and patiently waited for everything to calm down. I returned to the apartment building to see that its foundation was destroyed, and then I woke up. I realized that this was exactly the process I was going through. The foundations of the old me were collapsing. The changes were quite intimidating, but I knew that new foundations were being established at the same time. I also knew that once these foundations were fully in place, I would be safe forever.

If you ever experience any identity issues ask yourself, "What lies behind my identity?" Connect with that, and the identity crisis will soon disappear.

Feel Like the Ocean, Think Like the Sky

The ego is really like a wave. It rises out of the ocean, flexes its muscles to show its power, but it eventually settles back into the ocean.

I have in my office an interesting novelty you may have seen. It is a transparent plastic rectangular box, containing a blue liquid that moves slowly from side to side and mimics the motion of waves. I put it there for two reasons.

First, to demonstrate to my patients the real pace of life. We move so fast through life that we literally miss it. When a person sits in front of this novelty box watching the wave going from side to side ever so slowly, he or she relaxes considerably, because their thinking slows down and begins to operate at the speed of life.

The second reason is this: I ask the patient to look carefully at the motion of the waves and tell me which part of this "ocean" is most peaceful. It is not difficult to answer this question; the bottom layer seems much calmer.

We talked earlier in the book in detail about identification. If you want, you can choose to identify with the wave. In this case, expect to roller coast up and down, pushed forcefully forward and backward. When the first wave is through with you, a second one will then show up, repeating the process, followed by a third and a fourth, so you either get very tired or you drown.

When you choose to identify with the deeper layers of the ocean, with your true foundation that is always calm, you too become calmer. This simple metaphor has enabled me personally to deal with stress and turmoil in my own life. Whenever it occurs, I just remember that these circumstances are nothing but waves and I can connect with the bottom of my own ocean, which is peace, and allow the wave to calm down.

Going deeper does not mean that I am hiding, avoiding, or denying what is happening. However, I make every effort not to identify with negative states. This enables me to reduce the stress associated with life's "storms" and deal with them as calmly as I can.

Another metaphor I like is the sky. On a cloudy day, you cannot see the sky. But this does not mean that it is not there. It is just hidden behind clouds. Take away the clouds and the clear sky is there. I like to treat my thinking like that. When I realize that too many thoughts cloud my mind, I avoid identifying with them. I gently push them away while doing some deep breathing until I can see the sky again, so to speak. Just like an airplane takes you above the clouds, true inner peace can lift you to that high altitude where you can see the sky and the sun again.

Treat your thoughts like clouds and your emotions like waves while you identify with the sky and the ocean, and your life will be much more peaceful.

Transcending Outside Resistance

One of my patients gradually progressed to a deep sense of love and peace. She wished she could tell that to everyone she knew, although I cautioned her that this would not be easy to do. Sure enough, she faced some resistance, even ridicule, when she tried to share her new findings with others. She came to ask my advice. I told her that the only thing she could do was to enjoy herself and become a living example, and she indeed was able to do so.

> Inside myself is a place where I live all alone and that's where you renew your springs that never dry up.
>
> *Pearl S. Buck*

I encounter this frequently. People advancing in spiritual territory begin to feel fears. "What if my husband leaves me?" "What if I stay lonely?" Spiritual manifestation can go side by side with feeling lonely or even isolated, especially if people who have difficulty understanding surround you.

But who feels lonely? The ego, of course. Use that as a guide to deepen your spiritual connection even more. At some point you will stop feeling lonely forever!

Doing Things Differently

You have the freedom of choice. Choosing what you want to identify with, what you want to focus on, and how you want to spend your time can enhance or diminish your work in this realm. I like the saying, "If you always do what you always did, you'll always get what you always got." If you want different results you have to do things differently.

Examine your motivation. Are you operating out of a sense of fear? Action that is based on any fear—for instance, fear of loss such as control, comfort, power, or possessions—is always ego-based. Soul-based actions are always motivated and accompanied by peace and love. Here is a priceless question you can ask yourself in any specific situation, and it will always get you beyond the confinement of the ego: "If I was totally spiritual right now, how would I feel and what would I do?"

> God hasn't promised an easy way, but peace at the center of the hard way.
>
> *Dale Evans*

You will always get an answer to this question. You know why? Because you are totally spiritual right now. When you ask the question and are willing to go with the answer, you will never regret it. The only way you do not get an answer is if you are not willing to listen. But if you are genuinely interested, you will know the right thing to do in any situation. Of course, the answer will always include peace. You will forgo trying to win every argument; you will avoid criticizing or judging people. Instead, you will listen and try to better understand them, even if they challenge your convictions and patience.

You will do what's right. The spirit always wants to do what's right—this very moment, and the next moment and the one after. All you have to remember is one word: PEACE. That's the ultimate shortcut. Don't you think this significantly simplifies everything? Have peace be your guide and you will live life to its fullest.

Spirituality doesn't guarantee a perfect life, or a life free of trouble, only a peaceful one. Spirituality hides in every stone, every leaf, and every drop of water. You can't always see it and you need to refocus, at times, to connect with it. Have you ever seen those computer-generated graphics called stereogram? On the surface you can see colorful patterns that usually don't mean a lot. However, when you look through the picture, relaxing your eyes into a soft-focus, a three-dimensional picture emerges from the colorful depths. Get into the habit of looking deeper into the moment, and a wonderful, hidden, mysterious world will reveal itself to you.

You have an infinite reservoir of peace and love just under your nose. How would you like to use it? One of the true criteria of spiritual transformation is when we all realize that we are not here for ourselves but for others. Once we can integrate this with our actions, we have completed our transformation.

Summarizing It All

The following spiritual practices can sum it all up.
- Reduce processing.
- Identify with your spirit instead of your ego.
- Become aware of the games the ego plays with you.
- Make it okay to feel deeper feelings.
- Face issues you still carry from the past and let them go.
- Let go of your needs for control, attention, and approval.

There is as much within the heart as there is in the whole world outside. Heaven, earth, fire, wind, moon, lightning, stars: whatever is and whatever is not, everything is there.

Chandogya Upanishad

- Let go of the need to be right.
- Accept yourself unconditionally.
- Accept others unconditionally and be kind to them.
- Breathe deeply.
- Shake hands with the moment and accept it as is.
- Tell the truth (facts—sensory based), not your perception of it.
- Reduce attachments.
- Strive for simplicity.
- Practice humility.
- Be still, even when you move.
- Connect with people.
- Care.
- Exercise.
- Eat right.
- Cry.
- Smile.
- Experience.
- Want less.
- Find joy in simple things.
- Connect with nature.
- Observe.
- Slow down.
- Be patient.
- Practice generosity.
- Love.
- Laugh.
- Be peace!

Please remember to separate *who you really are* from your thoughts about who you are. At the same time, remember that life is not your thoughts about it but the actual moments that create it.

Now you know without any doubt, I hope, that deep below all the chaos, all the difficulties, and all the challenging emotions and conditions, always lies peace. Can you look for it? When things are tough, will you commit to work through adversity to find and connect with it? When you can find it during challenging times, the connection will stay with you forever.

You are spiritual NOW! Allow your spirituality to come completely out. Repeat the following message often: *I live in the now. I am complete. I am peace.*

Imagine

I believe the ultimate vision we all must strive to fulfill is described in John Lennon's song "Imagine." To me, it represents where we need to head as a human race.

Imagine there's no heaven
It's easy if you try
No hell below us
Above us, only sky
Imagine all the people
Living for today

> Nothing happens unless first a dream.
> *Carl Sandburg*

Imagine there's no country
It isn't hard to do
Nothing to kill or die for
And no religion too
Imagine all the people
Living life in peace

You may say I'm a dreamer
But I'm not the only one
I hope some day you'll join us
And the world will be as one

Imagine no possessions
I wonder if you can
No need for greed or hunger
A brotherhood of man
Imagine all the people
Sharing all the world

You may say I'm a dreamer
But I'm not the only one
I hope some day you'll join us
And the world will live as one.

On a personal level, realize that deep inside you, below all the masks, roles, and agendas, you can find beauty far more magnificent than the most amazing sunsets you have ever seen. Deep inside you is wisdom that transcends all knowledge. Deep inside lie the answers to all the questions, the solution to all problems. Below personality and identity lie your spirit and its earthly pal the soul that can bring joy, love, and fulfillment into your life—right where you are, right now.

To enjoy all that, you have to choose LIFE. Life, the way it was meant to be, the ice cream style, with all the trimmings. Just be quiet, be still, breathe deeply, be fully aware, and connect with the deep moment. Connect with people and help them reconnect with their own true being, not by forcing or urging them to do so, but instead, by accepting and loving them unconditionally.

This is a journey without any distance. You have arrived, and yet, you were always here. Now deepen this wonderful relationship to get to know your re-found essence, as soft as silk and as strong as a rock, to its fullest. You don't need any further knowledge, nor do you need any new information. You KNOW it—now just learn to BE it.

Oscar Wilde wrote, "'Know thyself' was written over the portal of the antique world. Over the portal of the new world 'be thyself' shall be written."

I wish you full and complete PEACE. Shalom!

A New Beginning

The Principal called the Student to his office. "Who are you?" he asked, staring into the Student's eyes.

The Student looked at the Principal and said nothing. He took in a series of deep breaths while exhaling them very slowly. Gazing in the direction of the Principal he kept breathing deeply.

"You haven't answered my question!" the Principal exclaimed after a few minutes of total silence.

"I certainly have," answered the Student softly.

"I didn't hear any answer!" the Principal insisted.

"In that case, I am sorry to say," the Student whispered, "you have not been listening."

The Principal smiled. "You have completed your studies here. Now go practice your work outside."

Appendices:

Who are you? List 1

Melissa- a mom, a daughter, a sister, a partner, a teacher, perfectionist, caring, empathetic energetic - really I don't know this is what I try to be.

Who are you? List 2

Who are you? List 3

Realizations:

Games the Ego Plays:

_____

_____

_____

_____

_____

_____

_____

Limiting Patterns You Would Like to Transform:

_____

_____

_____

_____

_____

_____

_____

Conditions for Peace

I Wished...

Notes:

PeaceTogether

Would you like to promote the principles of peace in your community by conducting or participating in regular meetings to discuss applications of the principles described in this book?

Would you like to be part of a network that promotes these principles?

A leader's guide to help in facilitating such meetings is now available.

Volunteers with good organizational skills who can help in organizing the regional chapters are needed.

For more information please visit:
www.ShortcutToSpirituality.com

For Professionals Only

If you are a mental health professional interested in learning more about Core Integration Therapy (CIT)—a four-dimensional treatment modality that can help you in identifying and clearing clients' psycho-emotional blocks to inner peace e-mail the author at: **bob@ACEclinics.com**

Please include some information about your professional background.

Other books by the author:

The Revolutionary Memory Course
Dramatically Improve Your Memory and Concentration in 6 Weeks or Less!

This course is one of the most advanced programs in enhancing memory and concentration and is based on extensive research and clinical experience in this field. Included in the course are:

1. A three part workbook that describes effective and easy to use methods to enhance your memory.
2. The Concentration Matrix™—a powerful tool to sharpen your concentration and ability to focus well.

3. The Memory Cards™—specially designed cards (320 total) that will help you to improve your short-term, working, and long-term memory.

To order please visit the publisher's site:
  www.DeeperDimension.com
  or call the order line: **416-222-0004**

Coming soon:

Teach Your Kids How to Deal with Feelings

This special set consists of a picture book titled *Max the Guard Dog*, intended for children (ages 5 to 12) as well as a manual for parents, which teaches the most important elements of dealing with feelings. Teaching such skills to children can eventually make parenting an easier job to do. It can also significantly enhance the quality of their lives as they grow up.

For more information please visit the publisher at:
  www.DeeperDimension.com

Projects:

We Are Looking for Participants for the Following Projects:

Couples
Who would be interested in participating in a program that incorporates a special approach that can help to significantly enhance relationships.

Parents
Who would be interested in participating in a program where they will be taught a specific approach that can significantly enhance their communication with their children of all ages.

- The programs will be conducted in the comfort of your own home, at no cost to you
- You will be sent special material, and will be required to follow the instructions mentioned in the material
- You will also be required to send us periodical reports

If you would like to participate in any of these programs, please send us an e-mail and give us some background information, specifying the difficulties you are currently facing in your relationship, or with your child, and why you would like to participate in the project.

Please e-mail us at: **projects@deeperdimension.com**
Subject: Relationship Program or Child Communication Program

Stories:
Do you have an interesting true story that can fit in one of these categories?
1. You dared to be yourself and it paid off
2. You beat the odds in some way
3. Telling the truth and paying for it
4. Life disappointments and how you solved them
5. Dealing with life's challenges in a creative way
   We will pay for stories chosen to be published.
   Please e-mail us at **stories@deeperdimension.com**
   subject: True Stories

GENERAL REPLY FORM

Name: _____

Address: _____

_____

Tel: _____ e-mail: _____

I am interested in the following:

___ keep me on your mailing list for special announcements

___ I am interested in becoming part of *PeaceTogether* in the

following capacity: _____

_____

___ I am interested in becoming a group leader

My background:

_____

_____

_____

_____

___ Let me know when the book *Teach Your Kids How to Deal with Feelings* becomes available.

Please fax this form to: **416-222-0020**

Or mail to: **Deeper Dimension Publishing**
148 Finch Ave. West
Toronto, ON Canada
M2N 2J2